Performance and Credibility

Performance and Credibility

Developing Excellence in Public and Nonprofit Organizations

Edited by

Joseph S. Wholey
University of Southern California
Washington Public Affairs Center

Mark A. Abramson
The Center for Excellence in Government

Christopher Bellavita
University of Southern California
Washington Public Affairs Center

Lexington Books
D.C. Heath and Company/Lexington, Massachusetts/Toronto

Library of Congress Cataloging-in-Publication Data
Main entry under title:

Performance and credibility.

Includes index:
1. Corporations, Nonprofit—Management—
Evaluation—Addresses, essays, lectures.
2. Public administration—Evaluation—Addresses,
essays, lectures. 3. Evaluation research
(Social action programs)—Addresses, essays,
lectures. I. Wholey, Joseph S. II. Abramson,
Mark A., 1947–   . III. Bellavita,
Christopher.
HD62.6.P47   1986   658'.048   85–50707
ISBN 0–669–11037–X (alk. paper)
ISBN 0–669–11680–7 (pbk. : alk. paper)

Published simultaneously in Canada
Printed in the United States of America
Casebound International Standard Book Number: 0–669–11037–X
Paperbound International Standard Book Number: 0–669–11680–7
Library of Congress Catalog Card Number: 85–50707

The paper used in this publication meets the minimum requirements of
American National Standard for Information Sciences—Permanence of
Paper for Printed Library Materials, ANSI Z39.48–1984.

Contents

Tables and Figures

Tables

Figures

Part I
Introduction

1

Managing for High Performance: Roles for Evaluators

Joseph S. Wholey
Mark A. Abramson
Christopher Bellavita

G overnment and nonprofit organizations, like their counterparts in the private sector, are under increasing pressure to achieve perfor- in a cost-effective manner. Improving organizational performance is difficult in the government and nonprofit sectors. These organizations must respond to multiple constituencies and lack clear surrogates for the profit-and-loss and return-on-equity criteria that influence activities in the business sector. Yet public and nonprofit organizations can improve their performance. The thesis of this book is that evaluators can play major roles helping those who manage government and nonprofit organizations. We argue that the talents of evaluators are likely to be of increasing value to managers as they are called upon to achieve higher performance with limited resources. The book presents examples of how evaluators have helped government and nonprofit organizations move toward excellence.

Some Assumptions about Evaluation

This book is based on a series of assumptions about the value of evaluation in helping organizations manage for high performance. We believe that:

1. In our increasingly complex and interdependent society, effective government and nonprofit organizations and programs will continue to be needed.
2. The performance of these organizations and programs can be improved.
3. In the years ahead, the public will continue to demand more effective services and to debate the level of resources that should be available to government and nonprofit organizations.
4. Effective leadership in the public and nonprofit sectors will be more in demand, more necessary, and more difficult to achieve than ever before.

We believe that the pressures for efficient, effective government and nonprofit organizations can increase the demand for the services that evaluators know how to provide. Managers in all organizations can use evaluators to help them manage better.

Management Leadership Functions

If government and nonprofit organizations at all levels are to solve complex problems within tight financial constraints, managers will need to perform four key leadership functions:

1. Define expected organizational and program performance and establish clear, outcome-oriented objectives for their organizations and programs.
2. Assess organizational performance and variations in performance in terms of specific performance expectations.
3. Stimulate improvements in organizational and program performance (in particular, in productivity and cost effectiveness) or maintain high levels of performance.
4. Communicate credibly the value of the organization's activities, within and outside the organization.

A central premise of this book is that evaluators have the talents—knowledge, skills, and abilities—that leaders in government and nonprofit organizations need to solve many of their most important problems. Evaluators are skilled at working with policymakers and managers to identify relevant organizational objectives and performance indicators. They have the ability to produce valid, reliable information on resources consumed, activities undertaken, and outcomes achieved. Evaluators can draw credible conclusions about organizational effectiveness and cost effectiveness. Evaluators can identify significant variations in performance within and among programs.

We believe that the competition for scarce resources can serve to increase the value of evaluators' talents. Managers of nonprofit and government organizations are showing increasing interest in obtaining credible information about what their programs and organizations are accomplishing. There is a greater tendency to use such information to make policy, program, and budget decisions. Evaluators are in a position to help managers guide, defend, and improve their organizations at a time when they face increasingly tough competition for scarce resources.

Over the past several years, we have been impressed by many instances in which evaluators have helped managers clarify program objectives and priorities, communicate the value of activities to skeptical audiences, and stimulate improvements in program performance. This book brings together a series of chapters describing how evaluators and evaluation have actually helped organizations make the transition toward high performance.

Organizing Evaluations to Improve
Organizational Performance

Before the evaluator can help a manager improve organizational performance, an effective organizational relationship between the evaluator and manager must be created. The three chapters in part II of this book describe how the evaluation function has been structured to facilitate high performance.

In chapter 2, Kenneth Bickel provides a case study of how a large nonprofit organization, Aid Association for Lutherans, began to change the way the organization managed its fraternal benefit programs. The organization's previous evaluation efforts had not made significant contributions to decision making. Evaluators and higher level decisionmakers were unhappy with this outcome and looked for ways to increase the utility of evaluations.

The organization selected several of its programs to experiment with a new evaluation effort that sought to link program goals, activities, and resources with the overall mission of the Aid Association for Lutherans. The evaluations involved teams of decisionmakers, administrators, program staff, and evaluators in the process of planning, implementing, and using evaluation. The success of this initial effort to improve how program resources were used encouraged the organization to extend its methodology for evaluation to all of its fraternal benefit programs. A new framework for managing the organization's benefit programs emerged from the evaluation process.

In chapter 3, Steve Lillie and Mike Jewell discuss how an organization's evaluation function is influenced by size, complexity, resources, and decisionmakers' information needs. The authors describe how the U.S. Department of Health and Human Services organized evaluation functions within the department to respond to policymakers' requests while also maximizing the way evaluation resources are used. The centerpiece of their approach is a contracting process that gives public organizations the immediate capacity to use skilled evaluators from the private sector who have demonstrated an ability to perform high-quality and useful evaluation.

In chapter 4 Martin Kotler discusses how a private contractor organized its evaluation capabilities. The author first reviews the common criticisms leveled against evaluation (untimely products, limited utility, and so on) and suggests that these complaints frequently are evidence that the evaluation function is not well integrated with its organization and policy context.

Kotler argues that evaluators need to separate myths from the realities about how decisions on policy matters are made, and to reconceptualize the evaluator's role and techniques accordingly. Kotler also discusses how the communication tasks of evaluators can be organized to improve the links among management, evaluation, and policymaking.

Establishing Performance Expectations

In the American political system, government often promises more than it can deliver. In attempting to reach agreement on policies and programs—whether for protection of air quality, deinstitutionalization of mental patients, or procurement of weapons systems—policymakers tend to focus on problems. Policymakers are less concerned with the specific chains of program activities, short-term outcomes, and long-term outcomes that will be needed to translate resource allocations into progress toward policy goals. Faced with ambitious, competing goals, government managers often seem to be placed in "no win" situations.

With input from political and operating levels, performance-oriented managers need to find ways to translate policy goals into ambitious, yet realistic, input, process and outcome objectives, and performance indicators. (We use "performance indicators" to signify the types of measurements and comparisons to be used in assessing organization and program performance.) Outcome objectives and performance indicators provide the basis for implementing programs and demonstrating results.

We will first discuss four examples from our own experience in working with organizations that have established performance expectations, and then describe the more detailed examples presented in part III below.

In the federal Community Health Centers program, managers, staff, and grantees worked for four years to identify appropriate program objectives and performance indicators. Their "priority output" objectives emphasized health services delivery and efficiency, but also included outcome objectives such as immunizing 90 percent of the two-year-olds receiving health services.[1]

At the Harlem Valley Psychiatric Center, line and staff organizations translated global deinstitutionalization and mental health care goals into the more tractable yet still ambitious objectives of rapidly reducing in-patient census, developing community-based services, and providing high-quality care for all patients in the hospital and in the community.[2]

Given the pressures they face, most public and nonprofit managers require considerable help in operationalizing policy goals. Evaluators can help managers identify and sort through policy goals, test possible program objectives against past performance in the program or in similar programs, and clarify what types of program performance information could be produced.

In the Tennessee Health Department's prenatal care program, for example, evaluators helped managers to agree on priority objectives related to the proportion of health department patients initiating prenatal care in the first trimester of pregnancy and the proportion of low-birthweight infants born to health department patients.[3] Such "intermediate outcome objectives" represented a healthy balance between process objectives (upon which managers frequently concentrate) and ultimate impact objectives (on which researchers tend to try to hold programs accountable).

In the National Institute of Mental Health Community Support Program, evaluators helped managers clarify an overly ambitious goal that called for the development of "comprehensive, coordinated, community-based care" systems for chronically mentally ill people, including those returning to the community from state mental hospitals. Those in charge of the program decided to drop the unrealistic objective of "nationwide" development of community support systems and obtain help from evaluators to develop the specific performance indicators needed to operationalize the remaining program objectives.[4]

Part III provides additional examples of how the clear delineation of objectives benefited organizations and programs. In chapter 5, Steven Kapp offers a case study describing how the Aid Association for Lutherans' All-College Scholarship program went through the process of establishing performance objectives. The program had not been changed for two decades and was measured by vague indicators such as reputation and prestige. Kapp describes how the evaluation team, composed of staff, administrators, and evaluators, conducted a performance-oriented "rapid feedback" assessment that resulted in reformulation of the program's performance objectives.

In chapter 6, Dennis Palumbo, Michael Musheno, and Steven Maynard-Moody discuss the concept of the public sector entrepreneur as an individual who takes the initiative to ensure that organizations and programs set focused, performance-oriented goals. They illustrate the concept with an example of a multistate criminal justice program, and demonstrate the contribution that agreement on objectives makes to successfully planning and implementing a program.

In chapter 7, John King discusses how evaluators can link their concern for performance expectations to broader organizational improvement efforts. He cites examples of strategic planning in a mental health department and in a state college to show how evaluators can use their expertise to help organizations recognize the connections among the diverse objectives they pursue.

In chapter 8, Tom Horan illustrates what can happen when organizations unquestioningly accept inappropriate performance objectives. He describes how the nationwide "rideshare" program used learnings from past failures to improve the program's ability to encourage commuters to share transportation. Evaluators recognized that the initial program design was premised on the inaccurate assumption that commuters would willingly share and offer rides to others once they knew who else was interested in ridesharing. But prospective participants had little incentive to alter their commuting behavior until a few programs, having learned from the past, took a more proactive approach to ridesharing. Managers in these programs used a variety of new tactics, including personally matching individuals who could share rides, encouraging employer vanpool programs, suggesting parking incentives, and making other modifications to the old program based on the unique characteristics and incentive systems of local areas.

In chapter 9, Alain Barbarie explores the issue of establishing objectives for difficult-to-measure research and demonstration (R&D) programs. It is often argued that R&D programs should not be held accountable to the same standards of performance as operating programs. While sympathetic to the argument, Barbarie disagrees with the conclusion that R&D programs cannot be measured on a performance basis. He recommends that evaluators ask whether a particular R&D effort is a legitimate activity for government to undertake and whether there is a client group likely to make use of the research results.

In these programs and in others, a key initial management task was to determine what services and outcomes could be realistically expected from the resources available. The next step for management is to translate policy goals into specific input, process, and outcome objectives and performance indicators that can be used to manage programs and to demonstrate program results. Evaluators can also help managers in this important work.

Assessing Government Performance and Variations in Performance

A second task for performance-oriented managers is to assess the outcomes for which they have implementation and operational responsibilities.

Public and nonprofit sector managers often lack reliable information on the performance, especially the outcomes, of programs for which they are responsible. Accounting systems may provide data on agency expenditures, though not often on "program" expenditures. Management information systems may provide data on clients served and on services delivered; but program outcome data frequently are anecdotal, of questionable validity and reliability, and low in credibility. Managers need credible information about program outcomes to communicate the value of what they are doing and to stimulate higher performance.

We have been impressed by a number of public and nonprofit managers who have developed monitoring and evaluation systems that provide credible evidence on the extent to which intended program results were achieved. In the federal Community Health Centers program, for example, the bureau chief monitored grantee and regional performance on service delivery, efficiency, and outcome targets. The bureau allotted additional staff and grant funds to high-performing regions, and regional offices then allocated additional funds to high-performing grantees.[5]

The director of the Harlem Valley Psychiatric Center used at least seven different monitoring and evaluation systems to assess line and staff performance. Line unit performance was measured against such indicators as the number of inpatients, the quality of inpatient service, length of stay, number of inpatients to be placed versus the number actually placed in community settings, quality and appropriateness of placements in the community, number of discharged patients followed in the community, and the current status of discharged patients. Staff units were assessed in terms of their responsiveness in providing needed services.

Data on the performance of line and staff units were used to identify problems, to initiate corrective actions, and to reallocate resources. The performance of all units was well publicized throughout and beyond the Harlem Valley Psychiatric Center.[6]

To produce quantitative data on important program outcomes at any single point in time or over a period of time, evaluators may have to develop new measurement schemes to summarize and to communicate information not readily amenable to quantification. Some data may be buried in case records. In other instances, evaluators may have to use sample surveys, observations, or open-ended interviews to get behavioral and attitudinal data on the quality of programs or on outcomes. Estimates of cost effectiveness or net benefits of program activities may require collecting data on appropriate comparison groups, conducting time series analyses, or using other tools in the evaluator's repertoire. In each situation, the central question is whether improvements in information about program performance will outweigh the costs and time to obtain and to use the information.

There are many instances in which evaluators have assisted managers in obtaining useful information about program performance. For the Tennessee Health Department prenatal care program, for example, evaluators compared the birthweights of infants born to other low-income women who had not received prenatal services, but who had been receiving food stamps and WIC (Women, Infants, and Children) nutrition vouchers.[7]

Job Corps evaluators conducted a five-year longitudinal study to determine whether the high-cost Job Corps program produced better results than other programs that served a comparable population of disadvantaged youth. Researchers estimated Job Corps program costs, estimated program outcomes such as client earnings and criminal behavior, and then estimated the total dollar value of the program effects identified.[8]

The chapters in part IV describe other conceptual and methodological approaches managers and evaluators can use to obtain credible performance information. In chapter 10, Mary Ann Scheirer uses an example of a fluoride rinse dental program to illustrate that there are several levels of implementation, and that each level has a different set of information needs, which require different monitoring systems and data collection techniques. For example, some managers may be interested primarily in identifying program outcomes, while others are more concerned with understanding the behavior of the program participants. Some managers may have a micro or single program focus, while others are interested in implementation questions from a macro, multiprogram view.

In chapter 11, Carole Neves, James Wolf, and Bill Benton describe how "management indicators" can be used to monitor organizational performance. A management indicator is a measure of some aspect of an organization or a program that significantly affects performance. Indicators rely largely on existing data and focus on issues over which the manager can exercise some influence. Neves and her colleagues discuss how federal human service agencies have used management indicators and illustrate how ratios and computer graphics increase the utility and communicability of performance data.

In chapter 12, Wayne Gray provides a comprehensive and integrated set of questions to ask when planning and building an information system to monitor implementation of a new program. Evaluators, using Gray's scheme, can rank the program components in order of importance, decide how the components fit in with the existing organization routines, assess likely implementation problems, and then devise strategies and tactics to treat the identified problems. The evaluation phase of the monitoring process consists of three tasks: determining how well the ideal of implementation fits with the reality; deciding how well the program works; and then examining the effectiveness of the strategy and tactics used during implementation. Gray illustrates his technique by describing the monitoring of an army training program.

In chapter 13, Anne Hastings and Larry Beyna report on a five-year evaluation designed to assess the performance of the Department of Health and Human Services in implementing the 1978 Civil Service Reform Act. The authors describe the methods the department used to evaluate the act's impact and discuss some of the problems associated with assessing complex organizational change.

Stimulating Improvements in the Performance
of Government Agencies and Programs

A third task for managers is to stimulate improvements in the performance of the agencies and programs for which they are responsible.

In government, intangible incentives such as public recognition for a job well done or the opportunity to present a paper at a conference can be important motivators. Removing constraints, delegating authority, and increasing control over resources are other incentives that can motivate managers. In some cases, modest increments of discretionary funds have been used to stimulate and to reward effective organizational performance.

The federal Office of Child Support Enforcement has long used both intangible and financial incentives to motivate better state performance in getting absent fathers to contribute to their children's support. This effort has reduced the number of children who would otherwise have to be supported by welfare. The Office of Child Support Enforcement tracks the success of each state enforcement agency on several performance indicators, recognizes high performance in their newsletter, and holds award ceremonies honoring states for outstanding performance.[9]

A number of government agencies have encouraged efficiency by allowing subordinate units to keep and reallocate a portion of the savings achieved in a given fiscal year. In the Internal Revenue Service, for example, instead of having to return all unspent monies, subordinate units are allowed to carry 50 percent of any savings over into the next fiscal year.[10]

Performance incentives are one important element in an overall strategy to stimulate improvements in organizations and programs. The authors in part V provide additional ideas about how performance can be improved. In chapter 14, Michael Knapp and Marian Stearns illustrate how evaluators can help build and sustain local reform efforts. They cite the nationwide movement to improve schools to support their argument that looking for positive changes in the overall system can be a more fruitful target for evaluators than looking for individual program impacts. Knapp and Stearns draw particular attention to the role evaluators play in disseminating information about system performance to appropriate audiences.

In chapter 15, Liese Sherwood-Fabre describes some of the characteristics that facilitate large system improvement. She examined efforts to achieve bail reform and to improve the federal civil service, and found that broad support and involvement of all affected interests are key features of successfully implemented reforms. She shows how implementation is helped when the personnel reward system and the structures of the relevant organizations are compatible with the proposed improvement.

In chapter 16, Alan Balutis describes how the Department of Commerce saved $15 million by identifying ways to improve its administrative functions. Savings were then reallocated to operational programs in the Department of Commerce. Balutis describes the management-by-objectives type system and the political and organizational strategy policymakers used to achieve the administrative savings. He also discusses the implications of the Department of Commerce's activities for the Reagan administration's

"Reform '88," an initiative designed to improve administrative management throughout the federal government.

In chapter 17, Anabel Crane describes a specific technique that can be used to monitor and to stimulate improvements in national or state social programs. The "program review" is a method that has been used by the Department of Health and Human Services' Health Resources and Services Administration to improve Health Careers, National Health Service Corps, Migrant Health, and Indian Health Service programs. Program reviews bring together top practitioners and other experts for a broad and systematic examination of significant program issues. The review process encourages organizational and professional renewal, and gives evaluators an opportunity to present their findings to a broader range of decisionmakers and in a more timely fashion than is normally available.

Credibly Communicating the Value of Activities

A fourth task of performance-oriented managers is to communicate the value of their organization's activities both within and outside of their organizations. This helps ensure that needed resources will be available for future program activities. It also helps people inside the organization realize that they are contributing to something that is effective and worthwhile.

In many instances, managers have difficulty demonstrating what results flow from their programs. The anecdotal evidence that may be sufficient for internal program management often proves to be insufficient for communicating with higher policy levels or with important publics.

Here again, evaluators can be very helpful. Though many factors affect budget decisions, we have seen programs of demonstrated effectiveness withstand pressures to reduce or to eliminate their budgets at times when other programs generally recognized as ineffective were sharply reduced or eliminated.

Program effectiveness data played a part in congressional decisions to continue the Community Support Program for the chronically mentally ill. There was evidence from federal, state, and local evaluations that participating states had redirected their service delivery systems to focus on the needs of chronically mentally ill adults, that Community Support Program funds attracted additional state and local funds, and that program participants required less hospitalization because of the program.[11] Although the Reagan administration made no effort to get appropriations for the program in FY 1982 or FY 1983, Congress decided to maintain the Community Support Program as a categorical federal program.

Credible information on program performance has also influenced policy and budget decisions at local levels. In Arlington, Virginia, evaluations were used to help justify continuing a number of programs when many other county programs were being reduced or eliminated. A successful robbery prevention program, an effective auto tag enforcement program, a successful police take-home patrol car program, and an effective child abuse prevention program were all retained in spite of the elimination of federal support.[12]

The chapters in part VI provide additional evidence about the benefits of communicating the value of an organization's activities. In chapter 18, Christopher Bellavita describes the political nature of communication in a public policy environment and suggests that evaluators can become more effective political actors without abandoning their traditional concerns for objectivity and accuracy. He sees a major role for evaluators in helping managers use data and communication to help programs and organizations accomplish the most they can with the resources they have available. Bellavita reviews the major barriers that prevent effective communication and identifies five elements of a communication strategy that can be used by managers and evaluators.

In chapters 19 and 21, Joe Wholey provides two examples of how evaluations have been used to influence legislative and budget decisions. An evaluation that demonstrated the effectiveness and value of the Job Corps, a federal job training program, helped the program maintain its budget and enrollment levels in the face of Reagan administration proposals for sharp reductions. Evaluations had shown that Job Corps benefits outweighed the program's high costs. The chairman of the Senate Committee on Labor and Human Resources, Orrin Hatch, used the evaluation to convince fellow conservatives that the program should be maintained.

Evidence of program effectiveness also played a part in congressional decisions to keep the Women, Infants, and Children (WIC) nutrition program separate from the maternal and child health block grant, to reject proposed reductions in program funding, and eventually to expand the resources available to WIC. Principal investigators on WIC evaluations have testified at congressional hearings on legislation and appropriations. Advocacy groups have also used WIC evaluations to support their efforts to defend the program in a harsh budget and political environment. Wholey's analysis illustrates that, although many factors influence legislative and budget decisions, evidence of program effectiveness can play a useful, constructive role in policymaking.

In chapter 20, Jean Smith describes how, at a time when other state programs were being cut, evaluation information showing the effectiveness of Tennessee's demonstration prenatal care program was used to justify retaining the program after a federal grant expired, and to expand it statewide. Smith's case study also illustrates how each of the four steps in performance-oriented management—establishing realistic objectives, assessing performance, improving performance, and communicating the value of the program's activities—can contribute to program excellence.

Toward Excellence

Government and nonprofit managers need help in the political and fiscal environment of the 1980s. Evaluators can play positive and constructive roles in helping managers move organizations and programs toward high performance.

Evaluators can help managers establish and communicate clear, outcome-oriented objectives and performance indicators for organizations and programs. They can help managers assess performance in terms of those objectives and indicators. They can help managers stimulate improvements in performance. Evaluators can help managers communicate the value of organizational and program activities to people who work inside the organization as well as to those who control needed resources.

The cases presented in this book illustrate how managers and evaluators used the proposed four-step strategy to help move their programs or organizations toward excellence. In some cases, all four steps were used. Other cases highlight in depth one or several of the steps. In chapter 22, the editors draw together the lessons learned from these cases and discuss the implications for evaluators of their changing roles.

In future years, policymakers and managers in government and the non-profit sector will have to allocate scarce resources among competing programs and projects. If we evaluators can work efficiently—we, too, face declining resources—our work is more likely than ever to be used at both management and policy levels.

Today's frontier for evaluators will be work aimed at the development of strategies and incentives needed to produce better public and nonprofit management, and better services in an environment of scarce resources. This book is intended to contribute to that effort.

Notes

1. See Joseph S. Wholey, *Evaluation and Effective Public Management* (Boston: Little, Brown, 1983), p. 21.

2. Ibid., pp. 23–25. For further information, see Murray Levine, *From State Hospital to Psychiatric Center* (Lexington, Mass.: D.C. Heath, 1980).

3. Ibid., pp. 76–86.

4. Ibid., pp. 66–76.

5. Ibid., pp. 190–191.

6. Ibid., pp. 23–25.

7. See Joseph S. Wholey and Margaret S. Wholey, *Evaluation of TIOP and Related Prenatal Care Programs: Interim Report* (Arlington, Va.: Wholey Associates, 1981); Joseph S. Wholey and Margaret S. Wholey, *Toward Improving the Outcome*

of Pregnancy: Implications for the Statewide Program (Arlington, Va.: Wholey Associates, 1982); and chapter 20 below.

8. See Charles Mallar et al., *Evaluation of the Economic Impact of the Job Corps Program: Second Follow-up Report* and *Third Follow-up Report* (Princeton, N.J.: Mathematica Policy Research, 1980 and 1982); and chapter 19 below.

9. Meetings with Office of Child Support Enforcement Staff, 1980.

10. Wholey, *Evaluation and Effective Public Management,* p. 191.

11. See Jack Katz, *Report on the NIMH Community Support Program (CSP)* (Rockville, Md.: U.S. Department of Health and Human Services, Alcohol, Drug Abuse, and Mental Health Administration, December 1981). See also U.S. Congress, House, Committee on Appropriations, *Department of Labor, Health and Human Services, Education, and Related Agencies Appropriations for 1984, Part 3: Health.* Hearings: 98th Congress, 1st session, 1983, pp. 725–726.

12. See Joseph S. Wholey, *Zero-Base Budgeting and Program Evaluation* (Lexington, Mass.: D.C. Heath, 1978), pp. 23, 39.

Part II

Organizing Evaluation to Improve Organizational Performance

I n a government or nonprofit organization concerned with results, there is agreement on realistic, measurable objectives. Performance is assessed in terms of those objectives, information is used to improve the way the organization operates, and the value of the organization is communicated to stakeholders inside and outside the organization.

A central argument of this book is that evaluators can encourage an organization's transition to excellence by facilitating performance-oriented management. An important ingredient in the transition to excellence is the role the evaluation function plays in the overall organization.

The typical criticisms of evaluation—that decisionmakers' needs are not met, products are not timely, and the information produced is only marginally useful—are symptomatic of an evaluation function that is not well integrated with the rest of the organization. The three chapters in part II suggest how the evaluation function can be organized to help improve organizational performance.

The authors in part II agree that a concern for results means that evaluators have to be prepared to change the way they view their role in organizations. Evaluators who adopt a service-oriented stance and who view themselves as participants rather than as outsiders in the organization's work, appear to have a greater impact than evaluators who view themselves as objective, uninvolved social scientists. The role change needs also to be accompanied by a reconceptualization of the evaluation task.

Kenneth Bickel describes how a large nonprofit organization embarked on a multiyear plan to make evaluation more useful to decisionmakers. The organizational core of this strategy relied on participation, incrementalism, and flexibility.

Evaluators first worked with managers and other staff to identify the purposes and activities of a variety of programs, the resources used, the desired outcomes, and the problems encountered by the programs. This information was used to clarify the overall goals of the organization and then to determine the relationship between individual programs and the organization's mission. The evaluation contributed to subsequent program and resource allocation decisions that strengthened the performance of the organization.

The lessons that Bickel reports from this experience can benefit other organizations interested in bolstering their evaluation component. He suggests that evaluators should start modestly and build on their successes before attempting major evaluation-based organizational or program changes. Policymakers, administrators, and program staff should be involved in the entire evaluation process. Evaluation plans should be rigorous enough to clearly direct and integrate evaluation tasks, yet be flexible enough to permit evaluators to modify what they are doing as experience requires.

Steve Lillie and Mike Jewell note that different organizations require differently structured evaluation components. A complex public or nonprofit agency needs the capacity to respond to the short-term as well as the long-range information needs of decisionmakers. Sometimes these needs can be met by internal evaluation staff. A problem arises, however, when the organization needs specific information quickly about an issue that is outside the expertise of the staff. Organizations that rely on external consultants often run into problems of lengthy contracting processes and other start-up costs that prevent timely completion of work.

Lillie and Jewell describe how a complex government department organized its evaluation function to respond to the realities created by the needs of policymakers and the resources available for evaluation. The centerpiece of their approach is an innovative contracting process that gave the organization the freedom and flexibility to use skilled evaluators from the private sector who had demonstrated their ability to perform quality work within severe time constraints.

Martin Kotler writes from the perspective of a successful and effective private-sector evaluation contractor. His message is that evaluators need to separate the myths from the facts of what makes evaluation effective. Policymaking, he argues, is a messy process that proceeds by increment, trial and error, and bargaining. There are always more data that could be collected, additional refinements that could be made to the methodology, and other interesting issues the evaluators could explore.

But evaluators need to be able to quickly identify the skills, personnel, information, and work strategies that will help them to maximize what they can do—as opposed to what it would be interesting to do—within the resource and time constraints they face. Beyond that, evaluators need the ability to communicate complex issues to busy decisionmakers in a concise, defensible, and understandable manner.

2

Organizing Evaluation to Improve the Performance of a Nonprofit Organization

Kenneth L. Bickel

It has been nearly twenty years since Sills' excellent case analysis of the interplay between means and ends in a large nonprofit organization—the National Foundation for Infantile Paralysis (commonly called the March of Dimes).[1] The "means-ends" problem is most evident when the focus of board, management, or staff is concentrated on the proper administration of programs, policies, and procedures rather than on the achievement of specific end results. Nonprofit organizations seem particularly susceptible to this tendency. Without profitability or other bottom-line measures as major decision criteria (as in for-profit organizations) or legislative service mandates to provide continuity of purpose (as in government agencies), nonprofit organizations often exhibit a proliferation of programs and an absence of a unifying mission. The process of *addressing needs* may receive more attention than *meeting needs*.

A *results orientation* is a critical element in achieving high performance. Nonprofit organizations having multiple programs are vulnerable to becoming *process oriented*. This chapter illustrates how one large nonprofit organization adapted its evaluation efforts to address the "means-ends" problem and moved toward a results orientation. The organization is the Aid Association for Lutherans (AAL), a large fraternal benefit society with a national membership of about 1.3 million. Characteristic of fraternal benefit societies, AAL provides life insurance and other financial services which, in turn, provide funds for noncontractual fraternal benefit programs. AAL's fraternal department is responsible for developing and administering these fraternal benefit programs. One division in the department is responsible for program development and evaluation. Another division administers the programs.

AAL's benefit programs are intended to serve AAL member families, Lutheran organizations, and various community organizations in the areas of personal health, family strengthening, quality education, leadership development, and the stimulation of grass roots volunteer service. Approximately $17 million is devoted annually to these causes through about forty distinct service, educational, and charitable programs. The wide range of AAL benefit programs includes, for example, preretirement planning workshops, a smoking cessation program, college scholarships for meritorious students, and programs of small grants for community projects conducted by member volunteers in AAL's 6,100 branches.

AAL's Results-Oriented Management Initiative, a three-year project, has sought to bring about a clearer definition and focus to overarching benefit program results, and a concentration of human and financial resources on individual programs most able to demonstrate achievement of these results. As of spring 1985, indications are that the Results-Oriented Management Initiative will have important and far-reaching positive effects for the performance of an entire enterprise. This chapter describes elements of the initiative that are most generalizable to other organizations that have multiple programs with multiple purposes.

1. The Emergence of a Result Orientation (Spring 1982)

As recently as 1982, AAL's benefit program effort was essentially process-oriented. It was difficult to determine what results programs actually accomplished. Indeed, there was little agreement concerning the results that the forty benefit programs were intended to accomplish. In spite of a fairly hefty commitment to program evaluation in the fraternal department, management's most far-reaching decisions (for example, those pertaining to budget allocation) were made largely without information about actual program results. Evaluations were only conducted for the largest benefit programs and only at five-year intervals. There was little that resembled an *ongoing* results monitoring system. The evaluation process was relatively slow (up to eighteen months). Evaluation reports usually documented that programs lacked clear objectives, did not have target performance levels, and had one or more apparent design flaws.

A fairly widespread staff interest in having results-oriented programs had existed for some time. What was missing were some additional tools such as *evaluability assessment*. Evaluability assessment is a preevaluation step, described by Wholey[2], Schmidt, Scanlon, and Bell[3], and Rutman.[4] It calls for carefully conceived definitions of program objectives (at the input, process, and outcome levels) using measurable and plausible indicators. The evaluator has the role of helping policymakers and managers develop consensus concerning program expectations (often documented in a device called a program logic model). The evaluator attempts to bring management focus to potential problems that may hinder program performance. Evaluability assessment also attempts to help decisionmakers recognize and prioritize their information needs. A successful evaluability assessment increases the likelihood that evaluation will be useful.

Early in 1982, benefit program staff and evaluators became familiar with evaluability assessment through special two-day training events, conducted at AAL, using AAL programs as examples. The evaluation unit conducted several successful evaluations that employed this preevaluation step. The method caught on with program staff who formerly perceived evaluation with some amount of skepticism. For a year and a half, movement toward results-oriented management via evaluation occurred primarily at the individual program level.

Evaluability assessment and evaluation were used mostly for formative purposes. Managers intended to use evaluative information to improve individual programs, not to decide on their ultimate worth or whether they should be funded for another year. Evaluators became partners with program managers in improving programs. They were shedding the image of the "prophets of doom." (In chapter 5 of this book, Stephen Kapp illustrates this development in his description of a series of evaluations of an AAL scholarship program for high-achieving students.)

2. Launching the Results-Oriented Management Initiative (January–February 1983)

Management's Concerns

While optimism was rising that individual benefit programs were gradually becoming focused on results, there was no mechanism to ensure that the forty distinct programs taken together would achieve overarching benefit programs results. This greatly concerned the vice-president of the division responsible for program development and evaluation.

In addition, there was a growing feeling among some middle- and upper-level managers that there were simply too many individual programs and that resources were spread too thinly across the forty programs. Furthermore, with such a variety of programs directed at so many purposes, it was difficult for AAL to generate a consistent image with its chief constituencies. Reducing the number of programs seemed sensible, but there was no systematic and objective decision process for concentrating resources on the best performing programs by eliminating lower performing programs. The Results-Oriented Management Initiative was conceived as a means to address this and other concerns of upper management.

Summative Decision Criteria

At the direction of the development and evaluation division head, supported by his counterpart in program administration, policy development work began on three fronts. The key decisionmakers were interested in concentrating resources on programs that were clearly *most effective* at achieving intended results, *most appropriate* relative to AAL's chosen lines of interest, and *most efficient* in use of resources. To do this, each of these criteria needed to be operationalized.

What top management had in mind ultimately was a summative process to help them decide which of the forty benefit programs to keep and which to phase out. In some respects it paralleled a form of "zero-base budgeting," in which policymakers reallocate resources from lower priority to higher priority program activities.[5]

In making these summative program decisions, the three decision criteria were weighted roughly as follows: *program effectiveness*—65 percent of decision weight; *program appropriateness*—25 percent of decision weight; and *program efficiency*—10 percent of decision weight.

It was clear early on that program effectiveness was not the only criterion for deciding whether a program should be kept. AAL had been moving toward identifying key "lines" for program work. In a separate process not discussed here, AAL's lines of benefits came to be focused on five areas or values; (1) personal health, (2) family strengthening, (3) leadership development, (4) quality education, and (5) volunteer service. The ultimate decision to keep or to phase out a program would be influenced by whether it addressed these chosen causes. "Appropriateness" could serve as a "swing" factor where a program was only marginally effective.

Efficiency was the least developed decision criterion. Research staff developed several approaches to efficiency, including a type of cost-utility analysis adapted from the work of Pitz and McKillip[6] and Edwards and Newman.[7] Because of the newness of the concept and the complexities involved, efficiency criteria would affect the summative decision process to a fairly limited degree.

It was obvious that a fair assessment of forty programs would not be possible unless decisionmakers were quite explicit about intended outcomes and the relative priority among them. To accomplish this, a decision was made to conduct an evaluability assessment of AAL's entire fraternal benefit program effort. This will be described in section 3 of this chapter.

Purposes of the Initiative

The Results-Oriented Management Initiative was launched early in 1983 with the following purposes in mind:

1. *Identify and achieve general agreement on key results for AAL's whole benefitting effort through evaluability assessment.* Not only were these results to become highly visible for staff and AAL's constituencies, it was

intended that by identifying and elevating a unifying set of outcomes, staff would view the forty benefit programs together as a "single benefit program."

2. *Consolidate and focus the array of individual efforts.* In order to achieve greater focus, upper management was prepared to shift resources from weaker to stronger benefit programs; discontinuing the weakest programs if necessary and holding down further growth in others.

3. *Learn a common vocabulary and "rules of the game" for discussing program performance.* Much frustration was generated in discussions where decisionmakers had different definitions for basic concepts like "objectives," "goals," "processes," "indicators," "measures," and so on. The head of benefit development was interested to see "the rules of debate reach a higher form," as he was heard to say on several occasions.

4. *Enhance data-based decisionmaking skills of managers.* There was interest in encouraging development of decisionmaking styles that were more data-based and less dependent on anecdotal information.

5. *Increase program conceptualization and measurement skills among program staff.* The mid- and long-range plan for staff development in the two fraternal benefit divisions was to develop evaluation capacity in line units so program staff could play a larger role in ongoing monitoring of programs.

6. *Produce the basic elements of ongoing performance monitoring systems.* Related to the fifth purpose and consistent with the vision within the evaluation unit, it was hoped that significant portions of ongoing performance monitoring systems would be created through the Results-Oriented Management Initiative.

The remainder of this chapter is devoted to describing the three main phases of AAL's Results-Oriented Management Initiative: (1) the evaluability assessment of AAL's fraternal benefit program arm, (2) the rapid-feedback evaluations of individual programs, and (3) the management decision process that led to summative dispositions for each of the individual programs involved.

3. Evaluability Assessment of AAL's Benefit Program (March–August 1983)

AAL retained Wholey Associates to conduct the evaluability assessment of the fraternal benefit program. It involved examination of mission statements, budgets, and various policy and strategy documents of AAL. One- to two-hour interviews were conducted with members of AAL's board of directors, the president of AAL, upper management in the fraternal department, and managers of units responsible for program development and administration— about fifteen interviews in all. These interviews sought to gain board and management views on benefit program purposes, evidence of goal achievement levels, and special problems and challenges. Following the analysis of the documents and the interview data, a number of illustrative models of AAL's benefit program were produced for discussion purposes.

Commonly the most useful descriptive document is the program logic model. Figure 2–1 is the logic model for AAL's benefit program, which emerged from several iterations of managerial review. Wholey concluded that despite a few variations of opinion among key AAL people, "There is a high degree of consistency in the expectations of AAL policymakers and managers."[8] The four benefit program outcomes identified are shown in figure 2–1 as Objective 7.1 (Meeting real needs of AAL's four primary target groups); Objective 7.2 (Contributing to enhanced awareness and approval of AAL among various internal and external constituencies: members, branch officers, field staff, Lutheran church officials, legislators, regulators); Objective 6.0 (High participation rates among targeted recipients); and Objective 7.3 (Strengthen AAL's local branches).

The assessment also confirmed that there were three serious challenges to achieving improved performance: resources were spread too thinly over too many small programs; resource constraints were likely in the future; and information was lacking on program performance.[9] The report went on to describe the basic elements of a plan to improve program performance by addressing these problems. The plan became the basis for the Results-Oriented Management Initiative.

4. The Rapid-Feedback Evaluation Process
Assessment of Forty Individual Programs
(Fall 1983–Spring 1986)

Following the evaluability assessment, a three-year plan for completing evaluations of all forty programs was developed. The plan called for evaluations of eight to ten programs in each of four rounds. Each evaluation round was to be followed by a formal, one-day conference in which the head of the program development and research division would make a decision regarding the future status of the program. (This decision process is discussed in section 5.)

Interim evaluations of the process were conducted following each of the first two evaluation rounds. Since virtually all staff were involved in the initiative, the division heads recognized the value of assessing the initiative as it got underway. Not too surprisingly, the original plan looked somewhat

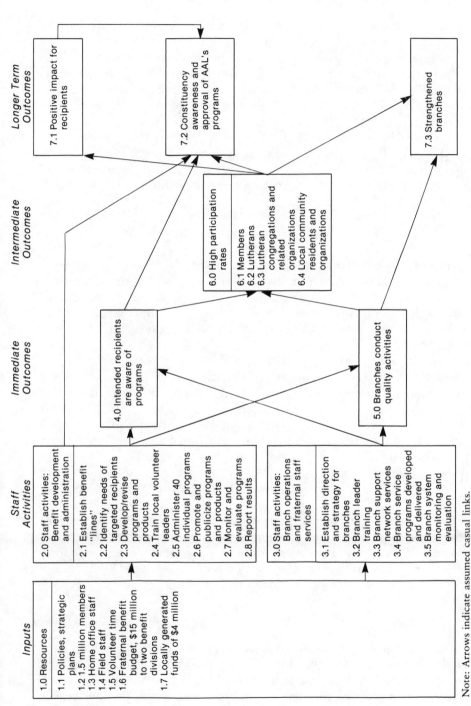

Figure 2–1. AAL's Fraternal Benefit Program—A Logic Model

Note: Arrows indicate assumed casual links.

better on paper than in application. The process evaluations led to a number of significant midstream process adjustments.

Evaluating forty programs in three years without significant new resources was only possible because evaluation designs were well focused, evaluation effort was broadly distributed across staff, and other projects were postponed. These evaluations incorporated many of the principles of what Wholey has called *rapid-feedback evaluation*.[10] Emphasis was placed on involving decisionmakers at several design development points; "mining" and synthesizing existing performance data; collecting the right information as opposed to a lot of information; using relatively small samples (N = 50) for original data collection; and completing each evaluation in as short a period as possible (four months or less).

The Evaluation Teams

Each program was evaluated by a team consisting of a program developer, a program evaluator, and a program administrator. Leadership of the team was provided by either a program developer or an evaluator. Teams were told to plan for thirty to thirty-five staff days per program, with team leaders expected to invest more time than the other two team participants. Time logs were kept by each participant.

Unit managers served as consultants to the team, helping in conceptualizing program outcomes, reviewing design ideas, and discussing preliminary findings on an informal basis. They were also responsible for redistributing the other routine work of team members.

Teams received additional support from other research and information units around the organization as necessary. Clerical staff became involved in various collection steps, including telephone interviewing and restructuring existing data sets.

Staff not trained in research were heavily involved. Although including somewhat less skilled and experienced staff in various research steps may seem cumbersome and inefficient, it was considered a necessity for the long-range success of this management initiative. Patton encourages including nonresearch staff by stressing that, "The personal [involvement] factor applies not just to utilization [of evaluation results], but to the whole evaluation process."[11] Wholey has made a similar argument.[12]

Technical Assistance

Technical assistance to evaluation teams and department management came in three forms. First, in September 1983, a day-long training and orientation event was held for all evaluation team members and managers. The agenda for this event included presentations on the definitions of the four benefit program outcomes identified in the evaluability assessment, orientation to the rapid-feedback evaluation process to be followed, explanations and discussion of roles and responsibilities, and practice sessions in developing measurable indicators for selected programs.

Second, the evaluation unit assisted teams in solving various data set puzzles and sampling problems. The evaluation unit also conducted and analyzed several surveys of constituent awareness of programs.

Third, for the first evaluation rounds, the charge was given to me to serve as consultant, facilitator, and technical resource person for evaluation teams and managers. I observed all evaluation presentations to managers and participated in management strategy discussions. In subsequent evaluation rounds, unit managers were expected to provide this support to teams.

Standard Evaluation Report Elements

To facilitate cross-program comparisons, evaluation teams followed a standard report outline that indicated the areas in which evaluation information was expected. After a few early adjustments, the twelve-part outline shown in table 2–1 became the standard. Parts IX, X, and XI form the core elements of the report, and proportionately more attention and coverage was devoted to these sections. Completed reports ranged from five to twelve pages, not including attachments. Appendices for additional tables, sample descriptions, and the like were used liberally, but the bodies of the reports were brief.

The Evaluation and Reporting Sequence

The evaluation and decision process was intentionally incremental so as to offer more opportunities for managers to adjust the plan or their expectations and to avoid doing more data collection and analysis than necessary.[13] The process involved the following sequence of events.

1. Program Evaluation Phase One. Over a four- to six-week period, teams occupied themselves with the tasks of evaluability assessment. Teams interviewed managers and reviewed program history, budgets, purpose statements, and administrative processes. They examined any existing program performance information pertaining to the four standard benefit results. Sometimes previous performance evaluation reports were available. Usually existing data sources were less focused, however, as in case files, annual reports, news articles, and correspondence.

Teams were encouraged to conduct small exploratory data collection efforts with a few "key informants" rather than samples of recipients. These

Table 2–1
Standard Reporting Outline for Evaluation Teams

I.   Program name and brief description
II.   Intended recipients
III. Constituencies (stakeholders) of interest
IV.   Conditions of eligibility
V.   Annual budget
VI.   Full-time equivalent administrative staff
VII. Vital program process information
      A.   Volumes, rates and trends
      B.   Implementation problems, challenges and assumptions
      C.   Record of program promotion and publicity
VIII. Availability of similar benefit or program from other sources
IX.   Conceptualization of outcomes (for four outcome areas)
X.   Indicators, findings, and sources for each outcome
XI.   Conclusions about overall program effectiveness
XII. Prospects for improving effectiveness

were done to gain a perspective of the feasibility and costs of pursuing certain types of performance information in a later phase.

The team would then set to work on completing the report outline through part X, indicating whatever information and conclusions were justified to that point. The most critical part of the work was conceptualizing outcomes and identifying alternative indicators (parts IX and X in the outline).

As an example, a team evaluating a college scholarship program might conceptualize the "positive impact" outcome in two ways: (1) enhancement of college choice for recipients, and (2) avoiding dropping out due to financial hardship. These concepts would then be operationalized in as many alternative ways as seemed reasonable. An indicator for the first "impact" concept might be the percent of recipients choosing the most prestigious (or expensive) of the three institutions they selected to receive their scores. The source of this data would be AAL's own records or a separate survey of recipients. A single program may have two, three, or four concepts for each outcome area, with ten to thirty separate potential indicators in total.

Since the four outcome areas were not considered equally important, teams were encouraged to allocate their efforts roughly commensurate with the priority weight of the outcome being considered. Thus, relatively more energy was applied to conceptualizing and measuring the "positive impact for recipients" (30 percent of the weight) than "branch strengthening results" (10 percent of the weight).

2. Management Review Session Number One. After managers had two or three days to review the team's report, a one-and-one-half hour meeting was held. In a formal hearing-like setting, the evaluation team discussed their initial findings and suggested the best measurement alternatives indicated in their report. Managers asked questions for clarification. The entire discussion served as input for the head of the program development and evaluation division, who was ultimately the decisionmaker. At the close of the meeting, he would request that the team pursue particular data collection alternatives and would indicate the indicators he most preferred for judging program performance based on existing data. Within seventy-two hours he would distribute a memorandum formalizing his instructions to the team for the next evaluation phase.

These management input sessions were critical to the credibility of the process and the eventual utilization of evaluation findings. Though this open style carried some risks for the top decisionmaker, it significantly reduced ambiguity around his decisions.

3. **Program Evaluation Phase Two.** Over the next eight to ten weeks, evaluation teams carried out data collection efforts in the areas requested. These efforts relied heavily upon carefully drawn, small-sample $(N = 50)$ surveys of program recipients, local branch officers, or other constituents. Although the sampling errors associated with samples of this size were relatively large (for example, plus or minus 12 percent with a 90 percent confidence level), managers were willing to make tentative conclusions about program performance. Again, the collection of data involved developers, researchers and administrators, and in some cases clerical staff. Collection of qualitative data was encouraged.

Drawing on the idea of service delivery assessment, used in the U.S. Department of Health and Human Services, a number of teams conducted site visits to learn how programs work in the field.[14] These visits were not expected to be representative from a sampling perspective, but were useful for suggesting hypotheses and appropriate methodologies.

Under the direction of the evaluation unit, special telephone surveys were conducted of members, Lutheran clergy, and branch officers to measure awareness and approval levels for all programs undergoing evaluation. This relieved each evaluation team of the cost and bother of conducting a series of two- or three-question telephone surveys. The "omnibus" surveys also facilitated standard cross-program comparisons.

Following the collection of original data, evaluation teams would return to the standard report outline illustrated in table 2–1. In preparing the final draft of the evaluation report, the team would review each part, correcting and updating elements based on any new information.

The "Conclusions" section (part XI of the outline) was also completed at this point. Teams were invited to suggest a summative effectiveness score for each of the four primary outcome areas on a ten-point scale. Scores could be multiplied by the priority weight of the outcome category, with the sum of these weighted scores serving as an indicator of overall program effectiveness. The scoring formula was not rigorously applied in reaching the final program disposition decision. Its primary value was that it encouraged teams and managers to articulate their rationale for how they moved from data through interpretation to conclusions.

Teams also added a relatively short statement (in part XII) suggesting administrative changes or evaluation activities that would improve program performance. These suggestions would be useful if it was finally decided that the program would be retained.

4. Management Review Session Number Two. This session was structured in a fashion similar to the first management review session. The evaluation team would highlight and clarify findings, discuss their conclusions, and offer recommendations for future outcome monitoring efforts. The management team members could then share their various interpretations, concerns, or issues, and share their opinions about the overall effectiveness of the program. All this served, once again, as counsel to the head of program development and evaluation who would make the final program status decision after all programs in that round had been evaluated.

Evaluation teams had officially completed their work at the end of this meeting, although several teams remained intact to complete other program improvement tasks, such as monitoring system development.

5. Summative Decision Conferences

After each wave of program evaluations, a day was set aside to announce formally and discuss the future status of that set of programs. All evaluation team members and managers were invited to attend.

Programs were given one of five classifications: (1) *"Promote"*—add significant resources at the earliest budgetary opportunity; (2) *"Promote but . . ."*—execute program improvement plan within the next two years, modest increases in resources should be allocated to the program in the meantime; (3) *"Revise"*—revise program elements considered problems for program effectiveness, appropriateness, or efficiency over the next one to three years, add no new resources until revision is complete, then reconsider for category status "1" or "2"; (4) *Phase out but . . ."*—execute a program phase-out plan within the next one to three years, but plans should include ideas for future programming to capture some recognized quality of the program; divert resources to status "1" or "2" programs as soon as possible; and (5) *"Phase Out"*—phase out the program within 9 months to 2 years; divert resources to status "1" or "2" programs as soon as possible. Responsibility for

Table 2–2
Example of a Program Decision Report

Results-Oriented Management Initiative *Decision Report*

I.   *Fraternal Benefit Program:* All-College Scholarship Program (ACSP)

II. *Summary of Findings:*

A.   Performance—According to the average rating of all raters, this program performed in the upper quartile of the 16 programs (that is, 5.91 in a range from 2.62 to 6.83) . . . The raters were quite consistent in their assigned values—ranging from 5.80 to 6.05 . . . The highest rating was consistently given to Constituency Approval while the lowest rating was given to the Branch Strenghtening outcome . . . Although its ratings were relatively high, all raters recommended a revision of the program on the basis of its outcome performance.

B.   Appropriateness—This benefit program received a perfect rating regarding goodness-of-fit with the proposed lines-of-benefits.

C.   Cost Analysis—This program received the lowest cost / utility score of the benefit programs in its category . . . Its administrative cost relative to benefit cost ratio places it in the top third (5th) in cost of administration.

III. *Decision:* Revise

IV. *Rationale:* This is one of AAL's most widely known and approved noninsurance benefit programs. We need to continue it; but, we should not promote it aggressively without addressing certain issues. For instance, we need to review the costs associated with administering the program. Can it be reduced? We also need to review the size and / or variability guidelines of the award, especially now that the program has been more clearly designated primarily as a recognition program and, secondarily, a financial burden reduction program. It is because of these issues and the need for our guidelines to be congruent with these purposes that the revised classification has been selected.

V.   *Areas of Improvement:* Impact (that is, recognition) appears to be the major outcome area that needs to be improved. The cost of administering the program should be studied in relationship to the consideration of new granting procedures (for example, level grants) which would honor the purpose (that is, recognition) of the program. It becomes rather clear that this program's clear shift to a recognition focus leaves our portfolio of benefits rather vacant with regards to *helping* members with career planning and meeting their real educational needs.

carrying out these decisions rested with line management. The decision would be captured in a one-page report for each program. An example is shown in table 2–2.

This conference was another example of decisionmaking conducted "in the open." After the initial announcement of decisions, the remainder of the conference was devoted to the following: (1) Staff were given the opportunity to ask for clarification, to question, and to debate the decisions. They could recommend altering decisions. (The head of benefit development amended three of eighteen decisions based on this input.) (2) Conference participants worked in groups to generate a prioritized list of ideas for improving their retained programs. (3) Closing presentations were made by the two division heads introducing their ideas for how each division would proceed in further developing results-oriented management.

6. Conclusions: An Assessment of the Initiative to Date

Recalling the purposes of the initiative discussed above, I would like to discuss some of our learnings and conclusions in six areas: (1) development of a "single benefit program" view, (2) program consolidation and focusing of efforts, (3) adequacy of the decision model, (4) capacity for ongoing program monitoring, (5) staff development, and (6) staff morale and motivation. These conclusions are based on data from two formal surveys of staff, an examination of program classification memos, review of time logs of evaluation teams and interviews with top management.

Development of a "Single Benefit Program" View

The Results-Oriented Management Initiative has made considerable progress in helping AAL staff identify and value a limited set of overarching benefit program outcomes. Remaining disagreements over purposes generally pertain to matters of outcome emphasis and measurability.

Concentration on these results has especially affected the development of new programs. Program staff have now experienced firsthand the frustration of evaluating programs with "evaluability" problems. New programs are being designed with systematically conceptualized outcome, many accompanied by performance indicators and target levels. Interdivision communication about outcomes has been affected as well. One program developer has noted, "Since administrators are using the same language, communication is easier."

Program Consolidation and Focusing of Effort

Five of eighteen programs evaluated to date are to be phased out. However, they amount to only $294,000 annually (about 3 percent) of the $10.0 million associated with the eighteen programs, and about 8 percent (one full-time equivalent staff person) of the thirteen full-time staff equivalent involved with all eighteen. Apparently, it is much easier to discontinue small programs.

The head of benefit development and evaluation has expressed more optimism about the results. He based his optimism on the belief that the cumulative effect of future budget and staff resource allocations following these phase-out decisions will bring the desired consolidation and focusing result *over time*. An anticipated shortfall in planned resource growth for

1985 and possibly 1986 may serve to legitimize more extensive consolidation and focusing of resources in remaining evaluation rounds.

Adequacy of the Decision Model

The adequacy of the three summative decision criteria—program effectiveness, appropriateness relative to AAL's chosen benefit outlines, and efficiency—was assessed. Staff felt most positively about how the program effectiveness criteria were defined and used. It was fairly clear through observation and reading the decision memos that the relative weights originally assigned to the outcomes were not rigorously adhered to. Furthermore, there was little to indicate that individual staff felt they should be adhered to rigorously.

Staff were somewhat less positive about how the "appropriateness" and "efficiency" criteria were defined and applied in the process. Efficiency (or cost-effectivenss) proved to be an especially difficult dimension to address systematically. With four diverse intended result areas (each with diverse sets of indicators), it was difficult to estimate the efficiency of one program, not to mention the difficulty of comparisons across programs. The evaluation staff's attempt to address this through cost-utility analysis seemed right, but it produced few converts. Efficiency will be a difficult concept to measure for the multiple-program, multiple-outcome organization.

Capacity for Ongoing Program Monitoring

Much has been achieved on this outcome at the individual program level. The process of carrying out rapid-feedback evaluations produced a range of measurement experiences that can be readily repeated or extrapolated for ongoing monitoring systems. The cost and logistics for such systems are also better understood. High priorities for the evaluation unit will be providing training activities and disseminating support materials pertaining to more technical aspects of monitoring system development.[15]

Top management also wishes to monitor results of the overall benefit effort. Progress has been made in developing standard indicators for the "Awareness and approval" and for "Participation" outcomes. The diversity across individual programs creates a greater challenge as far as deriving standard indicators for "Positive impact for recipients" and "Branch strengthening."

Staff Development

The most apparent gains in staff development were perceived by participants to have occurred in the areas of: (1) increased program conceptualization skills (able to think in terms of program results) and (2) technical evaluation skill development among team members. Almost half of the staff responding to the second survey felt "develop[ing] in some of the skill areas of interest to [them]" had contributed to their personal feeling about the overall worth of the effort.

In contrast, participants were somewhat less convinced that similar achievement had occurred in the area of "enhanced data-based decision skills among managers." It is more difficult for managers to demonstrate this capacity, since data-based decision making is fairly dependent on the individual's decision models, which are usually hidden from view. The purpose of the open forum elements of the initiative were to help managers make their models explicit.

Staff Morale and Motivation

Findings in this area suggest staff members are interested in seeing the Initiative through to its conclusion. Given a five-point scale asking "Overall, to what extent would you consider your *personal* involvement 'worth it' or 'not worth it'?" Sixty-six percent gave scores of "5" or "4" on the "worth it" end of the scale.

The factor most frequently mentioned (74 percent of respondents) as contributing to this overall assessment was that, "I feel the effort will eventually pay off for the department in an important way." Forty-six percent also checked this statement as the primary factor influencing their assessment, by far the most frequently cited item.

The effort was considered difficult and sometimes painful work for many participants. Roughly one-third felt that it was not appropriately built into work plans and/or was disruptive to other regular, "higher priority" work objectives. (This was a more noticeable problem in the administration division.) One staff member called the initiative "a necessary evil." However, a large majority felt the process should be applied to all remaining benefit programs. A minority called for decreasing the overall investment substantially. An analysis of the correlation of this suggestion (to reduce the effort) produced some very interesting findings. Respondents who felt that the effort should be cut back were noticeably: (1) *more* likely to have also indicated the effort was "disruptive to my regular, higher priority work objectives," (2) *less* likely to have indicated feeling "recognized for my efforts from others," (3) *less* likely to have indicated that they "enjoyed many pieces of the work," and (4) *less* likely to have indicated that they "had a lot of influence over developments and decisions along the way."

These latter findings are significant. They underscore the significance of carefully designed incentives and recognition for an initiative of these proportions. The development of incentives and rewards to encourage outcome-oriented thinking and behavior has been slow in coming. There are many possible ways to manage or influence the distribution of symbolic, tangible, and intangible rewards for individual and group effort. Given the high commitment of staff overall, one of the strongest incentives may prove to be simply carrying out the various program decisions made in the decision conferences, thereby showing their effort has had results.

The long-range goal of this initiative is that a results orientation become thoroughly ingrained into the culture of AAL's benefit program arm. The head of the development and evaluation division recently commented that, "My concern is that program developers and program administrators start asking the right questions to improve program performance, not just to supply information for some higher level (within the organization)." The initiative was a "special" project; something out of the ordinary. What we have hoped to achieve is a sufficient understanding and interest in results-oriented management so that these principles will find their way into many aspects of day-to-day operations. This will continue to be an enormous challenge and will require perseverance and long-term commitment on the part of management. Two years into the plan, development of results-oriented management in this large nonprofit organization still seems to be an achieveable goal.

Notes

1. David L. Sills, *The Volunteers: Means and Ends in a National Organization* (Glencoe, Ill.: The Free Press, 1957).

2. Joseph S. Wholey, *Evaluation: Promise and Performance* (Washington, D.C.: The Urban Institute, 1979). Also see Joseph S. Wholey, *Evaluation and Effective Public Management* (Boston: Little, Brown, 1983).

3. Richard E. Schmidt, John W. Scanlon, and James B. Bell, *Evaluability Assessment: Making Public Program Work Better* (Rockville, Md.: U.S. Department of Health, Education and Welfare, Project Share, Human Services Monograph No. 14, 1979).

4. Leonard Rutman, *Planning Useful Evaluations: Evaluability Assessment,* vol. 96, Sage Library of Social Research (Beverly Hills, Calif.: Sage, 1980).

5. Joseph S. Wholey, *Zero-Base Budgeting and Program Evaluation* (Lexington, Mass.: Lexington Books: D.C. Heath, 1978).

6. Gorden F. Pitz and Jack McKillip, *Decision Analysis for Program Evaluators* (Beverly Hills, Calif.: Sage, 1984).

7. Ward Edwards and J. Robert Newman, "Multiattribute Evaluation," Sage University Papers on Quantitative Applications in the Social Sciences, series no. 07–026 (Beverly Hills, Calif.: Sage, 1982).

8. Joseph S. Wholey, "A Results-Oriented Approach to Managing AAL's Noninsurance Benefit Programs," Report prepared for Aid Association for Lutherans (Arlington, Va.: Wholey Associates, 1983), p. III–2.

9. Ibid., p. IV–1.

10. Wholey, *Evaluation: Promise and Performance,* pp. 85–115.; and Wholey, *Evaluation and Effective Public Management,* pp. 118–136.

11. Michael Quinn Patton, *Utilization-Focused Evaluation* (Beverly Hills, Calif.: Sage, 1978), p. 68.

12. Wholey, *Evaluation: Promise and Performance,* 1979, p. 39.

13. Ibid., pp. 12–15.

14. See Michael Hendricks, "Service Delivery Assessment: Qualitative Evaluation at the Cabinet Level" in N.L. Smith, (Ed.), *Federal Efforts to Develop New Evaluation Methods, New Directions for Program Evaluation,* no. 12 (San Francisco: Jossey-Bass, 1981), pp. 5–24.

15. See, for example, Rhona Millar and Annie Millar, (Eds.), *Developing Client Outcome Monitoring Systems: A Guide for State and Local Social Services Agencies* (Washington, D.C.: The Urban Institute, 1981).

3
Organizing Evaluation in a Government Agency

Steve Lillie
Mike Jewell

T his chapter describes attempts in the U.S. Department of Health and Human Services (HHS) to make evaluation more supportive of efforts by policymakers and program managers to improve organizational performance. It focuses on the activities of the Division of Evaluation within the Office of the Assistant Secretary for Planning and Evaluation (ASPE). The division's responsibilities include oversight of evaluation activities throughout the department, as well as the execution of short-term evaluation studies responsive to the information needs of policymakers.

In section 1 of the chapter, key elements of a responsive evaluation program are described, and organizational approaches used by several components of the department are discussed. In section 2, the contracting mechanism used by the Division of Evaluation, ASPE for its short-term evaluations is described.

1. Organizing Evaluation for Responsiveness

Origins of the Approaches Used in HHS

Over the past several years, in recognition of the need to make evaluation more relevant and responsive to managers and policymakers, the Assistant Secretary for Planning and Evaluation has encouraged innovative approaches. Authority to approve projects anticipated to cost less than $135,000 has been delegated to the operating divisions of the department, and agencies have been urged to focus their evaluation efforts on serving the needs of program managers and policymakers at their own levels.[1] As a result of these actions, several units of the department have developed new approaches to evaluation. Some of these approaches are described later in this chapter.

Interaction: The Key to Responsiveness

Brush asserts that those carrying out short-term evaluations must involve policymakers in the planning, execution, and dissemination stages of studies.[2] She identifies the points at which the input of the study client is particularly important.

> At the outset, study questions must be established in accordance with client information needs.
>
> In the study design and execution, data collection must be in line with constraints established by policymakers, including time and resource limitations.
>
> At the conclusion of the study, findings must be presented in accessible form, and results must be translated into information to support policy and program decisions.

The need for client input requires a continuing interaction with the policymaker over the course of the study. In the studies conducted by ASPE, this interaction takes the form of periodic briefings of the policymaker during the study to obtain assurance that the study is on track and to redirect it as needed. Additional direction for the study is achieved through the establishment of a work group of program, policy, and evaluation staff, which meets to review study progress and acts as a surrogate for the policymaker between briefings.

A New Mode of Operation for Evaluation Offices

In order to serve policymakers successfully, the evaluation office must reorient itself, shifting from an analytic focus to an orientation in which client needs take precedence. This new mode of operation requires several changes in the organization of the evaluation office. Evaluators' perceptions of their role in the organization must change from "objective reporter/analyst" to "supportive problem solver." Although a solid background in evaluation techniques is needed, a new emphasis on communication skills—oral, written, and visual—arises. Effective working relationships with program staff and policymakers must be established and reinforced. Finally, a capacity to respond quickly to information needs must be established.

The Role of the Evaluator

Barkdoll stresses the importance of avoiding the role of program critic, and suggests that cooperation, openness, and timeliness are essential to achieving optimum results.[3] Shared responsibility for conducting the evaluation; continual sharing of findings, insights, and conclusions with program staff; and strict adherence to a well-defined schedule for the evaluation study all contribute to establishing and maintaining a supportive role for the evaluator.

Skills Needed for Effective Short-Term Evaluation. Resourcefulness may be the most important "skill" required of those who carry out short-term policy evaluations. The resourceful evaluator will have several traits, including the ability to acquire adequate program knowledge rapidly at the outset of a study, the ability to conceptualize program issues and translate them into study questions, the possession of analytic resources and an understanding of their applicability in a given situation, and skills in verbal and visual communications.

Establishing Effective Working Relationships. The development of a mutually supportive relationship with the program manager and staff requires a commitment of time and energy on the part of the evaluator. Some of the techniques used to establish such a relationship include: involving the program manager and staff in the initial stages of the study (defining issues, developing the approach, and so on); using program staff as part of the study team; and informing the program manager about progress as the study evolves and findings are developed. The role assumed by the evaluator, as described above, can contribute to the effectiveness of the relationship.

Developing a Quick-Response Capability. The last essential requirement for developing a capacity for short-term policy evaluation is perhaps the most difficult because the shift to shorter, smaller projects may place strains on the systems in place for planning, procurement, and study management.

The capacity for carrying out short-term studies may be developed in-house or may be a contracted capacity. Both approaches are used in HHS, as illustrated below.

An in-house capability offers the advantage that the programmatic expertise developed by evaluators becomes an asset of the organization. In addition, the close working relationships with program and policy staffs required for short-term evaluations may be easier to establish when in-house studies are the rule.

On the other hand, contracting for short-term evaluations avoids the pitfall of building a staff that may not be needed in the future, and provides greater flexibility in acquiring the requisite skills for specific projects. In the development of a contracted capacity for short-term evaluation, it is vital for the evaluation office to work closely with the procurement authority to explore the alternatives (task order contracts, basic ordering agreements, purchase orders, and so on) and to establish the ground rules for procurements.

Understandably, procurement offices often are uneasy about the appropriateness of innovative contracting mechanisms, and the evaluator must explore patiently how atypical program evaluation requirements may be met through atypical contracting mechanisms. Frank discussions of how competitive procurement can be assured under the new mechanism, desired timetables for award of projects, and likely changes in the workload of the procurement office may be fruitful in implementing a contracted capacity for short-term evaluation.

Short-Term Evaluation Approaches Used in HHS

The short-term evaluation approaches of several units of HHS are described below. The organizational levels of these units are illustrated in figure 3–1.

Division of Evaluation, Office of the Assistant Secretary for Planning and Evaluation (ASPE)

Level. Department staff.

Purpose of Evaluation. To identify and fulfill policymakers' information needs.

Mechanism for Short-Term Studies. Task order contract in four program areas, one contractor for each area, maximum eight months, $135,000.

Characteristics. Policy focus, intensive management of contracted studies.

Studies are selected in response to policymaker needs and are designed in consultation with policymakers and program staff.

Studies are executed by contractors, with a high level of in-house staff involvement in monitoring (via a work group of policy and program staff).

Briefings are routinely provided to policymakers in study progress, and study approaches are adjusted as necessary to assure that the client's questions are addressed.

Office of Health Planning and Evaluation, Office of the Assistant Secretary for Health (OHPE)

Level. Operating division.

Purpose of Evaluation. To provide a quick-turnaround evaluation mechanism for agencies in the Public Health Service (PHS).

Mechanism for Short-Term Studies. Task order contracts in technical areas, several contractors in each area, maximum eighteen months, $150,000.

Characteristics. Contractual mechanism for evaluation studies, available for use by PHS agencies.

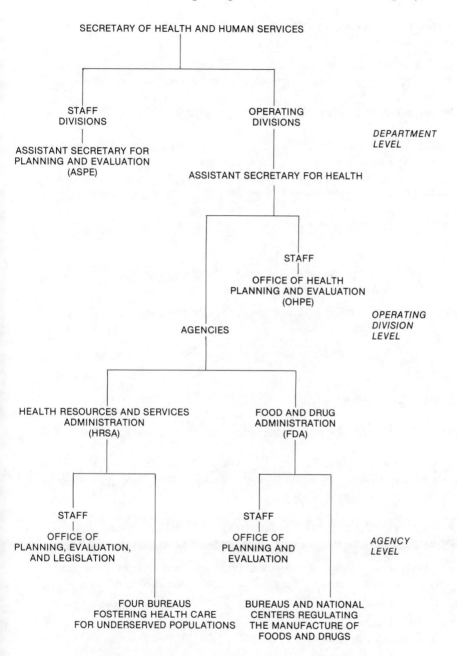

Figure 3–1. Organizational Levels in the Department of Health and Human Services

Studies are proposed by agencies for execution under the OHPE task order mechanism.

Studies are executed by contractors, with management by the agencies proposing the study. OHPE provides quality control for studies.

Health Resources and Services Administration (HRSA)
Level. Agency.
Purpose of Evaluation. To identify programmatic information needs and to design and contract for studies to meet the needs.
Mechanism for Short-Term Studies. Basic ordering agreements in technical areas, several contractors compete for award of each task order, maximum twelve months, $100,000.
Characteristics. Centralized focus, contracted studies, decentralized management of studies.

Each bureau within the agency has its own evaluation component and provides project officers for the contracted studies.

The agency evaluation office provides quality control, technical assistance, and support for studies.

Bureau or division directors are the primary clients for most evaluation studies.

Food and Drug Administration (FDA)
Level. Agency.
Purpose of Evaluation. To support and facilitate improved management and decision making.
Mechanism for Short-Term Studies. In-house staff of evaluators.
Characteristics. Centralized evaluators, in-house studies, strong working relationships with program managers.

Evaluators work closely with program staff to schedule, define, and execute studies, and to present findings to policymakers.

The evaluation process emphasizes cooperation between evaluators and program staff, openness of the study process, and timeliness.

*Distinguishing Characteristics of
Short-Term Policy Evaluation*

The approach employed at the department level differs from the other contractual mechanisms for short-term evaluation used in HHS in that a smaller "stable" of contractors is employed (four as opposed to fifteen to twenty).

The short-term policy evaluation tends to serve the information needs of one or perhaps two high level policymakers, although it sometimes fulfills technical programmatic information needs or provides the basis for improvements in program management. Although many contractors with excellent technical capabilities are available, use of the mechanism is selective, thus a smaller number of contractors is required. Because of the limited use of contractors, it is possible for ASPE to control the quality of briefings more easily. In 1983 and 1984, about 13 percent of ASPE's evaluation funds were spent through task order contracts.

Another distinguishing characteristic of short-term policy evaluation is its centralized nature. The other mechanisms tend to rely more heavily on program staff to manage or perform evaluations. In the policy evaluations managed by ASPE, program staffs are involved in design, execution, and dissemination through participation on the work group and in briefings, but responsibility for the study is not delegated to them.

2. The Task Order Contract: A Mechanism for Performing Short-Term Evaluations

The task order mechanism developed in the Office of the Assistant Secretary for Planning and Evaluation, HHS, has been used over the past several years to provide evaluative information to policymakers on departmental programs. This part of the chapter describes the task order contract generically and provides details on the characteristics of the mechanism used in ASPE.

Definition

The task order form of contract is not defined by statute or procurement regulations, but is derived from a number of requirements-type contracts which have been sanctioned by statute or regulation. Thus it is a "mix and match" of other mechanisms such as basic ordering agreements, time and materials contracts, and indefinite quantity contracts. The purpose of the task order contract is to provide for quick turnaround on predictable requirements for information from across a wide but definable set of programs and policy issues. Just as a time and materials contract might allow for periodic purchase of parts or munitions without competition for every order, the task order contract buys information, evaluation, or analysis of programs that are listed in the contract. Control over costs is provided by the initial competition as well as by periodic recompetition requirements. Critics argue that each task should be competed separately to achieve the maximum competition practicable. Advocates counter that additional competition not only defeats the quick turnaround purpose, but ultimately costs the government more in staff time, and needlessly so, since most study requirements have already been addressed in the initial competition for the overall contract.

The task order contract is an award for the purchase of an amount of effort, which may or may not be specified, limited by a ceiling for a specified period of time. In short, it is a level of effort, term-type contract. The mechanism established in ASPE consists of four competitively awarded contracts with a ceiling of $600,000 per contract and a limit of $135,000 on each study. The contracts are for twelve months each and contain two one-year options.

Structure of the ASPE Task Order Contract

Task order contracts have been used in ASPE since 1979. During this period, the vehicle has been used to test new evaluation techniques, to design large-scale evaluations of department programs, to conduct analyses of policy issues, and to provide quick turnaround responses to information requests from policymakers. These contracts have allowed ASPE to address urgent information needs in such areas as diagnostic related groups, welfare dependency, and health services for Indians.

Typically, four task order contracts covering major program areas in the department have been used: (1) Public Health Service programs (2) Human Development Service programs (3) Social Security and Health Care Financing Administration programs and (4) a "cross-cutting" contract for topics relating to multiple programs. The current set of contracts allows for three types of studies to be performed: performance assessments, evaluation designs, and evaluability assessments. These studies usually take four to eight months, with eight months being the maximum time allowed for a study. Historically, ASPE has spent between $1 million and $2 million a year for up to twenty short-term studies. In fiscal years 1983 and 1984, ASPE conducted twenty-three studies which cost about $2.3 million. Overall, evaluation expenditures in those two years in ASPE were $19.9 million.

The overall task order contracts are signed without an obligation of funds. Individual tasks are negotiated with budgets set on a fixed price basis, and it is these "delivery orders" that obligate funds.

Administration

Staff of the Division of Evaluation in ASPE serve as project officers for the contracts. "Delivery order officers" are selected to manage individual studies, and are usually from the relevant substantive policy office within ASPE. A staff member from the agency where the program being studied resides will often serve as a codelivery order officer.

Task order studies involve frequent interaction of staff from various departmental units through work group meetings. Frequent briefings are provided for policymakers to solicit their input. Study results and informational products are often developed iteratively; thus, critical information may be provided to the policymaker several weeks before the final report is submitted.

As a rule, management of individual studies is quite intensive. In addition to frequent briefings and work group meetings, telephone calls and additional meetings of substantive government staff with the contractor are common. These contacts provide opportunities for the contractor to test draft products and to obtain study direction in a less formal way than in fullscale briefings and meetings.

This style of contract management has evolved because of several factors. More extensive policy-level interest in a study naturally generates additional staff involvement to assure responsive and timely products. In addition, the somewhat controversial nature of the contract mechanism has provided extra incentive for ASPE to demonstrate that this "shortcut" procurement method provides good results. Finally, the time frames required for these studies necessitate careful management and frequent progress checks to meet delivery dates.

Start-up time for an individual task is between ten and forty-five days from the time the procurement office receives a delivery order package, depending on the urgency of the requirement.

Issues

From the evaluator's perspective, there are two significant issues regarding the use of task order contracts:

1. Does this method of contracting succeed in serving the "quick turn-around" information needs of policymakers seeking to improve program performance?
2. Will continued use of this controversial method of procurement be permitted?

The answer to the first question is yes. Strictly from a procurement perspective, the lead time required to launch a delivery order is dramatically shorter than with other procurement approaches. The procurement office has frequently done better than the agreed-upon award time of ten days minimum, forty-five days maximum. Many high-priority delivery orders have been awarded in five to ten working days. In exceptional circumstances, some tasks have been awarded in two or three days. By comparison, a 1982 study of procurement lead times for various contract mechanisms used in HHS found the following average processing times:

Task Order Contracts	30 days
Basic Ordering Agreements	90 days
Normal Negotiated Procurements	120 days

At least one agency in HHS has done much better than the average ninety-day processing time for basic ordering agreements, but it appears that about thirty days' lead time is the best that can be achieved with that mechanism, and then only for priority cases.

While the issue of procurement lead time is important, equally significant is that ASPE's experience appears to demonstrate that these studies succeed in meeting client needs in almost every case.

On the issue of the future use of the task order contract, the situation is less clear. Each time the ASPE task order contracts have been opened for new competition, an internal debate regarding the legality, appropriateness, and need for the task order contracts has taken place. These discussions have confirmed that the mechanism is legal and that it needs to be carefully structured and closely managed. Any uneasiness about the nontraditional nature of the mechanism has been outweighed by the need for a quick turnaround vehicle.

Various forms of the task order contract are in use in other federal agencies, notably in the Agency for International Development, the Department of Defense, and the Department of Housing and Urban Development. It seems likely that task order contracts will become more common as an evaluation vehicle in the years to come.

Conclusion

The experience in HHS over the past several years has been that short-term evaluation studies can provide *useful* and *timely* information to those who desire to improve organizational performance.

Usefulness is achieved by involving clients in the design and conduct of studies. Timeliness is achieved through development of an appropriate mechanism for executing studies and through rigorous adherence to a delivery schedule.

Notes

1. *Fiscal Year 1985 Evaluation Guidance* (Washington, D.C.: U.S. Department of Health and Human Services, April 1984).

2. Lorelei R. Brush, *The Short-Term Policy Evaluation: A Responsive Evaluation Strategy in a Political Context* (Washington, D.C.: Aurora Associates, 1983), pp. 5–6.

3. Gerald L. Barkdoll, "Downside Risk to Program Evaluation," *The Bureaucrat* (Summer 1983):16–18.

4
Conducting Short-Term Policy Evaluation Studies in the Real World

Martin Kotler

D issatisfaction has grown with evalution system efforts and results in federal departments.[1] A general consensus has emerged that the evaluation system displayed major shortcomings in achieving its goals of high-quality studies that provide useful and timely information for policymakers and program managers. This prevailing sentiment emanated from several studies including an assessment completed by Macro Systems in 1982. Overall perceived inadequacies focused upon the perception that policymaker information needs were not adequately met, that evaluation products were not timely, that evaluation information was not always useful, and that only limited audiences for evaluation information were being served.

The policy assessment, by its very nature, must often be completed within a compressed time period and under strict deadlines because congressional hearings are scheduled for a specific date or for other reasons, such as an Office of Management and Budget (OMB) deadline. In a recent assignment for the Office of the Assistant Secretary for Planning and Evaluation, Department of Health and Human Services (HHS), Macro Systems had policy assessment findings ready for distribution within fifteen weeks of the issuance of the evaluation contract. Rapid completion calls for demonstrated staff experience and enthusiasm and proven technical and managerial competency—adeptness at identifying and fielding a seasoned, experienced, and knowledgeable team with the utmost speed and beginning a study with limited opportunity for a review of available literature, underlying issues, relevant politics, availability of data, and other salient information. Prior knowledge of programs, departmental goals, and major issues, as well as a keen analytic capability on the part of the staff, coupled with sophisticated senior management, are required.

Consequently, as our firm became more heavily involved in conducting short-term policy-oriented studies, we reorganized our approach and our structure to meet decisionmaker needs. Rather than employ an academic approach emphasizing methodological purity, we used our organization structure and staff in a flexible manner to meet the demands of each assignment. We focused upon the potential utilization of evaluation information by framing study questions to meet policymaker needs and by rigorously excising peripheral issues.

Staff saw that evaluation results were increasingly used in policy debates, and their interest and enthusiasm increased. As multiple and concurrent assignments were undertaken, staff shared techniques, findings, and effective practices in a self-generating dissemination effort that improved each assignment.

Conducting Short-Term Policy Evaluations

In the conduct of short-term policy assessments, the contractor frequently finds himself in a maelstrom of a multiclient setting where sharply diverse and conflicting positions have been established, where data are difficult to obtain and to validate, where the driving criteria for proposed changes may be hidden or not articulated, and where time constraints preclude comprehensive data collection, elaborate analyses, and the luxury of contemplative reflection. Many powerful agencies and individuals feel threatened by the potential of an expanded departmental role and resist any attempt—including the assessment itself—that might reduce their independence. Fear of loss of independence, coupled with possible budget reductions, activate defensiveness and hostility and may create attempts to suborn, to control, or to redirect a study.

This hostility may translate into highly conflicting views of the issues to be studied and may include substantial disagreement on directions for a study. In this event, contractor staff, in conjunction with the Federal Work Group, must carefully delineate the opposing views to define with some level of clarity the nature and dimensions of the conflicting approaches. Once the divergence is specified, several steps may occur:

Develop succinct graphic models characterizing the conflicting views, and spell out the ramifications and implications of alternate perceptions of the areas in disagreement.

Interview each policymaker or manager and patiently walk him or her through each variant model to ascertain what is acceptable, what is anathema, and what common ground is shared.

Synthesize the results and, if the conflict is deemed bridgeable, attempt to consolidate views into a more harmonious approach or reach consensus.

Should these approaches fail because the divergence is too great, the hostility too pronounced, the animosity too heated, or the basic philosophies too polarized, the competing approaches will be brought to higher levels of resolution. In terms of conflicting views on the direction of the assessment, the client is the final arbiter. Where conflicts of this nature arise, and they have in the past, the conflicting views of study direction are carefully noted and documented, and these views, with Federal Work Group recommendations, are discussed with senior officials for resolution.

Small Samples

A common issue in policy assessments is small sample sizes and limited data analyses due to time and budget constraints. Clearly, a small sample, for example, eight sites when the universe may by fifty or one hundred, cannot be used in terms of statistical validity. However, many of the policy studies focus on qualitative issues. A key to solving or reducing this problem is to use the significant amount of existing data available on the sites that will not be visited: agency annual reports, planning forecasts, lists of grant guidances and grants/contracts issued.

The proper use of small sample sizes in short-term evaluations depends upon several factors, including the size of the population from which the sample is drawn, the nature of the sample, the method of selection, the extent and quality of available information about it and, just as important, the nature of the policy questions addressed.

In the case of very small samples, formal data reduction methods are usually not required. Frequently, these small samples are not randomly selected and, thus, do not meet the assumptions underlying traditional statistical inference techniques. Appropriate methods to use include ranking or sorting of the observations, arraying the information in tables, clustering, plotting, and other qualitative analysis methods. The inclusion or exclusion of information, the identification of outliers, and related inferential techniques often are done in a judgmental manner for these samples.

Larger samples frequently lend themselves to simple data analysis techniques including medians, averages, and similar analyses. However, even in these instances, Macro Systems often uses the qualitative techniques of ranking, arraying in tables, plotting, and graphing to display the total information set in structured ways. Our experience has been that drawing policy inferences from these very small sample sizes is not critically dependent upon precise estimates of central tendency, ranges, or structural relationships. Rather, inferences are more frequently drawn based on knowledge of the policy issue and information about the sample observations, which permit the drawing of informed judgments.

Working with Decisionmakers

Not every program manager or policymaker is acquainted with short-term assessment purposes, methodologies, or activities. As a result, it can be anticipated that some level of apprehension or defensiveness may be encountered. Some have unrealistic expectations of the scope, intent, and purposes of a proposed study. Sometimes it is incumbent upon the contractor to define what the study will *not* do, for example, act as an advocate to secure greater funding. Often, problems result from discrepancies in perceptions about the definition of the intended program or its stated goals among managers and policymakers; inability or reluctance of program management to delineate performance measures or to specify the use of evaluation information; or the sensitivity and defensiveness of some program managers and policymakers when plausibility issues surface. During the conduct of these assignments, special care has to be taken to avoid obscure terminology and arcane jargon that will interfere and mask the intent and purpose of the study.

Evaluation Management Focus

Short-term policy studies must focus on the issues at hand, the available data, and the prompt formulation of the right study questions. There is always a strong temptation to expand the study, to pursue peripheral queries, to include more and more data, and to employ stronger and more sophisticated analyses. All too many studies have been dissipated by a favorable response to "Wouldn't it be interesting to know . . . ?"

Short-term evaluations must be properly focused, and the temptation to explore or to follow interesting but peripheral issues must be carefully resisted. Time and budget constraints call for experienced management of the evaluation process to achieve the desired products. Throughout each policy study, *demonstrably strong and sometimes ruthless management* is required to keep up the momentum, to adhere closely to the established tasks and time-targets, and to preserve intended objectives through a focused approach.

Maximizing Utility of Evaluation Efforts

Traditionally, an evaluation study culminates in the submission of a final report. All too often the final report is a bulky tome, replete with many statistical tables, a thorough explanation of the methodology, a discussion of the findings, and perhaps some recommendations. Final reports with impressive density showcasing the thoroughness and erudition of the study team are likely to grace someone's bookcase, and the maximum utility anticipated may be the balancing of a rickety table. Not only do reports of this type obscure useful findings (where they exist), they ignore a major reality of the policymaker: limited time. They place an unreasonable burden upon a policymaker, asking him or her to plow through recondite verbiage before the report's payload is encountered.

With few exceptions, policymakers tend not to be interested in minute technical detail, in the subtleties of data collection, or in long-winded presentation of methodology. They tend to become bored, restless, or irritable when they are confronted with massive presentations of system design or abstruse reliability or validity issues. One must view the briefing and the final report as the culmination of the study, and the degree to which the briefing and report are concise, hard-hitting, defensible, and devoid of "red herrings" will largely determine the usefulness of results to policymakers and policy decision making.

Briefing Policymakers

An effective method of increasing the potential utility of evaluation results is a carefully prepared briefing for decisionmakers. The briefing for senior policymakers is becoming a more frequent occurrence in evaluation studies. The development of a briefing taxes to the limit the skills and experience of the contractor team and the Federal Work Group. In effect, the totality of the study has to be compressed within a twenty- to thirty-minute presentation, with an additional half-hour reserved for questions and answers.

The development of the briefing is an arduous but exciting process because it calls for the distillation of the study findings. Mastery of the facts and findings is a sine qua non. The art resides in how to pare ruthlessly extraneous findings or insights. The contractor must select unerringly policy-related findings that are defendable even when they may appear counterintuitive or flout conventional wisdom, must engage and maintain the interest of the policymakers, and must articulate the caveats and restraints inherent in short-term assessments without vitiating the thrust of the findings. The process of constructing effective briefings is iterative. Exhibits require revision and tightening; presentations after at least two "dry runs" call for significant elision; and the presentor tightens his or her remarks to a hard-hitting briefing that delivers the important findings to the relevant policy user within the allotted time period. Often, an ancillary briefing package is useful to present additional facts, analyses, or peripheral information; it may be useful for the question-and-answer period following the presentation.

Another major problem concerns the presentation of policy or management issues to policymakers. Poorly thought-out briefings will place decisionmakers in the awkward position of being overwhelmed by massive presentations and without adequate time to review the options, to fully comprehend the implications of each option (even when defined in the briefing documents), and to develop an action plan and obtain commitments from key executives or subagency units. Timing and careful allocation of evaluation contract resources are required to ensure that adequate time is available to develop an action plan with policymakers, to reinterview key officials to gain their *active* support, and to identify the series of steps necessary to turn the approved option(s) into operation. This key culminating activity all too often is left undone, and the approved options end up as "paper tigers." This neglect frequently vitiates the impact of a sound and carefully thought-out and potentially useful study.

A successful briefing calls for the study team to follow these key guidelines:

Mastery of the data and analysis.

Clear vision of the relevant findings and an iron resolve not to cloud the focus of the presentation with interesting but irrelevant facts.

Ability to present succinct and organized findings in exhibits and effective graphic displays.

Assiduous attention to identifying sources for critical data or findings.

Selection of the most appropriately skilled individual to conduct the twenty- to thirty-minute briefing.

The development of the final report often can use the briefing as a base for preparation. Because the briefing is oral and the exhibits used are anchors for presentation, the final report has to narrate the presenter's remarks and the exhibits, and provide written, clear bridges to project the main findings in an orderly and succinct manner. Final reports of a policy assessment should be designed not to exceed twenty-five or thirty pages and should present the findings in a clear, "reader-friendly" manner.

Generally, the findings and conclusions should appear at the beginning of the report. Methodology, program description, forms used, and other materials can be placed in appendices.

Gritty Aspects of Policymaking

Traditional evaluation methods, often wonderful models of a nonworld, frequently disconnect policymakers from the evaluation process. This disconnection results in policymaker perceptions that evaluation products are largely arcane, irrelevant, expensive, difficult to obtain—and ultimately useless. This disconnection results primarily from misperceptions by evaluators of the nature of policy decisions and from ignoring the sovereignty of usefulness as the principal hallmark of effective evaluation.

All too often, evaluators (and others) are remarkably uninformed about the grittier aspects of policymaking. It is often viewed in the abstract: policymakers exhaustively study issues, competing priorities, service gaps, and equity issues, and then painstakingly decide, on the basis of the best available information and moral principles, how to allocate finite resources against a great universe of needs. From this perceptive, better policy decisions depend upon the comprehensiveness and quality of available information and rigid analysis, and the evaluation function can be leveraged expansively.

The nature of real world policymaking in federal departments is considerably different. Policymaking is not clear-cut, but ambiguous. Decisionmakers try to distinguish relevant emphases and departmental priorities among a rapidly changing backdrop of conflicting objectives and shifting criteria. They seek to identify relative tendencies against a short-fused timescale. They deal with fluctuating probabilities rather than triumphant certainties. Rough correlation and patterns are the beacons, rather than clear-cut cause and effect relationships.

Policy decisions always strike some balance among many conflicting values, objectives, pressure groups, and political forces. Consequently, a policy decision will often appear inadequate, craven, or dim-witted from any single perspective within as well as outside of the department. By definition, policy decisions have some negative consequence for some of the groups or individuals involved.

Policymaking, at best, may appear to be a compromise, or even may be perceived as minimally adequate—rarely, if ever, are these decisions optimal, just, or Solomon-like.

In addition, policymakers are required at times to make decisions against the facts, against intuitive perceptions, and to flout conventional wisdom. Often there are no "right" answers to major problems. Evaluators who seek to amass huge databases and perform intricate analyses based upon a rigorous methodology will not often serve policymaker needs. Studies of this nature may serve other needs and audiences such as adding to the knowledge base, impressing other evaluators, and publishing impenetrable articles in arcane journals. The policymaker is forced to function in a killing ground of implacable forces, shifting support, multiple claims, demands, and loyalties; he is driven by administration priorities, congressional pressures, judicial decrees, advocacy groups, and potentially hostile media coverage. Above all, the policymaker has rigid time constraints and must act and decide before all the facts are known, all the data are analyzed, all the trends discerned, and before all the realistic options and their implications are analyzed.

One concomitant impact of the time lag between developing the idea for an evaluation project and its actual commissioning is the overall lack of policymaker input into the design of evaluation plans and the formulation of individual evaluation projects. Key evaluation questions specific to policymaker needs may never arise; consequently, policymaker needs may remain unmet. Therefore, policymakers at times criticize or demean evaluation products. One Deputy Assistant Secretary has been quoted as asking, "Why is this stuff so unusable?" Matching evaluation information with political or policy debate is a difficult process because of the inherent time lag and also because the appropriate questions have to be posed long before the debate in order to make sure that evaluation projects can be designed and implemented to provide relevant information.

Another source of dissatisfaction on the part of policymakers is that many projects are either not policy-oriented or, if they are, they are not packaged in a manner to capture the interest or need of policymakers. Instead of focusing upon implications for budget authorization or reauthorization, regulatory reform, or response to congressional inquiries, study results frequently present in exhaustive detail technical issues of reliability, validity, or fairly esoteric variants of system design. Thus, major consumers of evaluation information feel frustrated with evaluation results, and skepticism grows regarding the value of evaluation information. Another perception is that the system is "analyst driven" and is designed to expand a knowledge base primarily for the benefit and use of analysts, while policymaker needs (and those of managers as well) are at best only partially met. Thus, there is a persuasive consensus that the evaluation system does not, in general, provide enough useful information to policymakers.

Key Aspects in Conducting Excellent
Short-Term Policy Studies

The evaluation team performs to meet the informational needs of the policymakers. The job calls for providing important information that will be useful for policy debate and resolution. Evaluators need to know the policymaking milieu and to tailor the study to provide useful information, regardless of whether it appears positive or negative. Evaluators can contribute to the debate by framing the study questions appropriately, and by remembering they are there to illuminate—not to make the decisions.

To perform effectively, the evaluation manager has to:

select quickly an appropriately skilled and experienced team;

discern central issues from peripheral concerns;

hew relentlessly to the main tasks;

employ effective interviewing skills and data collection approaches;

assess and analyze data continuously to arrive at defensible conclusions; and

present conclusions precisely and succinctly through oral briefings and well-written reports.

Sharp focus, sensitivity, and responsiveness to client needs—rather than elaborate data collection and analyses—are the guides to follow. As evaluators, we should maintain our usefulness in providing important contributions to policy debate and resolution. Rethinking our role and focusing on useful service may reverse evaluation stagnation and bring renewed vigor to the frontier of social inquiry.

Note

1. This chapter reflects the particular viewpoint of an evaluation contractor and describes from this perspective some of the issues and problems in conducting short-term, policy-oriented studies. The author, chairman of the board of Macro Systems, has directed over thirty recent short-term evaluation studies, across a wide gamut of HHS and other program areas.

Part III
Establishing Performance Objectives

A major role of leaders in the American political system is to establish broad visions and goals for society to pursue. The incentive structure of the political process, however, encourages government to promise more than it can deliver, and to be relatively unconcerned with how goals will be translated into effective organizations and programs. Establishing performance objectives is a way for managers to make the link between broad goals and ambitious yet realistic input, process, and outcome objectives.

Steven Kapp discusses how establishing performance objectives helped an organization to improve its performance. In the organization he describes, evaluators were unhappy with the limited contribution their efforts made to decisions about a college scholarship program. The program had been unchanged for two decades. Performance was measured by such vague indicators as reputation, prestige, and testimonial letters.

Evaluators, working in conjunction with program staff, identified program activities, resources, products, and intended outcomes of the scholarship enterprise. These data were used to guide discussions about what goals were appropriate for the program and to find out what information management needed to assess performance. Evaluators then conducted a "rapid feedback" study to provide the required information in a short period of time. The evaluation led to the development of specific program performance indicators to measure how well the program was doing. Kapp's work illustrates how involving program staff in evaluating increases the likelihood that evaluation findings will be used.

Dennis Palumbo, Michael Musheno, and Steven Maynard-Moody discuss who is responsible for establishing performance objectives. Most organizations already have established routines for doing tasks, including evaluation. For many organizations, establishing realistic and measurable objectives is a departure from the normal way of operating. Palumbo and his colleagues offer the model of the public sector entrepreneur as someone who will take the initiative in helping organizations set focused, achievable goals.

Entrepreneurs may be the formal leaders in an organization, mid-level managers, or street-level workers. Entrepreneurship can be seen as a role as well as a personal characteristic of a particular individual. Entrepreneurs uncover opportunities, generate support for ideas, and play a central role in building an implementation coalition. In the process, they can infuse an organization with a common purpose.

The authors use criminal justice policy to demonstrate that where there is agreement about what the organization or program should be doing, there is a greater level of success. Agreement about expectations can also help people feel better about what they are doing, that they are working for something higher than their own day-to-day job routines. New programs and new directions in organizations are unlikely to occur unless someone is willing to be an entrepreneur.

Many organizations conduct strategic planning. John King describes how performance-oriented evaluators can become a part of their organization's strategic planning process. In two case studies, he illustrates how evaluators brought their expertise into the larger planning activities of an organization. King's message is that evaluators can assist an organization to recognize the connection among the diverse objectives it pursues. But for this to happen, evaluators must be willing at times to lead and to sustain the organization through its planning process to demonstrate the payoff from attending to performance objectives.

Thomas Horan illustrates what can happen when organizations unquestioningly accept inadequate performance expectations. The rideshare program was developed during the 1970s to promote carpooling and other alternatives to single driver commuting. This national program focused most of its efforts on developing computerized lists matching riders and drivers, and making those lists available to the public. The chief measure of program performance was the number of people on the lists.

The theory behind the program assumed that people would share rides with other people once they knew who lived close to them and who worked similar hours. The results of this program were disappointing until evaluators were able to convince some of the program managers to reexamine the theory.

A revised theory recognized that prospective rideshare participants had little incentive to change their commuting behavior. Simply having information about potential riders was not enough to make the program work. Some rideshare agencies took a more entrepreneurial promotion and advocacy role in the program. They personally matched individuals who could share rides, and encouraged employer vanpool programs, parking incentives, and other transportation management techniques. They relied on performance measures more realistically associated with the desired program outcomes.

A central lesson in this case is that evaluation can help translate public policies into effective programs by understanding how people actually behave, and then tailor programs to those local realities. This does not imply that micro levels can ignore macro policy directives. It does mean that allowing local levels to select specific methods of implementing program goals can make the difference between high performance and no performance. Horan highlights the role evaluators can play in this process.

Alain Barbarie examines the issue of how to establish performance objectives for research and development (R&D) programs. Evaluating R&D programs from a performance perspective is frequently difficult because, among other reasons, information generated by evaluators is rarely fed back into the program.

Typically, R&D efforts are evaluated on the basis of the quality of the research being done. Barbarie argues that the increased demand for accountability in government dictates that more performance-oriented criteria should replace the "quality of research" criterion. Evaluators should ask whether a particular R&D effort is legitimate for government to do and whether there is an audience likely to use the research results. Barbarie also calls for involving client groups in the construction of the R&D plans to increase the chances that the products of the research will be used.

5
Defining and Redefining Performance: AAL's All-College Scholarship Program

Stephen A. Kapp

Program evaluations can play a key role in the continuing struggle for effective program delivery. This chapter will describe the contributions of three efforts to evaluate the effectiveness of AAL's All-College Scholarship Program. Specifically, the chapter will illustrate: a process for utilizing evaluation findings to improve program performance; how the evaluation improved management's understanding of the program; and the evaluation's impact on the definition of program performance. This process should aid program managers and program evaluators interested in improving program performance.

Background

Aid Association for Lutherans (AAL) is a fraternal benefit society. The AAL All-College Scholarship Program (ACSP) is one of AAL's largest and oldest programs. The program's reputation typically had functioned as a substitute for objective information regarding program performance. Likewise, past program evaluation efforts did not consistently provide information to help improve program performance. Either evaluation efforts did not focus on program improvement or no process was developed to implement recommendations for improving program performance. Consequently, program managers were seriously questioning the ACSP's ability to perform effectively in an environment of escalating college costs and decreasing sources of alternative support.

The Fraternal Benefit Research staff recognized the need for an evaluation strategy that contributed to improving program performance. Evaluability assessment was marketed as an approach directed at improving the impact of evaluations on program performance. Evaluability assessment is a pre-evaluation tool designed to prepare programs for more useful evaluations.[1]

Evaluability Assessment of ACSP

In order to obtain a grasp of program management's perception of the program's resources, activities, products, and intended outcomes, two major tasks were initiated. All printed program materials (historical files, program documentation, and promotional materials) were examined. Additionally, a series of interviews with program managers revealed varying perceptions of the program's objectives. A subsequent set of program management interviews culminated in the documentation of an accepted version of the intended program. A logic model of AAL's All-College Scholarship Program appears in figure 5–1.

The graphic depiction of the program logic facilitated valuable discussions among program management and the researcher regarding the appropriateness of program purposes, the plausibility of program objectives, and management information needs. The most critical issue was the compatibility and the competing importance of the intended outcomes: (1) the recognition of high-achieving members (5.1, 5.2), and (2) the enhancement of college choice (5.4). These concerns evolved into recognition of a need for empirical information.

The Rapid-Feedback Evaluation

The rapid-feedback evaluation was conducted to address management needs for information. A rapid-feedback evaluation (RFE) is an evaluation aimed at providing preliminary measurement of program performance as part of the process of developing performance indicators and designing full-scale evaluations.[2] The RFE provided information regarding all the encircled items of the logic model (figure 5–1); however, the present discussion will be limited to the efforts focused upon the two immediate outcomes: recognizing semifinalist losers (5.2) and enhancement of college choice (5.4).

The time available for the project was not sufficient to permit inclusion of all evaluability assessment participants. However, it was still important to identify and to include the likely users of this information in the process. Michael Patton speaks to the importance of this component of evaluation:

> The personal factor refers to the presence of an identifiable individual or group of people who personally cared about the evaluation and the information it generated. Where such a person or group was present, evaluations were used; where the personal factor was absent, there was a correspondingly marked absence of evaluation impact. The personal factor represents the leadership, interest, enthusiam, determination, commitment, aggressiveness, and caring of specific, individual people. In terms of power of evaluation, these are the people who are actively seeking information to reduce

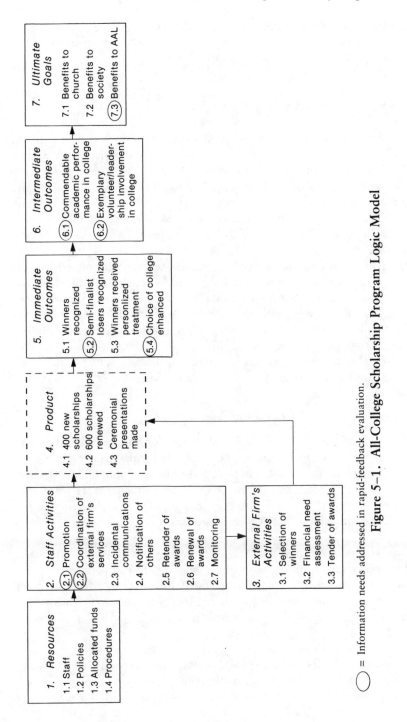

Figure 5–1. All-College Scholarship Program Logic Model

◯ = Information needs addressed in rapid-feedback evaluation.

decision uncertainties so as to increase their ability to predict the outcomes of programmatic activity and enhance their own discretion as decisionmakers. These are the users of evaluation research.[3]

The Rapid-Feedback Evaluation Team

A rapid-feedback evaluation team was formed that included two of the ACSP's front-line program managers and this researcher. Other team members provided critical consultation on the more pragmatic elements of the researcher's design of the RFE, for example, the appropriateness of proposed program performance indicators, and the in-house data collection procedures. The team members were also trained as interviewers for the small-scale telephone surveys ($N = 50$) of four samples (winners, semifinalist losers, field staff, and members at large).

The RFE team's most complex task was the development of performance standards. Performance standards are expected levels of performance for an effective program, stated in terms of specific performance indicators.[4] Performance standards were established through simulated decision making meetings, where the teams discussed the implications of dummy data tables. Although program managers found this task very awkward and time consuming, by the end of the process they were not only attached to the established standards, but also to the importance of the task.

Findings of the Rapid-Feedback Evaluation

The findings of the rapid-feedback evaluation for the intended outcomes "recognizing high-achieving members" (5.2) and enhancement of college choice (5.4) evaluation are listed in table 5–1. The format in table 5–1 shows performance indicators, actual results, and performance standards, highlighting effective performance (results exceed standards) and ineffective performance (results which do not meet standards).

Semifinalist/Losers Recognized (5.2). Becoming a semifinalist in the ACSP could be perceived as an achievement in this highly competitive program. Measurement of performance on this intended outcome was directed at determining whether semifinalists/losers shared this perception. For each performance indicator, actual program performance exceeded the performance standard for the ACSP.

Enhancement of College Choice (5.4). Significant attention was focused on the findings under this intended outcome. Low performance would strengthen the position of a group of program managers advocating smaller,

Table 5–1
Rapid-Feedback Evaluation Findings

Intended Outcome	Performance Indicator	Actual Results % Yes	Performance Standards % Yes
Semifinalist/losers recognized (5.2)	Reported the receipt of formal recognition (letter)	57.1	25
	Felt honored to be chosen as a semifinalist	85.7	57
	Felt it was not necessary for AAL to make arrangements for public recognition	65.3	24
Enhancement of college choice (5.4)			
Semifinalist/losers	Did college change when you did not win	6.1	49
	Compensated for not winning by changing college	2.0	30
Winners	Did your college choice change when you won	6.0	51
	Would have compensated by changing colleges	0	30

standard-sized recognition awards. Such a change was viewed as a more efficient approach, both financially and administratively.

Actual program performance was considerably below performance standards on this intended outcome, reflecting ineffective program performance. The consistency of the findings on the four measures strengthened the validity of the findings regarding ineffective program performance on the intended outcome of "Enhancement of College Choice" (5.4).

Utilizing RFE Findings

In the case of "Recognizing Semifinalist/Losers" (5.2), program management was pleasantly surprised to discover the program's respectable performance under this intended outcome—particularly when considering the modest efforts aimed at program performance on this intended outcome. ACSP's performance in this area was viewed as a "sleeper." A limited amount of discussion was focused on strategies for capitalizing on this program strength, such as gifts for semifinalist/losers.

Discussion was not as positive concerning the intended outcome "Enhancement of College Choice" (5.4). Perplexed program managers and this researcher considered strategies ranging from leaving the program in its present state to restructuring the award process and dropping this intended outcome. Discussions resulted in an agreement to change the program's intended outcome from "the enhancement of college choice" to "reducing the financial burden of higher education."

This major program revision was based predominantly on the findings of the RFE. The RFE documented the poor performance on the "Enhancement of College Choice," and led to program management's dismissal of the intended outcome as implausible. The program's objectives were adjusted in the interest of program improvement.

The RFE was very influential in deleting an implausible outcome from the intended program and, eventually, in the redefinition of effective program performance. The involvement of program managers throughout the process diminished the possibility that the evaluation would be viewed as the work of another "outside expert." All evaluation efforts were built on a common concept of the program (the logic model). Program management's involvement with the data collection enhanced the credibility of the findings. The development of performance standards provided managers with skills in the interpretation of evaluation findings, diminishing some of the trauma associated with the decisionmaking process.

The Results Oriented Management Initiative: A Second Evaluation

At the organizational level, an evaluability assessment of the entire fraternal benefit effort was initiated (see chapter 2). This process, the Results-Oriented Management Initiative, led to the reconvening of the RFE team. The mission of the team was to examine the ACSP's contribution to four departmental intended outcomes: (1) the ACSP's impact on recipients; (2) awareness and approval of the program by major constituencies; (3) participation in the program; and (4) the program's contribution toward the strengthening of AAL branches (local volunteer units).[5] The RFE results met the needs for information, except for the newest intended outcome, "Reducing the Financial Burden of Higher Education." The team saw this as an excellent opportunity to assess the program's performance on the new intended outcome. Consequently, they recommended such an evaluation to an upper management team.

At the first of two presentations to the management team, the vice president for fraternal benefit development declared the primary purpose of the ACSP to be the recognition of high-achieving members. The information collected in the RFE provided sufficient performance information on this intended outcome.

Assessing the ACSP's Redefined Program Performance

Program managers had described effective performance in "reducing the financial burden" as meaning the ACSP scholarship awards should "make a difference" in the financial aid packages of the winners. The team operationalized this concept as meaning that winners should have to rely less on "self-help" types of financial aid—work-study grants and loans.

To assess program performance in this area, we collected financial aid information on two separate populations of winners from 1980 to 1984: "renewable winners," receiving $500 to $1,750 annually for four years, and "nonrenewable winners," receiving one-time $500 awards. Within institutions, comparisons were made between renewable winners with financial need and nonrenewable winners with financial need. Financial need was determined by using the federal definition. Comparison groups were established at two Lutheran institutions, four private institutions, and three public institutions. These institutions represented historically popular choices of ACSP winners.

Table 5–2 presents our findings on the percentages of need met by various sources. Our expectations regarding "self-help" types of aid were not met. On the contrary, renewable winners had a greater percent of need met by loans than nonrenewable winners. Although the findings for work-study grants demonstrated a difference in the hypothesized direction, the difference

Table 5–2
Financial Aid Packages of Renewable and Nonrenewable Winners

Source	Renewable Winners (N = 30)	Nonrenewable Winners (N = 19)
Grants	9%	16%
Loans	24%	18%
Work Study	8%	11%
AAL Award	28%	3%
Institutional Aid	31%	43%
Other Aid	14%	11%
Unmet Need	6%	7%

was very slight. Perhaps the most telling finding was the similarity between unmet needs in the two populations. The remaining unmet need after the utilization of a variety of sources of financial aid was approximately the same for both groups.

These findings describe poor performance on the intended outcome of "reducing the financial burden of higher education." Whether looking specifically at "self-help" types of aid or generally at the entire financial aid packages, it is difficult to find differences. These findings forced us to reconsider the likelihood that the ACSP award could "make a difference."

Utilization of Results-Oriented Management Initiative Findings

At the second presentation, upper management was apprised of the ACSP's poor performance on the intended outcome of "reducing the financial burden of higher education." Despite the ACSP's adequate performance on two of the other intended outcomes, the program was classified as a program requiring revision. Additionally, the vice president for benefit development recommended dropping the program's intended outcome, "reducing the financial burden of higher education." This strategy would make "recognition" the program's primary purpose, calling into question the high cost of awards designed to "reduce the financial burden." The vice president's views on the program and the program's "public" classification increased the likelihood of the program being revised in a fashion that would accommodate program improvement.

Once again, the definition of effective program performance had changed for the program. On this occasion, the definition of effectiveness occurred at the department level. At the department level, the incentives for utilization were created by "publicity" documenting low program performance. The program logic is currently being adjusted since the evaluation revealed that the program performs poorly on the intended outcome "reducing the financial burden of higher education." The program now has the primary purpose of "recognizing high-achieving AAL members." Additionally, an effort is underway to address poor program performance.

Improving Program Performance

This chapter has discussed an ongoing process that assists program management at different levels in utilizing the findings of program evaluations. The process used evaluation to enhance program management's understanding of the ACSP, and to facilitate redefinition of effective program performance.

The impact of this process is best illustrated by the continued efforts to improve the ACSP's program performance. The front-line manager responsible for revising the ASCP has pursued a complex approach addressing the program's potential for improvement. Tentative directions for revision from upper management suggested giving the program a single purpose, simplifying the management of the program and reducing costs. Although the simplicity of this type of revision was attractive, the program manager was still committed to the importance of the program's secondary intended outcome, "Reducing the financial burden of higher education." Her commitment is being addressed through an experiment designed to hold financial aid officials accountable for "Reducing the financial burden of higher education" through the enforcement of additional program guidelines. If the results of this test are negative, the intended outcome "Reducing the financial burden of higher education" will be dropped.

In addition, a monitoring system is being designed to inform management of the extent of the program's success in "Recognizing high-achieving members." The monitoring system will use a qualitative approach to gain additional understanding of this intended outcome by asking winners and semifinalist/losers to "tell the story" of their recognition through the ACSP. Managers envision using learnings from this effort to emphasize the salient aspects of recognition to participants through customized promotional materials or relevant gifts. The planned monitoring system exemplifies the interative nature of the process of using evaluative information to attain a better understanding of program performance.

This chapter has described a process for utilizing the insights attained through evaluation to effectively manage a single program. The iterative process integrated different levels of program management into the evaluation. The management involvement enhanced credibility of the insights gained. This credibility facilitated management's use of the insights to attain a better understanding of the program. In this example, the higher level of understanding led to an improved definition of program effectiveness in terms of plausible intended outcomes. The process continues, with program management requesting further evaluation information in the interest of helping the adjusted program achieve higher performance.

Notes

1. Joseph S. Wholey, *Evaluation and Effective Public Management* (Boston: Little, Brown, 1983), p. 35.

2. *Ibid.*, p. 109.

3. Michael Q. Patton, *Utilization-Focused Evaluation* (Beverly Hills: Sage, 1978), p. 64.

4. Wholey, *Evaluation and Effective Public Management,* p. 10.

5. See Kenneth L. Bickel, "Organizing Evaluation to Improve the Performance of a Nonprofit Organization," chapter 2 above.

6

Public Sector Entrepreneurs: The Shakers and Doers of Program Innovation

Dennis Palumbo
Michael Musheno
Steven Maynard-Moody

E ntrepreneurship is recognized increasingly as an important determinant of innovation in the private sector. Innovations in the computer industry, biotechnology, and telecommunications have changed the face of the American economy, and entrepreneurs in these fields are credited with the business expansion associated with these technologies.[1] The entrepreneurs who pioneered these businesses are characterized as risk takers—individuals who are alert to new opportunities, have the knowledge to exploit these opportunities, and are able to combine a number of production modes in new ways.[2]

Although the idea of an "entrepreneur" is generally reserved for the risk-taking business person, researchers have recently focused on the importance of entrepreneurs in public agencies. A number of studies have pointed to the importance of entrepreneurs, particularly in the implementation and the innovation processes of public agencies.[3] Our research attempts to identify who these entrepreneurs are and to ascertain their importance in implementing new public programs. It is a study of public sector entrepreneurs in implementing community corrections in three states: Oregon, Colorado, and Connecticut.

This research is part of a larger project aimed at discovering the factors that account for successful implementation of community corrections programs. Entrepreneurship was one of several variables included; the others are: (1) degree of commitment to the programs by those responsible for implementing them, (2) the degree to which the program has been implemented, (3) the extent to which the program has been adapted to fit into local needs and circumstances, (4) the amount of perceived support given to the program by various groups such as elected officials, service providers, and the community, (5) the amount of access to decision making various groups have, and (6) the amount and type of training provided.

The main hypothesis of the research was the higher the programs scored on these seven factors, the more successful they would be in achieving their objectives. These objectives were: (1) reducing commitments of nonviolent offenders to state prisons, (2) lowering costs of corrections, (3) reducing recidivism, (4) receiving higher success ratings by implementors, (5) no lessening of community safety, (6) improving services such as drug and alcohol abuse treatment and job locating services, and (7) no widening of the net of social control.

Entrepreneurship was found to be an important factor in program success as measured by these seven impact variables. The other variables mentioned above (numbers 1–6) also were important. Because the variables were not being measured on the same quantitative scale, we did not obtain a quantitative measure of how important entrepreneurship is as compared to the other six variables. However, entrepreneurship was important, particularly in achieving coordination among the large number of criminal justice agencies and actors that are involved in implementing community corrections (for example, judges, courts, sheriffs, jails, prosecutors, public defenders, probation officers, counselors, community social service agencies, nonprofit service providers, and legislators); and also in getting agreement between upper- and street-level implementors about the goals that the programs should achieve. This latter, crucial role of entrepreneurs is the focus of this chapter.

Defining Entrepreneurship

The concept of the public sector entrepreneur is similar to that of business entrepreneurs. Championing an innovation, risk taking, setting bounded goals, and bringing together a support group of people are all characteristics of the effective public sector entrepreneur. Robert Yin discusses the bureaucratic entrepreneur as one who is able to mobilize the winning coalition of adopters, implementors, clients, and supporters needed to set the program implementation process in action.[4] Tornatzky et al. describe the role of the top-level administrator in championing an innovation and guiding it throughout the implementation process.[5] Eugene Bardach describes the role of the "fixer" in setting implementation back on track when it is in danger of faltering.[6] Eugene Lewis adds that ". . . entrepreneurs are not necessarily charismatic, but they do bring out zealousness in their subordinates; they inspire in them the belief that the task they serve has about it something much more than the self-interested humdrum of everyday life."[7] Finally, James Doig writes that the entrepreneur has the ability to set bounded and focused goals.[8]

Although the meaning of public entrepreneurship is clearly related to our common understanding of entrepreneurship in the private sector, the concept suffers from some inherent contradictions and has yet to be integrated with the dynamics of the policy process. Some scholars have argued that entrepreneurs emerge from positive organizational and social climates[9] while others conclude that individual entrepreneurs create these climates.[10] More critical to this study, the current literature on public-sector entrepreneurship has yet to be integrated with what we know about the activities of public employees in the policy process. The existing literature does not distinguish between entrepreneurs and leaders and ignores the role of entrepreneurs at the middle and bottom levels of bureaucratic hierarchies in the program innovation process.

Are entrepreneurs different from what we normally refer to as leaders? Lewis argues that the principal role of entrepreneurs is to expand the goals, mandates, and power of their organizations in ways unforeseen by others.[11] But leaders play the same role.[12] However, entrepreneurship and one's position in the bureaucratic hierarchy are not identical. Lewis writes:

> It does not necessarily follow that because a person dominates a public organization, he is by definition a public entrepreneur. On the contrary, many public organizations are run by people who are quite content to remain at the top in order to direct operations and maintain boundaries. The public entrepreneur, on the other hand, sees the organization as a tool for the achievement of *his* goals.[13]

The entrepreneur, therefore, has a high need for personal achievement and a different vision of the world. Entrepreneurs march to a different drummer. They do not see their activities as integral to their routines as bureaucratic actors.

The literature on public sector entrepreneurs also has a "big name" bias. Frequently, the only public sector entrepreneurs studied are the most visible figures in the public arena. For example, Eugene Lewis' study focuses on three powerful men: Hyman Rickover, J. Edgar Hoover, and Robert Moses. These highly visible entrepreneurs are presented as people who create or profoundly elaborate a public organization ". . . so as to alter greatly the existing pattern of allocation of scarce public resources."[14] However, the public entrepreneurship literature gives very little attention to those lower down in the hierarchy. Yet our research has found that people at the middle and even street level in an organization perform an entrepreneurial role, particularly in regard to the implementation stage of the policy process.

Clearly, the public policy literature has established that the implementation stage is crucial to translating new ideas into effective action.[15] And, some research is emerging that links entrepreneurship to this stage of the innovation process. For example, Wilken identifies three stages of entrepreneurship—(1) perception of the opportunity, (2) planning, and (3) implementation of the strategy for combining the elements of production. He concludes that a different person can perform each of these.[16] The literature on organizational behavior has established that street-level bureaucrats possess sufficient discretionary power to make or break a policy, particularly in regard to program delivery.[17] But the public entrepreneurship literature is based on the top-down model, which assumes that all important decisions rest with top management and ignores the potential of entrepreneurship at the street level. We shall show below that this is but a partial view of entrepreneurship.

Research Methods and Questions

This chapter examines three issues regarding public sector entrepreneurs. First, it describes the various roles they play and examines the question, "Is entrepreneurship better understood as a role set or an individual trait?" Second, we investigate whether entrepreneurship applies only to top management or is spread throughout the levels of the organizational hierarchy. Third, the chapter explores the impact of public sector entrepreneurs on the program implementation process.

As we said above, the findings are a part of a larger study of the implementation of community correction in Oregon, Colorado, and Connecticut. Community corrections is one of the recent programmatic innovations in criminal justice. Although it includes a wide variety of programs, the general thrust of community corrections is the use of community residences (that is, halfway houses) and services (that is, substance abuse treatment, educational programs, employment aid) as an alternative to incarceration of nonviolent offenders in state prisons. The general research design is described in detail elsewhere[18] and will be discussed here only as it relates to public entrepreneurship.

Triangulation

Determining how important an entrepreneur is in getting a program adopted and successfully implemented is not an easy task; the question does not lend itself easily to quantitative analysis. In fact, the activity of entrepreneurs and their relative importance compared to other variables affecting implementation probably cannot be measured through quantitative means alone.

We have used triangulation of qualitative and quantitative methods in an attempt to identify and to analyze the role of entrepreneurs in community corrections programs.[19] Specifically, we mixed field research based on open-ended interviews with mailed questionnaires, agency records, and data supplied by the agencies to analyze the implementation of community corrections. Entrepreneurial roles and activities were examined primarily through qualitative methods. We asked informants during our field visits if they could identify specific persons who were influential in getting community corrections started in their particular area and to identify the roles they played. In addition, we observed specific individuals during our field visits who were visible figures regarding community corrections in their area.

With the completion of the field research, we developed and mailed questionnaires that included open-ended items on entrepreneurship. This questionnaire was mailed to several hundred participants in community corrections in each of the three states.[20] Specifically, one question asked respondents to name and give the position of individuals who were influential in implementing the program in their area. We also asked respondents to describe the ways in which these individuals were influential and, using close-ended items, we developed other, indirect measures of their influence on the program innovation process (that is, promotion goal agreement).

Research Questions

One of our major goals was to explore the nature of public entrepreneurship in the implementation process. The specific questions we address here are: Do those involved in the implementation process identify only one, a few, or many individuals as crucial to program start-up and routinization? What positions and roles do those identified as entrepreneurs occupy in the community corrections network? Do high visibility administrators, such as the state-wide director of community services, dominate the entrepreneurship roles or do entrepreneurs come from a wider range of positions associated with community corrections? Does the nature of entrepreneurship vary according to the administrative structure developed to implement community corrections?

The ability to set clear goals, shaped by feasibility in terms of identified resources and known constraints, is one of the crucial roles associated with entrepreneurship. Doig identifies the following as important dimensions to the entrepreneurial role:

1. Identify (and create) short-term and long-term goals for their agencies.

2. Develop and nourish *external* supporting constituencies, while neutralizing existing and potential opponents.

3. Create *internal* constituencies (and neutralize opposition) through changes in organizational structure, recruitment of personnel, and reward structures.

4. Use planning staffs, and the data they generate, to support the manager's goals.

5. Systematically scan organizational routines to identify areas of vulnerability (to corruption, and to loss of individual power and position), and take remedial action.[21]

We attempted to verify one of these dimensions, promoting goal agreement, by measuring the degree of consensus about goals that existed between upper- and street-level implementors. Our reasoning was that if the entrepreneur was successful in gaining support for program goals, there would be greater agreement about goals between the upper- and street-level participants in community corrections, and this would be positively related to successful implementation. As indicators of program success for this particular research, we included: (1) how much reduction there was in the commitment of nonviolent offenders to state prison, (2) how successful implementors believed the program to be, (3) perceived changes in community safety, and (4) perceived improvements in various services such as probation, treatment, and community programs (that is, community service). Successful community corrections programs reduce commitments to prison, are viewed by those working in the criminal justice as effective, and provide better services without increasing the perceived threat to community safety.

This last research question can be stated as a hypothesis: The greater the level of goal consensus across the organizational hierarchy, the greater the level of program success.

Findings

Entrepreneurial Roles

The roles played by public sector entrepreneurs are varied. Our field observations revealed that the following is the rank order of importance in roles: (1) being a philosophical proponent of community corrections, (2) getting the program set up, (3) garnering local support, and (4) assuring that community corrections becomes an established component of the larger criminal justice process. These roles include a mixture of promotional networking and administrative activities, including efforts to convince skeptics of the value of the approach, making sure that viable programs emerge from the policy mandate, and linking community corrections with the larger process of administering justice. For example, one of the most recognized entrepreneurs, the director of community corrections in a county, was able to get sheriffs, prosecutors, judges, probation officers, and counselors to interact and to work together when they previously did not. Fortified by an incredible amount of energy, this entrepreneur spent of lot of time visiting and touching bases with all of these people to make sure they understood what was happening in the different parts of the program. As the sheriff put it, "Before Lou [the director] took over, none of us even got together, much less talked to each other. Now we have a common denominator." Many of the programs that composed community corrections existed before the county became a part of the state's system. Many of them were begun under Law Enforcement Assistance Act (LEAA) funds earlier in the decade. The pre-trial release programs were operated by the circuit court, the misdemeanant program consisted of only one probation office and was utilized primarily by the district court, a very small work-release program was operated through the sheriff's office, the state corrections division supervised felony probation and parolees in the county, and mental health services were available to offenders only upon the request of the county court. There were no volunteer services, drug counseling, or community service programs. However, under the director of community corrections, all of these programs were available and well coordinated.

The questionnaire responses confirmed our field observations that entrepreneurs play diverse roles in the innovation process. Each respondent was asked to rate a list of roles associated with influential persons from "very important" to "not important at all" on a seven-point Likert scale. For each questionnaire, a role was designated as important when a respondent rated it as important or very important.

In Colorado, the most important role played by entrepreneurs was that of getting the community corrections program established in the judicial district; 85 percent of our respondents stressed the importance of this role. The other roles identified by the respondents were: getting support for community corrections (83 percent), serving as a philosophical proponent (81 percent), and assuring that community corrections became an established component of the criminal justice system (74 percent). A surprisingly low 36 percent identified lobbying for the Community Correction Act as an important entrepreneurial activity. Hence, the respondents stressed the internal, as opposed to external, dimensions as being more important.

The roles played by entrepreneurs in Connecticut were similar. Respondents identified getting the community services program started as the most important role (80 percent). This was followed by being a philosophical proponent of community services (78 percent), expanding community service programs (78 percent), linking community service programs with other agencies (69 percent), developing effective treatment and service programs (68 percent), and building political constituencies for community corrections (55 percent).

Who Are Public Sector Entrepreneurs?

Rather than uncovering a single individual performing a variety of roles, our reputational analysis revealed a number of different people were entrepreneurs in each locale where successful implementation was evident. For example, in Colorado, the judicial district that had the most successful program had twelve different people as entrepreneurs, but one person was named ten times, another was mentioned six times, two others were each mentioned four times, and the remaining eight persons were only mentioned once each. This same pattern held for most other successful districts in Colorado. For example, in another district that successfully implemented community corrections, the two top individuals were each named by eleven persons as being the most influential, and the next three persons on the list were each mentioned five times apiece, with six others each being mentioned by only one person. Thus, one conclusion we reached is that entrepreneurship was spread over more than one person in any given locale where innovative outcomes emerged, although a few people often stood out.

Equally significantly we found a wide range of organizational participants named as influential in getting community corrections adopted and implemented. These included probation officers; county commissioners; judges; district attorneys; and state officials such as the regional manager, state director of community corrections, or the state director of corrections. In both states, many different types of individuals were named, but the type varied by program locale. For example, three judges were identified in one district, whereas in another the two most frequently identified entrepreneurs were probation officers.

Although upper-level administrators, such as judges, county commissioners, and state directors were named more often than street-level service providers, a number of the latter participants were also named. For example, of the seventy-four entrepreneurs named in the twenty Colorado judicial districts, sixteen (or 22 percent) were probation officers. Thus, although the entrepreneurial role is more likely to be occupied by an individual in middle- and upper-level positions, street-level workers play entrepreneurial roles in the implementation process as well.

Our findings are in agreement with those of Hage and Dewar who noted that " . . . the values of the elite inner circle are more important than those of the executive director or of the entire staff in predicting innovation. . . ."[22] The executive director's values were found by them to be an important predictor of organizational performance, but the values of the elite inner circle were more important. Our findings are similar in that the entrepreneurial role sometimes is filled by top-level individuals (that is, state director of community corrections or county director), but sometimes it is filled by a street-level implementor (that is, probation officer). The majority of people named as entrepreneurs were upper-level implementors, but they were not often the state, county, or district directors. Instead, they included officials such as judges, district attorneys, county commissioners, professors, public defenders, clerks, sheriffs, program supervisors, volunteer group organizers, deputy wardens, and ministers or priests. Thus, our findings support the conclusion that the role of entrepreneur is spread among many individuals rather than just one individual, and these individuals are middle- and street-level implementors, not just the top person. Hence, entrepreneurship is different from formal leadership, as Lewis has noted.

Hypothesis: Goal Consensus and Program Success

If, as discussed above, one of the primary roles of public sector entrepreneurs is to act as an internal program advocate, then we may assume that members of the organization where there is a high level of entrepreneurial activity will agree more about what the program is supposed to accomplish than in organizations with less entrepreneurial activity. Getting public workers crucial to the operation of community corrections to believe that they are working toward a common goal important to society, rather than simply meeting daily work requirements, is one of the most important tasks of entrepreneurs. Thus, we should expect the more successful organizations to have a greater amount of agreement between the upper- and street-level implementors about the goals of the organization. We tested this hypothesis in one of our study sites (Colorado).

The difference in agreement between upper- and street-level implementors was measured for the four most important goals of the program. These goals are to rehabilitate offenders, to save money, to promote community involvement in corrections, and to provide humane treatment of offenders. Respondents were asked how important they thought each of these goals was on a seven point Likert scale ranging from "very important" (7) to "not at all important " (1). The mean score of upper- and street-level implementors for each of these goals was computed. We then subtracted the average score of street-level respondents from the average of upper-level respondents and computed the absolute sum of the differences for the four goals for each of twelve judicial districts. These absolute sums are listed in column 3 of table 6–1.

Twelve judicial districts in Colorado were ranked on nine variables: average percent of work effort spent on community corrections, belief in effectiveness of community corrections, support for the program, changes in activities to adapt to local circumstances, availability of training, amount of reductions of offenders sent to state prison, perceptions of how successful the program is, perceptions of how well the program is implemented, and perceived increases in cooperation. The district that received the highest sum of ranks in these nine variables was ranked first, and so on down to the twelfth district. We then ranked the same twelve districts on the amount of difference in agreement about goals with the district having the least difference being ranked first (see table 6–1).

The Spearman rank-order correlation between the agreement on goals and implementation success is 0.43, meaning there is a high correlation between the extent to which there is agreement between upper- and street-

Table 6–1
Correlation between the Difference in Agreement on Goals of Upper- and Street-level Implementors and Implementation Success

Number of the Judicial District	Rank on Implementation Success (Highest to Lowest)	Difference in Agreement between Upper- and Street-Level Implementors on Four Goals	
		Absolute Difference	Rank[1]
20[2]	1	0.51	1
4	2	1.35	3
8	3	1.57	5
6	4	2.62	10
12	5	2.00	7
14	6	2.25	8
17	7	1.55	4
1	8	2.73	12
21	9	2.37	9
2	10	1.33	2
18	11	1.89	6
10	12	2.72	11

$r_s = 0.43$

1. The numbers in this column are the rank order of the difference in agreement about goals with the smallest difference ranked first.

2. The numbers in this column refer to specific judicial districts in Colorado; for example, judicial district number 2 (ranked 10) is Denver.

level implementors on the one hand, and successful implementation on the other hand. *In other words, where the two levels agree about which goals are important, the organization does better.* We take this to be indirect evidence that the entrepreneurs in the more successful districts were doing a better job of getting the members of their organizations to work toward a common goal.

The goals most often identified in Colorado was rehabilitation. This was the goal that was selected by the largest percent of all respondents as being very important. Fifty-three percent of all respondents gave this goal a rating of 7 on the 1-to-7 scale; whereas only 25 percent gave "save money," 22 percent gave "promote community involvement" and 37 percent gave "provide humane treatment of offenders" such a rating. This fits in with the idea that entrepreneurs make the members feel they are working for some high-order purpose (that is, rehabilitating offenders) rather than simply putting in their time as public employees.

As we pointed out above, the broad aim of the research on which this chapter is based was to discover what implementation factors were associated with the most successful programs. We found that a large number of different implementation factors contributed to better program performance. In addition to entrepreneurship, we found that the more successful programs had a higher degree of commitment to the program by implementors; more support by elected officials, the community, and service providers; more training for staff; and more adaptation to local conditions. But as we said above, it is not possible to quantitatively determine which of these variables contributes most to successful implementation, nor to determine the relative contribution of each variable.

Nevertheless, we can say that an entrepreneur can overcome obstacles to successful implementation. For example, we found that support by street-level implementors, who are the key to successful routinization of the program, is an important ingredient in program success. In Oregon, we found that the street-level implementors were not as supportive of the program as the street-level implementors in Colorado or Connecticut. Almost 50 percent of the Oregon street-level implementors said they supported the program moderately, little, or not at all, whereas in Colorado only 7 percent of street-level implementors and in Connecticut only 9 percent said this. Part of the reason for the lower level of support in Oregon is the opposition of the probation officers' union to the program. Probation officers comprise the majority of street-level implementors in Oregon and Colorado, but not in Connecticut. The opposition of probation officers in Oregon stems from the fact that to become a full participant in the program, all probation officers must give up their state positions and become county employees. This threatens the statewide union and lessens their job security. As state probation officers, they not only have higher status, but they can transfer from one county to another if a cutback occurs in the county in which they work. As county employees, they cannot do this. But in the successful counties, entrepreneurs have been able to overcome this obstacle and to infuse the street-level implementors with a sense of mission and high level of support for the program.

Turning Entrepreneurs Loose

Entrepreneurial activity is crucial to successful program implementation. New programs will not get adopted or become an established part of an agency's routine without entrepreneurs. The principal activities of entrepreneurs are to uncover opportunities for new programs, to become philosophical proponents for the program, to generate support and zeal for the program among those who must implement it, and to put together the winning coalition of adopters, implementors, clients, and supporters needed to set the implementation process in action.

Entrepreneurs are able to generate support because they know how to get agreement among diverse groups about what the goals of the program should be. In the area of community corrections, for example, setting bounded and focused goals is a crucial entrepreneurial function. But there is a dilemma here. If the emphasis of the program is placed on rehabilitation alone, the more conservative groups and individuals will not support it. If the emphasis is strictly to save money, the people who believe in rehabilitation and humane treatment will be turned off. Balancing these goals and groups is not an easy task and it takes entrepreneurial skill to do so.

Entrepreneurial skill is not restricted to those at the middle and top of an organization, although they tend to be most identified with this activity. Street-level implementors play a greater entrepreneurial role in decentralized than in centralized programs. Without the zealous involvement of street-level implementors in these settings, successful implementation is unlikely.

But how can entrepreneurship be fostered and encouraged? For example, finding that entrepreneurial activity is crucial to successful implementation of a program does not, by itself, lead to a prescription for action. It does not do much good simply to tell officials, "Go find some entrepreneurs in order to better achieve what you want."

But some prescriptions still emerge. It is possible to create organizational conditions that encourage entrepreneurship. For example, public agencies should decentralize their operation or at least encourage broad involvement in developing adoption and implementation strategies so as to create the opportunity for street-level and middle-level personnel to function as entrepreneurs; in this way new and better program approaches are more likely to become a routine part of the agency or service network. Also, giving recognition, rewards, and positive inducements to those who function as entrepreneurs is another way to improve program performance. Finally, implementation research is a good way to discover the factors that help optimize program performance, including identification of the role that entrepreneurs are or are not playing in the organization. As indicated in this study, a triangulated research methodology which draws upon both quantitative and qualitative methods is essential to discovering the importance of public-sector entrepreneurs in the implementation process.

Notes

1. David A. Silver, *The Entrepreneurial Life* (New York: John Wiley, 1983).
2. See, for example, Sidney Greenfield, Arnold Strickon, and Robert Aubey (Eds.), *Entrepreneurship in Cultural Context* (Albuquerque: University of New Mexico, 1979); and Israel Kirzner, *Perception, Opportunity and Profit: Studies in the Theory of Entrepreneurship* (Chicago: University of Chicago Press, 1979).
3. See, for example, Eugene Lewis, *Public Entrepreneurship: Toward a Theory of Bureaucratic Political Power* (Bloomington, Ind.: Indiana University Press, 1984).

4. Robert Yin, *Changing Urban Bureaucracies* (Lexington, Mass.: Lexington Books, 1979).

5. Louis G. Tornatzky et al., *Innovation and Social Process: A National Experiment in Implementing Social Technology* (New York: Pergamon, 1980).

6. See Eugene Bardach, *The Implementation Game: What Happens After a Bill Becomes Law* (Cambridge, Mass.: MIT Press, 1978).

7. Lewis, *Public Entrepreneurship: Toward a Theory of Bureaucratic Political Power,* p. 24.

8. James Doig, *Resources, Strategies and Constraints of the Policy Entrepreneur: Lessons from the (Somewhat Peculiar) World of Public Authority,* unpublished paper, 1981.

9. Paul Wilken, *Entrepreneurship: A Comparative and Historical Study* (Norwood, N.J.: ABLEX, 1979).

10. See, for example, Joseph Schumpeter, *The Theory of Economic Development* (Cambridge, Mass.: Harvard University Press, 1949).

11. Lewis, *Public Entrepreneurship: Toward a Theory of Bureaucratic Political Power,* pp. 230–238.

12. See, for example, Fred E. Fieldler and Martin M. Chemers, *Leadership and Effective Management* (Glenview, Ill.: Scott, Foresman, 1974); and William R. Lassey and Richard R. Fernandez, *Leadership and Social Change* (La Jolla, Cal.: University Associates, 1976).

13. Lewis, *Public Entrepreneurship: Toward a Theory of Bureaucratic Political Power,* p. 237.

14. Ibid., p. 9.

15. See, for example, Eugene Bardach, *The Implementation Game: What Happens After a Bill Becomes Law* (Cambridge, Mass.: MIT Press, 1978); Jeffrey Pressman and Aaron Wildavsky, *Implementation* (Berkeley, Cal.: University of California Press, 1973); and Laurence J. O'Toole and Robert S. Montjoy, "Interorganizational Policy Implementation: A Theoretical Perspective," *Public Administration Review,* 44(6) (Nov./Dec., 1984):491–503.

16. Wilken, *Entrepreneurship: A Comparative and Historical Study.*

17. See, for example, Michael Lipsky, *Street-Level Bureaucracy* (New York: Russell Sage Foundation, 1980); Gene E. Hall and Susan Loucks, "A Developmental Model for Determining Whether the Treatment is Actually Implemented," *American Educational Research Journal 14* (Summer 1977):263–276; and David E. Aaronson, C. Thomas Dienes, and Michael C. Musheno, *Public Policy and Discretion* (New York: Clark Boardman, 1984).

18. Dennis Palumbo, Steven Maynard-Moody, and Paula Wright, "Measuring Degrees of Successful Implementation," *Evaluation Review 8* (February 1984):45–74; and Dennis Palumbo, Michael Musheno, and Steven Maynard-Moody, *Final Report: Evaluating the Implementation of Community Correction in Oregon, Colorado and Connecticut* (Washington, D.C.: National Institute of Justice, 1985).

19. See T.D. Jick, "Mixing Qualitative and Quantitative Methods," *Administrative Science Quarterly* (1979):602–611; P. DeLeon, "Policy Evaluation and Program Termination," *Policy Studies Review* 2(1) (1983); Dennis Palumbo and Michael Musheno, "New Methodological Perspectives on Process Evaluation," (Unpublished paper presented at the 1984 Western Political Science Association Meetings, Sacra-

mento, California); Charles Reichardt and Thomas Cook, "Beyond Qualitative Versus Quantitative Methods," in C. Reichardt and T.D. Cook, *Qualitative and Quantitative Methods in Evaluation Research* (Beverly Hills, Cal.: Sage, 1979), pp. 7–33; and Patton, *Qualitative Evaluation Methods* (Beverly Hills, Cal.: Sage, 1980).

20. Connecticut: N = 478 with a response rate of 33 percent; Colorado: N = 280; Oregon: N = 264 with response rates of 45 and 55 percent, respectively.

21. Doig, *Resources, Strategies, and Constraints of the Policy Entrepreneur: Lessons from the (Somewhat Peculiar) World of Public Authority*, p. 5.

22. Jerald Hage and Robert Dewar, "Elite Values Versus Organizational Structure in Predicting Innovation," *Administrative Science Quarterly, 18*(3) (1973):287.

7

The Role of Evaluation in Strategic Planning: Setting Performance Expectations at a State Mental Health Authority and a State Institution of Higher Education

John P. King

The question of how the talents of evaluators can be effectively used to improve organizational performance has perplexed evaluators and managers alike. Observations that the results of evaluation studies are either not used, ineffectively used, or misused are widespread. Guba and Lincoln (1981) note that many managers and decisionmakers have grown wary of evaluation research because they perceive its findings to be trivial and the knowledge it generates to be irrelevant to the problems at hand.

Although there are examples of evaluation research that fit these perceptions, the fact remains that even those studies that are substantially significant and amenable to effective utilization are not used to the extent that is either possible or desirable. The reasons for this may lie in the ways in which evaluators have conceptualized and carried out their roles and, alternatively, the ways in which others have cast them in these roles.

Let us think for a moment of the image of the hardworking, number-crunching, report-writing evaluator. Such an individual often produces good, solid, and even eloquent sets of data and data analyses. However, the data and its analyses are often reported as is, without being selected, organized, and substantively analyzed. Data, rather than information, have been presented. Therefore, the manner in which the evaluation findings can be applied is not conveyed. The assumption that those invested with the authority to make and implement decisions will follow a model of rational decision making and further examine and analyze the data before using to to make decisions is, at best, misguided (Tetlow, 1983). If the talents of the evaluator are to be used to improve organizational performance, two points must be kept in mind. Information rather than mere data is the objective of evaluation research and such information must be developed and presented in a way that is "designed to catalyze and inform action" (Buhl & Lindquist, 1981).

The strategic planning process is an important arena in which evaluators can have an impact by developing information and by playing facilitative and action-oriented roles in the decisionmaking and problem-solving processes. Evaluative information on organizational characteristics and performance can identify strategic objectives and action plans that will move the organization toward attainment of its goals and will further define performance expectations for both the organization and the individuals who are a part of it.

A discussion of the role of evaluation research in strategic planning will touch upon many of the same issues, concepts, and processes found in the CIPP—Context-Input-Process-Product—model (Stuffplebeam, 1983) and the responsive evaluation models (Guba & Lincoln, 1981; Stake, 1983). We will not focus, however, upon a model of evaluation or even upon evaluation itself, per se. Rather, our focus will be upon a dynamic organizational process, strategic planning, that fully encompasses and includes evaluation research as a basic component. Evaluation is not set off as a separate activity and only assumes importance to the extent it contributes to the strategic planning process and defines performance expectations.

Strategic Planning

All organizations and institutions, be they academic, public/human service, or business, are faced today with rapidly changing circumstances and demands. The hackneyed call for accountability has given way to the call for performance, achievement and, yes, excellence. Organizations and institutions face both internal and external pressures and no longer have the luxury of either sitting back and letting things work themselves out or of dealing with them in a piecemeal manner. The ability to identify, to analyze, and to assess internal and external factors related to organizational performance, and to make timely, critical decisions about future courses of action in the light of these factors is called for.

In order to undertake such a process of identification, analysis, assessment, and action-oriented decision making, the organization must know what its business is, where it stands in relation to similar organizations, where it is headed, and what factors will either facilitate or inhibit its movement in the desired direction. Strategic planning is the process that enables an organization to accomplish all of this and, therefore, to establish performance expectations. (Steiner, 1979; Jedamus, Peterson and Associates, 1980; Cope, 1981; Caruthers, 1981; Keller, 1983; Uhl, 1983).

Strategic planning is not a process detached from ongoing organizational dynamics where individuals passively think about where they would like their organization to be and what extra features might enable it to get there. It is, instead, an active process in which the organization's performance is continually monitored and evaluated. Assessments of internal strengths and weaknesses, along with assessments of external opportunities and threats, are made and form an initial basis upon which judgments about the level and quality of the organization's performance are made. These assessments and judgments are then examined in light of existing organizational values, goals, and external demands. Clarification of existing goals and/or development of new organizational goals are accomplished in these initial stages of the strategic planning process and are immediately followed by the development of objectives and strategies.

Objectives and strategies resolve the question of how to move the organization in a desired direction and are developed from information produced in the planning process to set priorities and to allocate resources. Objectives establish specific goal-related results, and strategies describe how those results are to be attained. Objectives and strategies, therefore, further specify performance expectations for the organization.

The emphasis in the entire strategic planning process is upon developing information that will allow action-oriented decision making. In examining the question of how the information crucial to strategic planning can be developed and gathered, we should immediately recognize that evaluation research plays a basic and fundamental role. As the strategic planning process works to specify and establish indicators and expectations for organizational performance, evaluation activities are continually being undertaken and fed into the process. Assessments of strengths and weaknesses, of the effectiveness of organizational operations in meeting priorities and goals and resulting indicators of alternative courses of action to enhance organizational performance are all standard features of evaluation research. What, perhaps, is not a standard feature of evaluation research (although it is paid lip service) is the detailed study of external environmental factors and their impact upon organizational performance expectations. These, indeed, are factors that have assumed greater importance for evaluators. They have, however, often been removed from the influence of the evaluator due to the limited data-gathering role the evaluator plays in the organization. In the strategic planning process, however, the evaluator's role is not limited in this manner. The evaluator has an impact upon decisions that set priorities and allocate resources because his or her information-gathering activities are continually guided by the need to establish performance expectations. Obviously, decisions are not made by the evaluator alone. However, the importance of evaluation research and the use of the products of evaluation research, take on dimensions in the strategic planning process that are often diminished or not possible in standard evaluation research activities. Evaluation research products become valuable because they have been fully incorporated into a dynamic decisionmaking process.

In order to illustrate the role of evaluation research in the strategic planning process, and therefore in establishing organizational performance expectations, I will present two examples. In both examples, the evaluation process evolved as a part of a dynamic decisionmaking process that sought to address how organizational goals could be translated into specific objectives and strategies that would enable the organization to attain its goals and to improve its organizational effectiveness.

The Role of Evaluation Research in Strategic Planning at a Mental Health Authority

The development, delivery, and funding of mental health services have come under increasing scrutiny over the past decade. Millions of dollars have been poured into mental health services, and yet we still have large state institutions filled with patients who receive very little treatment. Likewise, the promise of effective, community-based treatment has failed to be fulfilled. A handful of patients receive services, while large numbers are relegated to the new back wards of single room occupancy hotels and homes for adults. Legislators ask where the money is going, community representatives decry the presence of seemingly unattended mental health clients in their midst, and advocacy groups demand a humane, effective service delivery system. Executive decisionmakers in mental health are therefore under extreme pressure to demonstrate that responsible and effective steps are being taken to meet the mental health needs of the public.

This was the situation facing the Virginia Department of Mental Health and Mental Retardation, where the author previously served as an assistant director in the evaluation office. The department had strategically assessed its position in terms of its long-standing goal of what it called "communitization," a deemphasis upon institutional treatment and increased emphasis upon community treatment, and found that it had not moved very far toward attaining that goal. Practices and policies in the past had done little more than move clients from one setting to another, and had done so without determining how those clients could best be served in their new setting. Performance expectations in the form of specific, quantifiable objectives and strategies had not been established. In order to operationalize the goal and to establish performance expectations, a number of decisions had to be made: Which clients are most appropriate for movement to community services, and what types of services will they need once moved into the communities? What types of services are needed for clients remaining in the institutions and, most importantly, what services will be most effective in preparing them for "communitization?"

Questions were also asked about services to clients already in the community. What are their service needs, and how will these services enable them to remain in the community? How will the transfer of large numbers of clients from institutions into the community affect the delivery of services to those already in the community?

In order to answer these questions, and to determine the most appropriate course of action for the department, information about the current operations of the institutional and community service delivery systems and their future needs was needed. The department, in other words, was faced with establishing performance expectations and developing operational objectives and strategies tied to the communitization goals. The classic setting for the implementation of a strategic planning process was therefore present.

The Virginia Department of Mental Health and Mental Retardation did, indeed, implement a strategic planning process, but it did not consciously and explicitly identify it as such. The evaluation office was called upon to develop assessment procedures that would determine performance expectations for the communitization process and further enable institutional and community programs to establish objectives and strategies to implement that process. The evaluation office responded with the development of the Virginia Community Level of Care—or CLOC—survey, and activities commonly associated with the strategic planning process were begun. The CLOC survey was developed and designed to provide specific information on client levels of functioning, client service needs, and the service delivery setting most appropriate for the client. Furthermore, it allowed for comparisons of actual, current services with those identified to be most in need. (For a further description of the CLOC survey, see King, Gouse, & Avellar, 1983). The CLOC survey was used to assess all publicly institutionalized mental health, mental retardation, and substance abuse clients in the state of Virginia—approximately 8,000 individuals—and a stratified random sample of community mental health, mental retardation, and substance abuse clients (sample size of 6,000).

Analyses of the data gathered through the CLOC assessment instrument provided the department with information on clients' physical care needs, degree of psychological impairment, and community potential, that is, the ability of the individual to perform those functions of daily living that allow one to be socially competent and to maintain oneself, or be maintained, in a community setting. A determination of the clients' overall functioning levels and the most appropriate services and service delivery settings could then be made on the basis of three indicators—physical care needs, degree of psychological impairment, and community potential—examined in relation to one another. These determinations could then be examined in relation to specific institutional and community programs and the nature of the resources available and currently utilized within them. This was done and served to establish goal-related performance expectations and to pinpoint where and how resources should be allocated and utilized in the future.

At the conclusion of the CLOC survey, it was possible to establish performance expectations related to the department's goals of a community-based treatment system. Each institution was provided with a profile of each resident client, and the same profile was provided to the community service system from which the client came. Performance expectations were established through determinations of the appropriate services and service delivery settings for the clients and the types of programs needed to effect the transfer of clients from institutional to community settings. The community service systems also received information describing their existing community client populations (from the sample survey) and performance expectations for them were similarly established.

The results of the CLOC survey provided the department's central office with systemwide information at a level of detail that never before had been available. Information that would allow one to make concrete, action-oriented decisions and to establish specific goal-related performance expectations was available. Decisions about the allocation of resources of institutions and community programs based specifically on client needs were possible. Decisions about the nature and types of programs to be delivered in institutions and community settings were possible. Priorities for the establishment of new programs could be established. And, perhaps most important, it was possible to look at previous and current practices and to determine alternative courses of action for the future that would enhance the performance of the agency in line with its proposed future direction.

Upon dissemination of the findings from the CLOC survey, a number of strategic decisions establishing performance expectations were immediately made. Target reductions for the number of clients served in each institution were developed on the basis of findings that identified clients who would most appropriately be served in a community setting. A number of the community service systems began to develop strategies to meet the needs of future deinstitutionalized clients and to maintain clients already in the community in that setting. Work with other agencies (such as Social Services, which has control over homes for adults in Virginia) was also undertaken in order to develop strategies to meet the needs of mental health clients in community settings.

Based upon the activities described above, we could say that the Virginia Department of Mental Health and Mental Retardation experienced a good deal of success in using evaluation research in the strategic planning process. Indeed, performance expectations for the state's mental health system were much more clearly established than before the process began. However, after a flurry of initial activities, the process began to stall.

Although the relationship of the strategic planning process based on the

CLOC survey to the future course of the department was clear and evident, it had never been explicitly integrated into the overall strategy of the department nor had the strategic planning process been given the type of sustained leadership and support it needed. Communities and institutions were left on their own to set directions and strategies in isolation from the executive leadership of the agency's central office. The executive leadership had devoted its energies to other areas of concern and ceased to play an active role in integrating the other various activities of the department into those activities surrounding the strategic planning process for communitization. Because the department failed to fully examine its overall strategic profile and to determine how its activities could relate to one another, what could have been a single, unified, and ongoing strategic planning process became separate, discrete activities. One major consequence of this was a loss in the clarity of the performance expectations established during the CLOC evaluation process.

The Role of Evaluation in Strategic Planning at a State Institution of Higher Education

This example is provided to illustrate how the problems in the mental health case can be avoided. The pressures facing public institutions of higher education are well known and documented: declining numbers of individuals in the population of traditional college age, increased facility and instructional costs at a time of fiscal constraints, increased competition in the traditional higher education marketplace, declines in liberal arts enrollments, and so on. The impacts of these factors upon institutions of higher education have been as varied as the responses to them. Institutions of higher education, however, have been particularly amenable to the strategic planning approach.

The strategic planning process at Longwood College is being undertaken in a very determined and explicit manner. The determination to establish performance expectations and strategies that will move the college toward attaining its broad educational and community service goals has been the driving force behind the strategic planning process and has served to legitimize the planning activities.

In the example from the state mental health authority, the strategic planning process based on the CLOC survey was never explicitly recognized as a strategic planning process and was undertaken with very little forethought as to how it would fit into the overall strategic management of the agency. One consequence of this was the apparent abandonment of the strategic planning process in one area to begin it in others, without any recognition of the possible relationships between those areas.

The college strategic planning process has begun by clearly laying out the nature of the relationships among the various components of the college (for example, enrollment as related to facilities utilization, allocation of faculty slots, and so on) and has guarded against the type of situation encountered by the mental health authority. Constituency groups also have been involved differently. Although the process used by the mental health authority involved the full array of constituency groups, it was done in an almost after-the-fact manner without these groups fully participating in laying the groundwork for the process. Constituencies were consulted but never included in activities that contributed to establishing performance expectations. This may be another reason why the process fizzled after its initial successes. The college, on the other hand, is fully involving each of its constituency groups—board, administration, faculty, staff, and students—in every phase of the strategic planning process. Clarification of policy goals and their translation into objectives and strategies are being accomplished through each group's participation in formulating evaluation questions, gathering information, and establishing performance expectations.

To illustrate the evolution of the strategic planning process and the manner in which evaluation research contributed to that process, I will discuss one particular area of concern at the college: enrollment. Enrollment concerns relate to a wide variety of issues and to several of the college's broad goals. Longwood, as a state institution in Virginia, is funded and allocated faculty positions through an enrollment-driven formula. The ability to accurately project enrollments and to develop strategies that will enable those projections to be met is crucial for ensuring the continued viability and stability of the college. Enrollment concerns also relate to desired outcomes regarding the quality and characteristics of the student body. Evaluations of enrollment trends and patterns in this context, then, can be seen as attempts to establish performance expectations as they relate to the broad goals of the college.

In attempting to establish enrollment objectives and strategies, initial evaluation activities addressed the question of the "WOTS"—weaknesses, opportunities, threats, and strengths. Internal college strengths and weaknesses in attracting students—both in quantity and quality—were addressed and external threats and opportunities either inhibiting or facilitating their attraction examined. Evaluations of the admissions process examining the volume of applications from first-time freshmen and transfers, acceptance rates, and enrollment rates, were undertaken in conjunction with evaluations of institutional policy on day and evening course scheduling, general education requirements, comparisons with other colleges, and so on. Evaluations of the quality and characteristics of enrolling students were similarly conducted. On the basis of these evaluation activities, a strategic evaluation profile of the college (its mission, clientele, expected outcomes, program offerings and priorities, geographic service areas, competitive advantages) is now being developed and alternative courses of action evaluated in relationship to directions established by this profile.

Evaluation and strategic planning activities related to the basic issue of enrollment, therefore, have touched upon all spheres of the college. For the first time in the experience of this author, evaluation research activities are being conceptualized and undertaken in a fully coordinated manner with the other operations of the institution.

Results from the evaluation studies noted above have been presented to various levels of decisionmakers and used by those decisionmakers to develop objectives and strategies to meet the college's broad enrollment goals and to establish performance expectations for those involved with projecting, generating, and maintaining enrollments; actors who range from institutional researchers, admissions officers, and custodians to residential counselors, administrative policymakers, and instructional faculty.

Conclusion

The information generated by the enrollment evaluation studies is, or course, quite basic, much like the basic information generated by the mental health CLOC survey. The two sets of studies, however, will be utilized in different ways. In the case of the mental health authority, the utilization and benefit of the evaluation will be temporary and fleeting. In the case of the college, it will be much more long lasting and meaningful. In the mental health authority, evaluation research was isolated from the general management functions of the department. At the college, evaluation research is used to inform all decicion-making activities. In the mental health authority, the establishment of performance expectations was limited to a particular time frame defined by the length of the evaluation activities. In the college evaluation activities are part of a larger strategic planning process, and the establishment of performance expectations transcends any boundaries that might be artificially imposed by the completion of the evaluation.

References

Avellar, J.W., King, J.P., and Gouse, A.S. "Evaluating a Human Service Delivery System: A Case Study in Diffusion." Presentation to "Evaluation 83," Evaluation Network/Evaluation Research Society Joint Meeting. Chicago: October 1983.

Buhl, C.C. and Lindquist, J. "Academic Improvement Through Action Research." In Lindquist, J. (Ed.), *New Directions for Institutional Research,* no. 32 (pp. 3–26). San Francisco: Jossey-Bass, December 1981.

Caruthers, J.K. "Strategic Master Plans," In Poulton, N.C. (Ed.), *New Directions for Institutional Research: Evaluation of Management and Planning Systems,* no. 31 (pp. 17–28). San Francisco: Jossey-Bass, September 1981.

Cope, R.G. "Environmental Assessments for Strategic Planning." In Poluton, N.C. (Ed.), *New Directions for Institutional Research: Evaluation of Management and Planning Systems,* no. 31 (pp. 5–16). San Francisco: Jossey-Bass, September 1981.

Guba, E.G. and Lincoln, Y.S. *Effective Evaluation.* San Francisco: Jossey-Bass, 1981.

Jedamus, P., Peterson, M.W. and Associates. *Improving Academic Management.* San Francisco: Jossey-Bass, 1980.

Keller, G. *Academic Strategy.* Baltimore: Johns Hopkins University Press, 1983.

King, J.P., Gouse, A.S., and Aveller, J.W. "The Virginia Community Level of Care Survey." Presentation to "Evaluation 83," Evaluation Network/Evaluation Research Society Joint Meeting. Chicago: October 1983.

Steiner, G. *Strategic Planning.* New York: The Free Press, 1979.

Stake, R.E. "Program Evaluation, Particularly Responsive Evaluation." In Madaus, G.F., et al., (Eds.), *Models: Viewpoints on Educational and Human Services Evaluation* (pp. 287–310). Boston: Kluwer-Nijhoff, 1983.

Stuffplebeam, D.L., "The CIPP Model for Program Evaluation." In Madaus, G.F., et al., (Eds.), *Evaluation Models: Viewpoints on Educational and Human Services Evaluation* (pp. 117–142). Boston: Kluwer-Nijhoff, 1983.

Tetlow, W.L., "The Pragmatic Imperative of Institutional Research." In Firnberg, J.W. and Lasher, W.F. (Eds.), *New Directions for Institutional Research: The Politics and Pragmatics of Institutional Research,* no. 389. (pp. 3–10) San Francisco: Jossey-Bass, June 1983.

Uhl, W.P. (Ed.). *New Directions for Institutional Research: Using Research for Strategic Planning,* no. 37. San Francisco: Jossey-Bass, March 1983.

8
Symbiontic Evaluation: The Nature of Rideshare Agency Change

Thomas A. Horan

T he field of program evaluation has become increasingly interested in the issue of program improvement.[1] Scriven, in his articulation of formative evaluation, first highlighted how evaluations could be geared to assist in the improvement of program operations.[2] Since then, a considerable amount of research has been devoted to demonstrating the utility of evaluation techniques, both formative and summative, in the improvement of program performance.[3,4] This chapter seeks to contribute to this growing body of knowledge by describing how program evaluations can have a "symbiontic" (that is, the smaller member of a symbiotic pair) relationship with program objectives, with the result being the increased effectiveness of both functions.

The substantive focus of the chapter is on Rideshare Agency (RSA) change. The chapter will commence with a discussion of the original RSA program model. It will then outline the evaluations and related research that have led to a reformulation of RSA objectives. The last section of the chapter will describe the parameters of this new RSA program model, drawing upon a range of evaluation and applied research findings to assist with the conceptualization of both the new program objectives and the new evaluation framework.

Background: Rideshare Agencies

Rideshare Agencies (RSAs) are the designated governmental agencies responsible for the promotion of ridesharing (for example, carpooling, vanpooling, buspooling). They were born with the passage of the Emergency Highway Conservation Act of 1974.[5] This act, passed in response to the 1973–74 oil embargo, authorized highway funds to be used for the promotion of ride-

The author would like to thank Gary Edson for his thoughtful review of an earlier draft of this chapter.

sharing as a fuel conservation and highway efficiency measure. In the ensuing decade, RSAs have been established in every state in the country.[6] The general program goals of these RSAs are in keeping with the enabling legislation: promote the primary goal of increased ridesharing in order to obtain the consequent goals of reduced vehicle miles traveled, reduced fuel consumed, reduced pollution emitted, and reduced commuter costs.

The Mainstream Program Model

In 1978, Wagner conducted a nationwide review of RSA strategies used to promote ridesharing.[8] He found a surprising degree of similarity in their approaches. At the time there were 106 RSAs established in thirty-four states. All (ninety) of the RSAs that participated in the review had an employer-based focus. Though there was also widespread use of activities geared toward the general public (for example, billboards and call-in information services), this aspect was generally considered to be of secondary importance. Such homogeneity of approach provided strong evidence that employer-based rideshare marketing had become the "mainstream model" for RSA rideshare promotion.

Wagner noted that the employer-based approach consisted of two basic elements: carpool matching and promotion. The matching service generally involved conducting matchlist surveys of the company's employees (to obtain the necessary home/work information), processing the information using a computer program, and then returning to employees a "matchlist" of other interested potential ridesharers who lived nearby.

As for promotion, Wagner found that RSAs relied heavily on using personal meetings with company personnel in order to gain their support for marketing ridesharing to their employees. Specific marketing practices used by the RSAs at the employment site, included posters, brochures, bumper stickers, and form letters signed by upper management.

A schematic model of the "mainstream" approach is presented in figure 8–1. The intended outcomes of the RSA efforts are in keeping with the enabling legislation: to promote the primary goal of increased ridesharing in order to obtain the consequent goals of reduced vehicle miles traveled, reduced fuel consumed, reduced pollution emitted, and reduced user (for example, ridesharer) costs.[7] The primary goal of increased ridesharing has two components: increased ridesharing service awareness and increased ridesharing behavior.[8] Ridesharing awareness is included as a goal because it is considered to be an important precondition for obtaining program induced ridesharing behavior.[9]

As Wagner noted, under this model are the provision of matchlist surveys and promotional assistance at the company site. The guiding RSA program

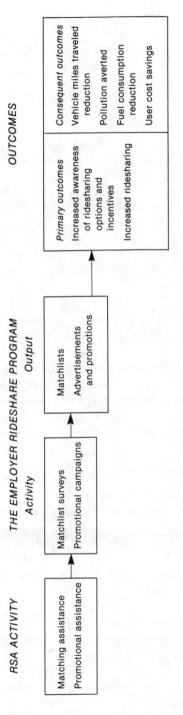

Figure 8-1. The Mainstream Model

hypothesis is that by providing matchlists and promotions to companies, ridesharing will increase at the company level. Thus, the immediate RSA objective is to maximize matchlist and promotional output at the company sites.

Evaluation Framework

Impact Assessment. Evaluations of programs operating under the mainstream model have focused on measuring the amount of increased ridesharing and determining the mileage, pollution, fuel, and cost savings.[7] At the heart of this impact framework is the applicant survey.[10] This is a survey of matchlist applicants designed to assess the "placement rate," that is, the percentage of ridesharing applicants who start or continue ridesharing as a result of receiving a matchlist. Often this survey can collect data pertaining to rideshare program awareness and vehicle miles traveled. Vehicle miles traveled can also be used to estimate the other consequent impact figures—pollution, fuel, and cost savings.

Performance Monitoring. As mentioned, the immediate program objective of RSAs operating under a mainstream model is to generate as many matchlists and promotions as possible.[11] Consequently, the performance monitoring aspect of mainstream evaluation usually entails reporting matchlist and promotion production levels for given time periods (for example, on a quarterly basis). The federal funding agencies usually require the following "penetration figures": the number of employers reached, the number of employees reached, and the number of matchlist applicants.[8]

Criticism of the Mainstream Model

Though the mainstream model represents the most prevalent approach to RSA rideshare promotion, increasing evidence suggests that it might not be the most effective approach. This section briefly summarizes three types of criticisms that have been levied against the mainstream model. Most of the evidence that forms the basis of these criticisms comes from a variety of evaluation, research, and demonstration projects that have been conducted during the last decade.

Low Placement Rates. Though evaluations of programs operating under the mainstream model have reported varying degrees of effectiveness, the general finding has been rather low placement rates.[11] The average placement rate of programs reviewed by Wagner was 16 percent.[8] (That is, 16 percent of those who received matchlists started or continued ridesharing as a result of the matchlist.) Other evaluations have also reported low placement rates. Both Andrle and Dueker, and Scheiner and Kieper reported under a 6 percent placement rate for employer-based matching and promotional efforts in their respective catchment areas.[12,13]

These impact findings are the basis of the most common criticism made against the mainstream model: the matching and related promotional activities place only a small percentage of potential ridesharers into ridesharing arrangements. As Geller, Winnett, and Everett concluded in their review of RSA evaluations: "It appears that without special incentives to carpool, carpool matching and organizational efforts are relatively ineffective" (p. 237).[14]

Effectiveness of Rideshare Incentives. A second line of mainstream model criticism has centered around the reported effectiveness of various "special incentives." These incentives are typically not promoted by RSAs operating under the mainstream model, but there is accumulating evidence supporting their effectiveness in getting employees to rideshare. Because these incentives form the basis of the emerging replacement model, they will each be briefly discussed.

Personalizing Matching. The most widely advocated complement to the matchlist survey is personalized matching. Personalized matching entails any of a number of activities that involve bringing potential ridesharers together to discuss the possibility of ridesharing. Examples of personalized matching techniques include "Meet Your Match" parties and follow-up phone calls to matchlist applicants.

Several RSA programs have demonstrated the effect that personalized matching can have on the placement rate.[15,16] For example, Commuter Computer conducted a demonstration project that involved training in-house coordinators to provide personalized assistance to employees. The evaluation of this project found that demonstration sites had a higher ridesharer formation rate than the control sites and that a sizable percentage of new ridesharers directly credited the coordinator as having influenced their change.[15]

Vanpool Programs. Vanpool programs are a second successful organizational inducement for ridesharing. There are a variety of ways that an employer can sponsor vanpools, ranging from an indirect administrative subsidy for employee-owned or third-party vanpools to outright ownership of the entire program. Evidence supporting the effectiveness of vanpool incentives is widespread; hundreds of companies nationwide run successful programs.[17] Indeed, it was the early success of company vanpool programs (particularly the 3M program) that provided optimism for the notion that ridesharing could be effectively promoted through companies.[5]

Parking Incentives. Parking incentives are perhaps the most popular organizational technique that can be used to encourage ridesharing.[14] Jacobs, Fairbanks, Poche, and Bailey conducted a study of preferential parking and parking subsidy incentives.[18] Both were found to significantly affect carpool rates, with preferential parking being noted by riders as the more influential incentive. On a more macrolevel, Hirst evaluated the impact of parking incentives introduced in Washington, D.C., and similarly found that these incentives significantly influenced the rideshare rate, especially when they were combined with a drive alone parking disincentive (that is, a $2-per-day parking fee for solo drivers.)[19]

Transportation System Management. Finally, the area of Transportation System Management (TSM) is emerging as an effective approach for improving the commuting conditions of employees. TSM entails a variety of techniques that can be implemented to increase traffic efficiency. Examples of TSM include flextime, park-and-ride lots, and high-occupancy vehicle lanes.[20] Most of these TSM techniques require public policy action. A notable exception, however, is flextime. Flextime is a proridesharing policy that can be implemented at the company level.

The concept behind flextime is to allow flexibility in employee start and end times so that potential rideshare arrangements would not be hampered by work time constraints. Although early investigations into the rideshare effects of flextime produced equivocal results, recent evidence supports the use of flextime as a proridesharing measure.[17,21] In particular, Jones studied the effectiveness of voluntary flextime policies introduced by twenty-three San Francisco companies.[21] In his evaluation of this demonstration project, Jones found that the ridesharing rate significantly increased for those 6,000 employees who participated in the program. Moreover, he found that the flextime participants, even those not ridesharing, changed their commuting times to more off-peak hours.

In sum, the research on incentives suggests that increased effectiveness would be achieved at the company level if RSA efforts were expanded to include promotion of these various incentives. Wagner succinctly summarized the state of affairs as follows:

> Ideally, rideshare encouragement programs should be multifaceted, composed of a wide range of actions including not only carpool matching and promotion but also various incentive measures to attract commuters to higher occupancy modes of travel. The carpool demonstration projects implemented to date have fallen considerably short of the ideal in that primary emphasis has been aimed at carpool matching and promotion with sig-

nificantly lesser emphasis devoted to developing and implementing other facets. (p. 38)[8]

Performance Pressure

Since the time of Wagner's review, the effectiveness of promoting a wider range of incentives has been increasingly recognized by RSA program managers.[11] However, many program managers are reluctant to change the emphasis of their programs because they feel pressured to maximize matchlist output. Jones, articulating this third line of mainstream model criticism, suggests that mainstream model evaluations are counterproductive to the development of more effective rideshare programs.[11] He argues that the consistently low placement rates documented in RSA evaluations commonly result in a perceived productivity problem by RSA managers, who respond by further intensifying the matchlist and promotional efforts of RSAs. Jones suggests that in order for RSAs to more comprehensively promote ridesharing at the company level, productivity should be recast in terms of constituency-development, rather than matchlist production.

The Constituency-Development Program Model

The model that emerges from the various lines of mainstream model criticism is one that stresses developing constituent-based programs.[11] The programmatic elements of a "constituency-development" model are presented in figure 8-2. The primary goals of the constituency-development approach remain the same as in the mainstream model: increased ridesharing awareness and behavior. The consequent goals of reduced miles traveled, fuel consumed, pollution emitted, and user costs remain unchanged. The intended output of the RSA's assistance to catchment area employers is, however, expanded to include various other promotion techniques, including: personalized matching, vanpool program, parking incentives and TSM.

The constituency-development program hypothesis is that by developing multifaceted in-house rideshare programs, ridesharing awareness and behavior will increase at the company level. Thus, under this model, the immediate RSA objective is to develop multifaceted in-house rideshare programs.

Though several RSAs have adopted the concept of a constituency-development model, both the detailed specification of the broadened RSA objective and a systematic assessment of RSA effectiveness in achieving its objective remain to be accomplished.[11,22] Fortunately, social science research pertaining to organizational innovations and their assessment can provide

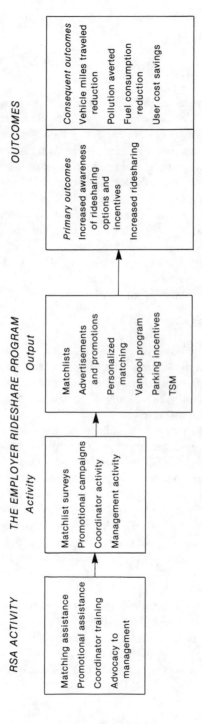

Figure 8-2. The Constituency-Development Model

useful insights in considering this broadened objective and its consequent evaluation.

Innovation Perspective

The study of organizational innovations is a burgeoning field of inquiry within social science. Some of the major findings of this research are that innovations will often be modified to fit the unique requirements of the host organizations, that innovations will be implemented in stages, and that various dimensions of a given innovation can differ as to their rate of implementation.[23,24] For rideshare promotion, the innovation perspective suggests that the in-house rideshare program can be conceptualized as an innovation, consisting of a number of possible dimensions: matchlists, promotions, personalized matching, vanpool programs, parking incentives, and TSM.

The innovation perspective also suggests that, for each company, the various possible rideshare program dimensions will differ as to their appropriateness and rate of implementation. Thus, the RSA objective, under the constituency-development model, is to implement to the fullest extent possible those rideshare program dimensions that are most appropriate to the client organization's needs and requirements. That is, beyond the relatively generic matchlist surveys and promotions, other aspects of in-house rideshare promotion should be implemented as they are appropriate to the organization's situation. For example, parking subsidies are generally considered to be more appropriate for those companies located in central business districts where parking is sparse.[25] The same incentive would not be as attractive when implemented in a suburban setting where parking is abundant.

Evaluation Framework

Impact Assessment. Because the primary goals of the RSA effort under the constituency-development model remain essentially unchanged from goals of the mainstream model (that is, increased ridesharing awareness and behavior), impact evaluations (such as the applicant survey) remain an important component of constituency-development evaluations. However, because the constituency-development model posits the development of an effective in-house rideshare program as an important intervening process between the RSA's efforts and the resulting ridesharing behavior, it becomes critical to assess the degree to which this intervening process is implemented.[26,27]

The measurement of an intervening process, though new to the rideshare field, has been the subject of systematic inquiry in several other fields, most notably education. Several major educational studies, particularly those by

Berman and McLaughlin, have demonstrated the importance of measuring the degree that new educational programs were implemented in the school settings.[28] Hall and Loucks have outlined a methodology for measuring implementation in an educational setting and, more recently, Leithwood and Montgomery have broadened Hall and Loucks' methodology, making it applicable to a variety of substantive areas.[29,30]

At the core of the Leithwood and Montgomery methodology is a procedure for developing an innovation profile that can be employed to measure the degree of implementation. A first step in the development of this profile is to specify the dimensions of the innovation. With regard to rideshare promotion, the relevant dimensions of the "in-house program" innovation are matchlist surveys, promotions, personalized matching, vanpool programs, parking incentives, and TSM. Each of these represent various aspects of an in-house rideshare program that can be implemented.

The second step in developing this profile is to specify the levels of possible implementation along a continuum from low to high, with "high" representing the ideal degree of implementation. The result of such a ranking would be the natural implementation progression for each of the dimensions.

Table 8–1 presents a basic format that can be used to develop an innovation profile for in-house ridesharing programs. The specification of dimension level (for example, low, medium, and high implementation) involve input from the incentive literature, from rideshare experts, and from various other stakeholders in the rideshare promotion process.[30] In keeping with the dual rideshare awareness/behavior program goals, the levels of each dimension would include both promotional and program activities.

Including a measure of in-house program implementation would allow the evaluation framework to assume a "theory-driven" approach to program assessment.[26] That is, the evaluation could be aimed at comprehensively assessing the constituency-development program hypothesis, rather than just providing an overall impact assessment of ridesharing behavior. One of the advantages to a theory-driven approach is that the explanatory power of the evaluation would be enhanced.[27] For instance, high or low employee ridesharing rates could be understood in terms of what activities were done at client companies. This represents a considerable improvement over the impact focus of the mainstream model evaluation framework, which posited no causal explanation regarding ridesharing promotion effectiveness.

Formative Implications. The innovation profile also has possibilities for improving the formative uses of rideshare evaluations. On a macrolevel, the innovation profile could be used to assess catchment area rideshare program activity levels. By aggregating the client company "user scores," an overall picture of the level of implementation for each in-house rideshare dimension could be obtained.[30] RSAs could use this information to help target specific

Table 8–1
An Innovation Profile for the In-house Rideshare Program

Level of Implementation

Dimension	LOW	MEDIUM	HIGH
Matchlist Survey: Matchlist advertising Matchlist activities			
Promotion: General rideshare advertising General promotional activities			
Personalized Matching: Personalized matching advertising Personalized matching activities			
Vanpool Program: Vanpool advertising Vanpool activities			
Parking Incentives: Parking incentive advertising Parking incentive activities			
TSM: Flextime advertising Flextime activities			

promotional campaigns in their catchment areas. Moreover, differences among company implementation patterns could be analyzed to see if any client market segmentation would be possible.

The macropicture would have formative implications since it would contribute to setting catchment area expectations and strategies. However, given the contextual thrust of the constituency-development model, the innovation profile probably has greater formative potential at the microlevel. For each client company, the innovation profile could assist RSAs in planning in-house program development. Initial program measurements could be used as part of an assessment of a particular client company's situation, and as such, could help form the basis for setting specific company rideshare program objectives. For example, if a client company has on-site, limited parking, but no preferential parking spaces, a goal could be set to implement the next level of preferential parking (that is, several preferential parking spaces).

Performance Monitoring. The innovation profile does not provide a process measure that can completely replace the matchlist production figure as the primary performance monitoring figure. Process measures tend to assess effort as opposed to impact.[31] Development of in-house rideshare programs represent an intended *effect* of RSA technical assistance activities. Consequently, monitoring under the constituency-development model would probably entail some service unit measure that tracked technical assistance and training provided by the RSA.

As Jones has argued, recasting productivity measures in terms of the constituency-development model is an important task, for the matchlist production emphasis keeps RSAs from working more extensively with companies to develop in-house programs.[11] The implementation of a constituency-development process measure is also warranted on a more conceptual level. A corollary to the constituency-development hypothesis is that RSA technical assistance will lead to greater in-house program activity. Such a process measure would allow for an assessment of this hypothesis.

Conclusion

This chapter has described the interplay that is possible between RSA program evaluations and RSA program objectives. The evaluation component of the mainstream model has, in combination with other research and evaluation on incentives, led to the development of a new program model. Within this new program model, the evaluation framework can be reformulated to increase its explanatory and formative uses. Hence, the relationship between program evaluations and program objectives has symbiotic qualities.

The role of evaluation is symbiontic (as opposed to symbiotic) because it is not necessarily the dominant factor in the determination of new program objectives. The extent to which RSAs ultimately adopt a constituency development focus and related evaluation framework has been and will be influenced by a variety of social, political, and economic factors over which the evaluation enterprise has no control.[5,32] Such an "important but limited" function for evaluations is consistent with the evaluation role advanced by several proponents of policy focused evaluations. For example, Cronbach et al. state, "Those who shape policy should reach decisions with their eyes open; it is the evaluator's job to illuminate the decision, not to dictate the decision" (p. 11).[4]

The purpose of this chapter has been to outline a symbiontic role that evaluations can play in the reformulation of objectives. Traditionally, the field of evaluation has focused on assessing established objectives.[33] Working within the realm of reformulating program models is relatively new ground.[1] Nonetheless, as this chapter has demonstrated, the evaluation enterprise can indeed contribute to the reformulation of objectives, and can also provide a comprehensive framework for the assessment of these new objectives.

Notes

1. M. Fleischer, "The Evaluator as Program Consultant," *Evaluation and Program Planning* 6 (1986):69–76.

2. M. Scriven, "The Methodology of Evaluation." In R.E. Stake (Ed.), *AERS Monograph Series on Curriculum Evaluation,* pp. 39–83. (Chicago: Rand McNally, 1967).

3. P. Horst et al., *Evaluation Planning at the National Institute of Mental Health* (Washington, D.C.: The Urban Institute, 1974).

4. L. Cronbach, S. Ambron, S. Dornbusch, R. Hess, R. Hornik, D. Phillips, D. Walker, and S. Werner, *Toward Reform of Program Evaluation* (San Francisco: Jossey-Bass, 1980).

5. R. Bradley and E. McCarthy, "Management and Organizational Issues of Ridesharing Program," *Transportation Research Record* no. 193 (1981):50–61.

6. L. Glazer, "Ridesharing Evaluation," *Transportation Research Record* no. 193 (1981):75–79.

7. C. Cohen, L. Gelmont, B. Goodman, and C. Oken, "Rideshare Performance Measures: An Evaluation," prepared for California Department of Transportation, 1983.

8. F.A. Wagner, "Evaluation of Carpool Demonstration Projects," FHWA, U.S. Department of Transportation, 1978.

9. N. Klein and D. Amdur, *Procedures for Evaluating Marketing Programs* (Oakland, Calif.: National Ridesharing Group, 1981).

10. L. Glazer and P. Webb, "Procedures for Carpool Program Evaluation," *Evaluation Kit No. 1* (Menlo Park, Calif.: Crain and Associates, 1981).

11. D. Jones, "Two Ways of Thinking About Productivity and Ridesharing," *Transportation Research Record* no. 193 (1981):32–34.

12. S. Andrle and K.J. Dueker, *Attitudes Toward and Evaluation of Carpooling* (Technical Report No. 32) (Iowa City: University of Iowa, Institute of Urban and Regional Research, 1974).

13. J.L. Scheiner and S.A. Kieper, "Carpool Information Project: Innovative Approaches Improve Results," *Transportation Research Record* no. 619 (1976): 16–18.

14. E. Geller, R. Winnett, and P. Everett, *Preserving the Environment: New Strategies for Behavior Change* (New York: Pergamon Press, 1982).

15. Commuter Computer, "Final Report: National Ridesharing Demonstration Project," prepared for California Department of Transportation, 1983.

16. W. Hershey and A. Hekimian, "Measuring the Effectiveness of Personalized Ridesharing Assistance," *Transportation Research Record* no. 614 (1983):14–21.

17. R. Plum and J. Edwards, *Carpooling: An Overview with Annotated Bibliography* (Minneapolis, Minn.: Center for Urban and Regional Affairs, 1979).

18. H. Jacobs, D. Fairbanks, C. Poche, and J.S. Bailey, "Behavioral Community Psychology: Multiple Incentives for Encouraging Carpool Formation on the University Campus," *Journal of Applied Behavior Analysis* 15 (1981):141–149.

19. D. Hirst, "Transportation Energy Conservation Policies," *Science* 192(15) (1976):20.

20. M. Misch and J. Margolin, "The Organization and Operation of Ridesharing Programs," prepared for the National Cooperative Highway Research Program, 1980.

21. D. Jones, *Off Work Early: The Final Report of the San Francisco Flex-time Demonstration Project* (Berkeley, Calif.: Institute for Transporation Studies, 1983).

22. T. Horan, *Rideshare Promotion and Evaluation: A Literature Review* (Garden Grove, Calif.: Orange County Transit District, 1985).

23. G. Downs and L. Mohr, "Conceptual Issues in the Study of Innovation," *Administrative Science Quarterly* 21 (1976):700–714.

24. L. Tornatzky, J. Eveland, W. Boylan, W. Hetzner, E. Johnson, P. Roitman, and J. Schnieder, *The Process of Technological Innovation: Reviewing the Literature* (Washington, D.C.: National Science Foundation, 1983).

25. J.P. Womack, P.A. Bowman, and H. Lum, *Employer Perceptions of Ridesharing* (Contract No. DOT–FH–11–9438) (Washington, D.C.: U.S. Department of Transportation, 1979).

26. H. Chen and P. Rossi, "Evaluating with Sense: The Theory Driven Approach," *Evaluation Review* 7 (1983):283–302.

27. J.C. Thomas, " 'Patching Up' Evaluation Designs: The Case for Process Evaluation." In pp. 91–98 *Implementing Public Policy,* D.S. Palumbo and M.A. Harder (Eds.), (Lexington, Mass.: Lexington Books, 1981).

28. D. Berman and W. McLaughlin, *Federal Programs Supporting Educational Change, Vol. IV: The Findings in Review* (Santa Monica, Calif.: The Rand Corporation, 1975).

29. G.E. Hall and S.F. Loucks, "A Developmental Model for Determining Whether Treatment is Actually Implemented," *American Educational Research Journal* 14(3) (1977):263–275.

30. K. Leithwood and P. Montgomery, "Evaluating Program Implementation," *Evaluation Review* 4(2) (1980):193–214.

31. T.H. Poister, *Performance Monitoring* (Lexington, Mass.: Lexington Books, 1983).

32. C.E. Lindholm and R.K. Cohen, *Usable Knowledge* (New Haven, Conn.: Yale University Press, 1979).

33. G. Glass and F. Ellett, "Evaluation Research." In M.R. Rosenzweig and L.W. Porter (Eds.), *Annual Review of Psychology,* (Palo Alto, Calif.: Annual Reviews, 1980).

9

Evaluating Government R&D: Beyond "Quality of Research"

Alain J. Barbarie

In Canada, as elsewhere, government research and development (R&D) is beginning to receive considerable attention by those asking for accountability in government. For one thing, in recent times there has been an increase in demand for accountability in general. For another, science and research are slowly being demystified. And, finally, countries everywhere are looking for ways to increase their national productivity, and in so doing are turning to R&D as a possible source of beneficial innovations. More than ever, R&D programs have to be evaluated, and evaluated well.

In spite of the fact that, in the federal government of Canada, R&D is generally mission-oriented in nature, it becomes quite clear when one examines the evaluation efforts in this area that evaluation studies have focused almost exclusively on the process of R&D rather than on its outcome. As evaluators will attest, approaches to measure the impacts and the effects of R&D program outcomes are fraught with difficulties. First, long time lags exist between R&D expenditures and the acceptance of any resulting technology. By their very nature, research activities are not repetitive, and by the time an R&D program outcome can be properly assessed, the program has usually moved on to new research. Second, R&D work usually contributes only a small part of the total effort required before new knowledge, or a new product or process is fully developed and institutionalized in the marketplace or organization for which it was developed. A number of external factors can intervene to diminish the potential impacts and effects of good research. And third, there are many examples where the major R&D outcomes were completely outside those anticipated. The whole field of radio astronomy, which developed out of research done to eliminate background static noice picked up by antennas, is a case in point. As a result, most evaluations to date have been limited to an assessment of the quality of the research done; and more often than not, the evaluation approach has been a peer review of the performance of the research team associated with the R&D program.

In times of increasing scrutiny of public spending and decreasing availability of resources, it obviously becomes more difficult to continue justifying funding R&D programs simply because they produce quality research. Currently, R&D programs are expected to achieve outcomes that will effectively contribute to the attainment of government policy goals. Essentially, quality research, although necessary, is no longer a sufficient criterion for program effectiveness, and quality research must now be pursued in the context of a clearly defined purpose.

Technology push (that is, do research and the applications will take care of themselves), even though it sometimes works, is not believed by policymakers to be generally operative today. Instead, R&D is now thought more likely to yield socioeconomic benefits in the presence of strong *market pull* (that is, where there are clients able and willing, even eager, to acquire and use the R&D results). And "market pull" will be strongest where R&D can be closely linked to the client.

As a result, two issues now emerge as being much more significant in the evaluation of government R&D programs. One is *legitimacy:* Is it appropriate for government to be doing this research? and the other is *relevance:* Is there a client intent on making use of the results of the research? For the purpose of this discussion, the R&D programs covered are those that are either carried out in-house (that is, in federal laboratories by government researchers) or contracted out to universities or private industry on a project-by-project basis. Specifically, grants and contributions programs, tax incentive programs, and procurement programs in support of industrial or university R&D are not included in this discussion, even though in some instances some of the points made here apply to them as well.

The Legitimacy Issue

The evaluation approach suggested here to address the issue of legitimacy for R&D programs is based on the premise that only a limited number of reasons can truly justify government doing research. And, as was noted earlier, doing quality research work does not by itself constitute a valid reason. For example, in Canada, a recent federal task force[1] concluded that it is appropriate for government to support research that improves a government department's or agency's capacity to:

Test or monitor.

Establish codes, standards, or regulations.

Maintain data bases.

Operate a national facility, such as a wind tunnel or a particle accelerator.

Address a national or regional problem, such as acid rain.

Carry out federal obligations in areas of national security or under various international agreements.

Provide, in conjunction with universities, a "window" on the international scientific community.

Maintain a national competence in certain key scientific sectors.

Help support the goals of private industry when the risks and expenditures involved with the R&D are too high or the potential payoff too small or too far down the road to attract private industry.

Help support the goals of private industry when the industry is too fragmented to undertake the necessary R&D.

Government must, in the national interest, perform certain scientific or technical tasks that no other organization can or is willing to do. It is therefore perfectly legitimate for government to support research that clearly enhances the accomplishment of recognized and accepted tasks such as those listed above.

The role of evaluators, in the context of this approach to the legitimacy issue, is to demonstrate, using the many evaluation techniques at their disposal, whether the R&D program being evaluated is designed to support one or more of a government's recognized and accepted tasks, and whether the associated R&D work must be and can only be done by government. In this demonstration, evaluators might assemble and question a panel of experts or survey researchers, managers, or clients of the R&D program. They might perform a file review, look at the department or agency act, other pertinent legislation, cabinet decisions and memoranda, original planning documents, or they might even interview the policymakers responsible for the program. Evaluators might also ask program managers to suggest other pertinent sources of information.

Evaluators might also find it necessary in some instances to demonstrate that the policy goals being supported by the R&D program are themselves valid. This is obviously a fundamental requirement for the program to be legitimate. However, the extent to which evaluators need to address this question will depend on the specific set of circumstances surrounding the evaluation. Policy goals are sometimes clear, but not always, and R&D can and does arise in many different ways. In this sense, each R&D program is probably unique, and its link to the policy goals complex.

Finally, evaluators should keep in mind the need to examine, in the context of the legitimate issue, the level of resources devoted to the R&D program being evaluated. If these resources are small in relation to the program's expected contribution to government policy goals, is the program still legitimate? In other words, if the amount of research done is limited, can it have, from a program design point of view, any real impact on the policy goals it is expected to support?

The Relevance Issue

The first step to address the issue of relevance is to identify all the clients of the R&D program. The clients, who will include actual and potential users, may range from university or industrial researchers, who use the publications and reports produced by the R&D program, to senior managers in a department or agency, who might use the results of the program to develop new policies. Probably the best way to identify the clientele is to interview program managers and researchers, as well as representatives from various groups or organizations (for example, companies, universities, or associations) in related fields.

The second step is to determine to what extent the various clients are satisfied that the program is producing or is likely to provide R&D results that will be useful to them. One way of doing so is to do a survey. However, experience has shown that unless such a survey asks the right questions, the survey response will almost always be positive. Whether they are for internal use or for more general consumption, government-produced R&D results are usually free. Accordingly, it will be in no one's interest to put the utility of the R&D effort in doubt. So what evaluators must do is develop a series of penetrating questions that will force the clients to reveal whether the program's R&D results are or can be of use to them; and if so, why and how.

The list of generic questions given below might be a useful guide in developing a specific set of questions to ascertain the true level of utility of the results of the R&D program being evaluated. These generic questions are the result of a review of numerous R&D program evaluation studies. Some apply to private sector clients, others to public sector clients, and many apply to both.

Has the R&D added to your knowledge of a scientific area or field of application in an incremental or "breakthrough manner?

Has the R&D raised important theoretical issues, resolved a scientific controversy, or advanced research techniques?

Will the R&D enable new lines of research to be explored?

Has the R&D developed a new generation of highly-qualified professionals, contributed to the maintenance of the scientific expertise of older staff; or through staff/student interchanges, has an R&D capability been developed in your organization or anywhere else?

Has the R&D resulted in products or processes that prove the feasibility of a scientific application?

Has the R&D resulted in products or processes which have led to savings or profits for you?

Has information resulting from the R&D solved any of your problems, or added to your knowledge of how to apply scientific information to a technical problem?

Are requests by you for R&D information or assistance increasing or decreasing?

Has the information resulting from the R&D contributed to the formulation, design, or conduct of other research, or has it been incorporated into government policy or regulations?

Are the R&D findings potentially relevant to future policy debates or international agreements?

Are the R&D findings communicated to the general public by means of publications or reports?

Has the R&D program successfully transferred new technology to the private sector, and has the transfer resulted in new products or processes being marketed nationally or internationally?

Has the technology transfer had any negative effects?

Are you actively monitoring the work of the R&D program to seek out commercial opportunities?

It should be noted that the perception of usefulness or potential usefulness of R&D program results might vary considerably as one goes from the top to the bottom of the organization being surveyed. Accordingly, all the relevant management levels of the client organization, from the president to the researcher, should be included in the survey, and each level should be queried as to how they see the R&D results being beneficial to their organization.

A related way of determining program relevance is to assemble a panel of knowledgeable persons representing the clientele of the R&D program. The panel might then be in a position to give an opinion of just how much the R&D program results are or will be useful. This approach might be used to corroborate the client survey findings and possibly to reinforce them by adding a qualitative dimension they might otherwise lack.

The Evaluation of the Minerals Program: An Example

The Minerals Program is a Canadian federal government program whose objective is to ensure an adequate supply of mineral resources and to promote their effective uses. The program involves a number of research activities first to promote a knowledge base for the development of policies and programs for the exploitation of minerals, and second to ensure the availability of technology for the supply and use of minerals.

The evaluation of the Minerals Program is singled out here for illustrative purposes because in addition to assessing the quality of the research done this evaluation, inter alia, also addressed the issues of legitimacy and relevance in a way quite similar to what has been proposed here.

There was consensus among potential beneficiaries of the Minerals Program that the technical work was of high quality, and that the professional standards and facilities were comparable with any in Canadian industry. The program's output was, in general, considered to be satisfactory from a technical standpoint. The quality of research was not, therefore, an issue.

However, by addressing the legitimacy issue, it became apparent that the objectives of the Minerals Program did not properly reflect the current interpretation of the role of the department. Furthermore, it also became clear that the policy goals supported by the program lacked clarity, and that a policy for the security of supply of strategic minerals needed to be made explicit as a basis for continuing research on such materials.

The relevance issue was addressed by means of a survey of the Minerals Program clientele. By soliciting the views of many levels of management, and not only those of researchers, it became obvious that a significantly greater amount of industrial R&D (that is, R&D done outside government) concerns mineral processing. This was also found to be the case in the Minerals Program. Given that both mining and processing have been shown to have an equal economic impact, it is evident that government R&D should redress this imbalance by conducting more research in the mining area.

The evaluation of the Minerals Program was highly successful. Not only did it provide senior management with the assurance that the program was doing good research, it also provided them with useful information for possible program design improvements as well as for the clarification of program objectives and policy goals.

Conclusion

The example given illustrates the advantages of the evaluation framework suggested here for R&D programs. For one thing, the framework goes well beyond the traditional "quality of research" evaluation which, in times of increasing scrutiny of public spending and decreasing availability of resources, is seriously inadequate. For another, the framework successfully circumvents the difficult task of having to evaluate an R&D program by attempting to directly measure its outcomes. And, finally, and perhaps most importantly, the framework promises to provide useful and timely information to decisionmakers because it is designed to determine first whether it is appropriate for government to be doing the research it is doing, and second whether there is a client intent on making use of the results of the research. Indeed, such information can enable a government to determine when substantial changes to its R&D programs are required. Other evaluation approaches, in particular those associated with "quality of research" issues, can only point to marginal changes. By addressing the issues of legitimacy and relevance, evaluators can be of great assistance to a government called upon to do more with less.

Note

1. See "Ministry of State, Science and Technology Canada," Report of the Task Force on Federal Policies and Programs for Technology Development, July 1984, pp. 26–28.

Part IV
Assessing Organizational Performance

Public and nonprofit managers frequently lack reliable information on the performance, especially outcomes, of programs they are responsible for implementing or monitoring. Managers need credible and valid information about program results to understand what works, to know where performance can be improved, and to communicate the value of what they are doing. Assessing organizational and program performance is a second task for results-oriented managers.

Mary Ann Scheirer maintains in her chapter that implementation assessment is not a single line of research nor a unified set of prescriptions for all researchers to follow. She identifies four domains of implementation assessment. Two focus on microissues, and two ask questions at the policy or macro-level. Each domain has a different set of information needs.

One type of implementation assessment explores the issues of what has to be done in a particular locale or organization to implement a new activity, who is responsible for doing it, and whether the activity was accomplished. A second type seeks explanations for the behavior of participants in implementation. The third assessment strategy focuses on the extent to which implementation occurred over a larger system—for example, multiple organizations, locales, or states. The last type looks for explanations about what did or did not happen in the macro-system during implementation.

Scheirer discusses how her framework can assist evaluators to plan for implementation and to select the appropriate methods of implementation assessment.

Carole Neves, James Wolf, and Bill Benton describe how *management indicators* can be developed and used to monitor organizational performance. A management indicator is a measure of some aspect of an organization that significantly affects performance. Management indicators rely largely on existing data, and focus on program concerns over which the manager can exercise some control or influence. A major value of indicators is to help managers identify priority areas where their attention and judgment can benefit performance.

Neves and her colleagues demonstrate how indicators can be used in human service agencies. A key feature of their pragmatic approach is the reliance on ratios and computer graphics to increase the communicability, understandability, and utility of management indicators. The authors also discuss the generic problems of data collection and use in complex organizations.

Wayne Gray looks at the issue of monitoring the implementation of new programs. Evaluators currently have a disparate collection of rules and warnings about how to plan for and monitor implementation efforts. Gray offers a comprehensive and systematic way to approach implementation tasks.

Evaluators must first have (or gain) knowledge about the new program, the implementing organization, and theories of implementation. This knowledge is used to rank in importance the components of the program, to determine how the components fit with existing organization routines, to anticipate implementation problems, and to devise strategies and tactics to treat the identified problems.

The last step in Gray's approach involves three types of evaluation: assessing the fit between the ideal and the reality of implementation, determining how well the program works, and examining the effectiveness of implementation strategies and tactics. Gray's framework provides evaluators with an integrated set of questions to ask when planning and building an information system to monitor implementation.

Anne Hastings and Larry Beyna's case study illustrates an extended effort to assess organizational performance. Their topic is the Civil Service Reform Act (CSRA) of 1978. The authors first review the intent of the law and the initial implementation barriers. Next they describe the methods used by the Department of Health and Human Services (HHS) to conduct a five-year evaluation of the CSRA's impact on HHS management practices.

The evaluation concluded that the reform was a short-term success, but that the long-term prospects are less certain. HHS successfully implemented the structure of the CSRA. However, the management tools made available by the act were used sporadically and not always appropriately. Also, civil servants' challenges to the legitimacy of the reform act have not been adequately addressed by CSRA advocates. The authors conclude by discussing some of the problems associated with assessing complex organizational change.

10
Managing Innovation: A Framework for Measuring Implementation

Mary Ann Scheirer

Stimulating higher organizational performance by focusing on improved implementation is an appropriate new role for evaluators. Organizations frequently attempt to improve their operations via innovation; that is, they initiate or import new equipment, new management techniques, or new processes to revamp their performance. Yet, the initial decision to adopt a technical or social innovation does not, in itself, produce the intended organizational benefits. The innovation must be *implemented,* in other words, integrated within the daily work routines of users at several organizational levels. Assessing the extent of implementation, as well as analyzing the mechanisms for achieving such change, both call for a variety of skills that evaluators could contribute.

In addition, planning for the changes to be brought about by an innovation often requires considerable organizational analysis by managers. Users' backgrounds and skills must be compared with the abilities assumed by the technical designers of an innovation. The motivations and incentives for front-line users are frequently not the same as the objectives motivating an adoption decision. For these reasons, planning for implementation processes should be a management activity separate from the decision making that determines *what* technical innovation or new social program will be attempted.

The complexity surrounding implementation processes, along with the growing recognition of their importance, has stimulated a large body of research. Previous analyses include theoretical and prescriptive essays, many case studies, and some across-site empirical studies. These studies suggest a wide variety of ideas for facilitating implementation but are not yet organized into a coherent framework. The dimensions of a framework are needed to permit synthesis across individual implementation studies, and to provide guidance to evaluators in planning what type(s) of implementation assessment might be most useful in a particular situation.

This chapter discusses two cross-cutting dimensions that should help to organize the present state of implementation assessment.[1] By use of the four-fold table generated from these dimensions, researchers can select the particular methods for implementation assessment that are needed for a particular evaluation study. Innovation managers can also use these dimensions as a guide to planning for the implementation process itself: what feedback information should be monitored about the processes occurring, and what cast of players should be involved in implementation considerations? The answers to such questions depend heavily upon the position taken along each implementation dimension.

The Dimensions Defined

Previous implementation researchers have generally oriented their studies along each of two dimensions: a theoretical perspective focused on either micro or macroimplementation and a measurement focus on either the extent of implementation or implementation processes. The micro-macro distinction has been discussed previously by Berman, who defined macroimplementation as the process by which the federal government (or other umbrella organization) executes policy so as to influence local delivery organizations in desired ways.[2] Macroimplementation studies most frequently examine the deployment of a new law or federal funding program. In macroimplementation, the originating policy source usually does not have coercive control, but instead operates in a loosely coupled system of actors with diverse interests, each of whom may change the policy or program as it is transmitted. In contrast, microimplementation studies focus on the individuals within one or more organizations to examine the nature of behavioral and/or organizational change involved in putting an innovation into place. The innovation involved may be either new technical equipment or a social program intervention.

Cross-cutting this macro versus micro theoretical perspective has been a polarity in the types of measurement employed, between examining the degree or extent of implementation, and illuminating the processes by which implementation occurs. Measurement emphasis on the extent of implementation addresses the question, "*How much* implementation occurred?" This measurement emphasis usually draws from the extensive psychometric tradition for creating an operational definition of a construct. For example, the innovation might be operationalized as requiring a number of components, with subsequent measurement of users' behaviors on each component used as the measure of extent of implementation.[3]

Conversely, process measurement focuses on the question, "*How* did the changes needed for implementation take place or fail to take place?" This research tradition has frequently used applications of field research techniques such as ethnography and naturalistic inquiry to illuminate processes occurring over time. Yin's work on the routinization of innovations, for example, used both case study and survey methods to trace ten organizational "passages and cycles" hypothesized to characterize the changes needed to ensure long-term use.[4]

Four Perspectives on Implementation Research

Intersecting the two dimensions yields the four-celled table shown in figure 10–1, with each cell suggesting a useful perspective for examining implementation. The implications of each perspective will be illustrated, particularly with reference to ongoing research on the adoption and implementation of a specific dental health innovation into public schools.

This innovation is the weekly use of a fluoride rinse for cavity prevention by all participating children within a classroom setting. Data on the use of the fluoride rinse program were collected in 1979 by Silversin and Coombs; further analysis of the 1979 data and a second-wave survey to study the long-term institutionalization of the program are underway.[5]

The focus on this fluoride rinse program is particularly illuminating for implementation questions for several reasons. First, its efficacy has been well-documented in controlled experimental studies: full use can prevent 20 percent to 50 percent of cavities among children living in areas without fluori-

| | | Measurement Focus | |
		Extent of Implementation	Implementation Process
Theoretical Perspective	Micro	Accuracy I	Individual or Organizational Change II
	Macro	Scope III	System Change IV

Figure 10–1. Research Foci Suggested by Dimensions of Implementation
            Assessment

dated water.[6] This previous experimental testing permits questions of theoretical efficacy to be separated from analysis of implementation issues.

Second, the characteristics of the fluoride rinse program are rather simple and not costly, thus alleviating the necessity for implementors to learn complex new skills. Analysis of this program thus separates implementation issues from staff training needs.

Third, the process of implementing a preventive health measure in public schools does involve the complex macroimplementation issues regarding the autonomy of local school districts, the proper role of schools in health promotion, and the coordination of fluoride program delivery among multiple classroom teachers. Thus, examining in some detail how implementation research on this program was or could be conducted will illustrate the possibilities and comparative strengths of the four perspectives.

Implementation Accuracy

Returning to the discussion of figure 10–1, the intersection of a microimplementation perspective with measurement of extent (cell I) suggests a research focus on the *accuracy* of implementation. This requires the detailed conceptualization of the innovation into measurable components, preferably behaviorally specified. For example, the components of the in-school fluoride rinse program recommended by the National Institute for Dental Research are that each participating child (1) should rinse for 60 seconds, (2) should rinse with a 0.2 percent sodium fluoride solution, (3) should not eat or drink for thirty minutes after rinsing, (4) should rinse once each week, and (5) should participate in the program for nine months of the school year. For these individual components to be carried out, the program further specifies school level components: that grade levels from kindergarten through grade 12 should participate; and that there be a systematic method for supervising the mixing and distribution of the rinse solution. In spite of the extreme simplicity of these components, Silversin and Coombs' 1979 survey found that among districts that had adopted the program, only 24 percent fully implemented the three components for which information was requested.[7]

For many other programs or innovations, describing the components of an innovation is a more lengthy process, partly because the innovation is more complex, but frequently because its developers have not completed the specification of "the innovation" into terms usable by the intended implementors. In this case, the researchers' work to develop indicators of the accuracy of implementation may require considerable time with developers to pin down program specifications or to define alternative acceptable uses of a new technology. The work of Hall and Loucks on analyzing innovation configurations, as well as its application in a recent extensive study of innovations in criminal justice and educational agencies, shows that such behavioral specification of the components of an innovation *can* be done.[8]

In the absence of agreement on the behaviorally defined components, researchers, program managers, and change agents frequently work at cross purposes because each is oriented toward different possible definitions of the innovation's requirements when translated into daily routines. Further, assessing the accuracy of implementation is now becoming recognized as a necessary intervening variable for quasi-experimental designs in outcome evaluations. Thus, defining and measuring the components of an innovation is frequently a prerequisite for other types of implementation assessment.

Individual Change

Moving next to cell II of figure 10–1, using a microperspective with an emphasis on implementation processes suggests a focus on individual and organizational change processes and/or on the sources of resistance to change. The research question becomes, how can implementation be facilitated among these individuals, or within these organizations? This question was not directly addressed by the prior research on the fluoride rinse program. Some evidence was collected, however, showing that accurate implementation was more likely if there was *not* turnover in the position of program supervisor, if the supervisor had visited another district to view an operational program, and if the supervisor had consulted a journal or magazine article about fluoride rinses. In short, from this study it appears that both individual and organizational variables are needed to explain the extent of implementation.

There is, of course, a vast literature on both individual and organizational change that can be applied to implementation issues. In my previous work, several theoretical perspectives are placed into an organizational framework for assessing implementation processes, along with two case studies illustrating the use of the framework.[9] Others have examined the extent to which individual attitudes, values, or perceptions about an innovation can predict the extent of individual level implementation. Perhaps the essential prescription to note about this research focus is the empirical connection logically linking cells I and II: research examining the processes of individual or organizational change ought to include measurement(s) of the accuracy of implementation as the dependent variable. Even qualitative or case study research on these issues should relate a process-focused narrative of events to indicators of *how much* change actually occurred.

Implementation Scope

Moving to the macroimplementation perspective, its intersection with a measurement focus on the extent of implementation (cell III) suggests an assessment of the *scope* of implementation over a wider sector of society. For some innovations, this perspective is identical to examining the extent of diffusion and adoption, perhaps using classical theory concerning the characteristics of an innovation that predict adoption. For example, Silversin and Coombs' nationwide survey of school districts found that by 1979 about 24 percent of all districts had adopted the fluoride rinse or a fluoride tablet program in at least some of their schools. This adoption decision was *not* related to the presence or absence of fluoride in the community's drinking water. Instead, adoption was more likely when district superintendents had received their first information about the program from health personnel, thus supporting a "linking agent" as an important influence on adoption.

For other innovations, particularly those whose implementation involves compliance with a law or federal policy, measuring the scope of implementation requires assessing which features are or are not being carried out in which local jurisdictions. Such assessments of the scope of implementation may require collecting information from several jurisdictional levels, usually federal, state, and local levels, to understand even the extent of program involvement at each level. Questions concerning the scope of implementation of a law, for example, school desegregation or equal employment opportunity, thus may involve examining the range of jurisdictions complying, as well as the numbers of individuals affected by the types of jurisdictions most likely to comply.

System Change

The testing of causal hypotheses concerning the scope of implementation or adoption is within the domain of cell IV, research on system changes to examine implementation processes at the macrolevel. Researchers with this perspective have, for example, studied the conflicting incentive systems hampering smooth linkages among federal, state, and local levels.[10] Full exploration of implementation from this perspective often requires an investigation of the multiple environments surrounding any specific change: the economic climate, other crosscutting political issues, pressures from other priorities impinging on major actors, and so forth.

Some examination of such issues was incorporated into the study of the fluoride rinse program, by asking what individuals or groups had been a major influence for or against local adoption. The hypothesized resistance from "antifluoridationists" was *not* supported; perhaps these individuals had diverted their attention to other issues by the late 1970s. Whether or not funding was available was cited as a major difference between adopters and nonadopters. This finding suggests the importance of both the prevailing financial support systems for health interventions within a public school setting and the likely negative influence of changes in the economic climate for such a program.

Implications

These four quite different orientations illustrate the diversity of research questions that have fallen under the rubric "implementation assessment." This wealth of approaches means that implementation study is not a single line of research. Further, there is not a unified set of prescriptions for other implementation researchers to follow. Like the six blind men examining an elephant, there are frequently as many different ways to assess implementation as there are researchers to work on a particular project. And they may all be "correct," that is, scientifically sound and potentially useful!

From this observation it follows that developing a research plan for implementation assessment may require extensive negotiation between a research sponsor, such as a federal agency or organizational manager, and the researcher or research team. Each participant is likely to bring to such discussions quite different perceptions of the definition of implementation assessment, and of the research resources needed for this task. This will probably be particularly true if the implementation assessment is originally considered as only a minor part of an outcome evaluation plan. Simply measuring the accuracy of implementation across some population of users often requires considerable research effort in itself. If more complex questions are of interest to the research sponsor, such as the effectiveness of various mechanisms to increase the accuracy of implementation, then the complexity of the data required increases accordingly.

A further implication of this analysis is that data collection using just one of the four perspectives is frequently inadequate. Careful measurement of either accuracy or scope of implementation may seem to be all that is required, but when the data show less than anticipated accuracy or scope, questions are inevitably raised concerning *reasons* for low accuracy or *what types* of people are high or low users. Conversely, a process investigation alone at either macro or microlevel lacks examination of the necessary dependent variable, the extent of implementation. Even a subjective assessment of the extent of change occurring is better than no assessment at all. However, such judgmental measures may be quite biased without careful enumeration of program components and some means for systematically finding an average level of use among many individuals. Further, knowing the extent of *adoption* of a program of technology, at the macrolevel, particularly if the adopter is an organization, does not reveal the accuracy of implementation by the front-line users.

The complexity of implementation assessment further implies that multidisciplinary research is frequently needed for full understanding of these issues. For example, an attitudinal assessment of individuals involved in a change effort may bring to bear the latest techniques from this branch of social psychology, but will be inadequate to encompass the forces impinging on these individuals when they work within an organization. Further, an economic-based cost-benefit analysis may be useful to decision making from a federal perspective, but may not include the political priorities or even budgetary constraints operating on program adoption decisions at a local level. Given that current graduate training for evaluation researchers usually draws from a single disciplinary approach, it is valuable for implementation assessment to be planned and carried out by multidisciplinary teams.

A final implication of this four-fold analysis is that there are no simple rules for evaluators to follow when designing the implementation portion of a larger-scale evaluation. Much will depend on the nature of the program, policy, or piece of equipment that is the subject of study. Are its components specifiable in advance or must they be defined during the course of field-based data collection? How complex are its components and how extensive is the change likely to be required of organizations or individuals? Is the study to be undertaken from a federal or local perspective? How extensive is the data collection effort included in the research budget? Which of the many research questions falling under the general topic of implementation assessment have high priority to the research sponsor? To the evaluator? The answers to each of these questions may suggest divergent approaches to implementation assessment design.

Conclusion

Consideration of each cell of the four-fold table introduced here should help to clarify the pros and cons of each approach in application to a specific implementation project. The performance of innovations in individual organizations will certainly be strengthened by careful assessment and feedback of implementation data. Such measurement is necessary even at the innovation development stage, to separate questions of ideal innovation efficacy from the issue of obtaining implementation in practical applications.

After the development and dissemination of an innovation, implementation assessment can provide the feedback information for program managers to monitor the actual changes taking place and any obstacles hindering full implementation. Finally, further rigorous measurement and cross-study synthesis by implementation researchers should help to consolidate the findings from individual studies into a more coherent body of tested prescriptions for future action.

Notes

1. The preparation of this chapter was supported in part by Grant No. 1 R01–DEO6895–1 from the National Institute of Dental Research. The conclusions

expressed here are those of the author and do not necessarily reflect the views of the NIDR.

2. Paul Berman. "The Study of Macro- and Micro-Implementation," *Public Policy,* 26 (1978):157–184.

3. M.A. Scheirer and E.L. Rezmovic, "Measuring the Degree of Program Implementation," *Evaluation Review,* 7 (1983):599–633.

4. Robert Yin. *Changing Urban Bureaucracies: How New Practices Become Routinized* (Lexington, Mass.: Lexington Books, 1979).

5. J.B. Silversin, J.A. Coombs, and M.E. Drollette. "Adoption of Dental Preventive Measures in United States Schools," *Journal of Dental Research,* 59 (1980): 2233–2242.

6. American Dental Association, Council on Dental Therapeutics, "Council Classifies Fluoride Mouth Rinses," *Journal of the American Dental Association,* 91 (1975):1250. See also A.J. Miller and P. Brunelle, "Fluoride Rinses," in R.E. Stewart et al. (Eds.), *Pediatric Dentistry: Scientific Foundations and Clinical Practice* (St. Louis: C.V. Mosby, 1982).

7. J.A. Coombs, J.B. Silversin, E.M. Rogers, and M.E. Drollette. "The Transfer of Preventive Health Technologies to Schools: A Focus on Implementation," *Social Science and Medicine,* 15 (1981):789–799.

8. G.E. Hall and S.F. Loucks. *Innovation Configurations: Analyzing the Adaptations of Innovations* (Austin, Tex.: Research and Development Center for Teacher Education, University of Texas at Austin, 1978). See also C. Blakely, J. Mayer, R. Gottschalk, D. Roitman, N. Schmidtt, W. Davidson II, and J. Emshoff, *Salient Processes in the Dissemination of Social Technologies,* Final Report submitted to the National Science Foundation (Lansing, Mich.: Michigan State University, 1984).

9. M.A. Scheirer, *Program Implementation: The Organizational Context* (Beverly Hills, Calif.: Sage, 1981).

10. J. Pincus, "Incentive for Innovation in the Public Schools," *Review of Educational Research,* 44 (1974):113–144.

11

The Use of Management Indicators in Monitoring the Performance of Human Service Agencies

Carole M. P. Neves
James F. Wolf
Bill B. Benton

*M*anagement indicators are selected measures of agency performance. Unlike more sophisticated research techniques that attempt to provide definitive or normative assessments of how well or how poorly an agency is performing, management indicators attempt to be indicative of an agency's performance. Management indicators are intended to be provocative, to suggest to managers a few areas where it may be appropriate to investigate further why a particular indicator shows up the way it does.

The distinctive features of the management indicator approach include its emphasis on:

Exploiting existing data wherever possible rather than requiring the generation of new data.

Focusing measures on the priority concerns of agency management, concerns over which the manager has some control.

Enabling the user to manage the system on an ongoing basis without additional staff or expensive investments in data processing.

The essence of management indicators is comparison. Specifically, indicators provide a basis for comparing the performance of one agency with the performance of similar agencies, the performance of the same agency with itself over time, and the performance of an agency against established norms, standards, and objectives.

This chapter addresses ways in which management indicators can be used to improve organizational performance. The authors present an introduction to management indicators, including a review of relevant literature and a description of recent work with eight local human service agencies across the country. The learning gained from the work, the utility of management indicators, and the potential problems with introducing management indicators into human service agencies are then discussed.

An Overview of Management Indicators

Definition of Management Indicators

In general, management indicators are measures of organizational phenomena. The term management indicator encompasses a broad range of tools used as reference points against which one can compare the results of other programs, historic data, information from other jurisdictions, goals and standards, or a combination of the above. The essence of a system of management indicators is comparison. The purpose of management indicators is to provide managers with practical information that can help them decide how to solve problems in their organizations.

A standard definition of the term management indicators does not exist. Management indicators are often defined by what they are not. Indicators are not definitive statements about what aspects of an organization's program are doing well or poorly, nor do they of themselves provide solutions to problems. They are not solely intended to be control mechanisms, nor should they be designed to be primarily regulatory or restrictive measures. Management indicators should not be used slavishly as the only measures of performance for a program or office.

Management indicators are intended to act as pointers to relevant questions for management to ask and as clues to where management may wish to focus its limited time and attention. Indicators can encourage managers to ask *why?* In the process of answering this question, managers are provided with diagnostic information about the possible need for policy clarification, training, corrective action, and opportunities to share best practices or useful alternative approaches to shared problems.

Bowers and Bowers define management indicators as: "selected items of data that focus management attention on those areas critical to efficient and effective program operations."[1] For Elkin and Molitor, key dimensions of a management indicator are that:

> It addresses one of a limited number of areas designated by top management as critical to the continuing successful functioning of the organization that will be monitored on a regular basis; it is made up of a ratio of operational statistics; there exists a criterion or standard against which the actual indicator values can be compared; it is displayed in graphic form and is analyzed as a trend over time (preferably over four or more time periods); and it is given a descriptive title.[2]

Kamis-Gould distills the concept of management indicators in terms of four vectors: appropriateness, adequacy, efficiency, and effectiveness.[3] Kamis-Gould explicitly recognizes indicators in systematic terms of input, process, and output. This characterization outlines several legitimate ways to bound the term management indicators, but it does not reduce the ambiguity of the term and contributes little to our understanding of exactly what pieces of data serve as indicators. Kamis-Gould's explanation of indicators is supported by several authors who formulate operational definitions of management indicators. Indicators are often used in three areas: assessment of effort (input); assessment of effects or results (outputs or outcomes of effort); and assessment of process (an analysis of why and how a result was achieved). Suchman proposes five categories to which indicators may be applied: effort, performance, adequacy of performance, efficiency, and process.[4] Although Suchman and others provide us with classification schemes that prove useful once indicators are considered in detail, clear-cut definitions of the term are not usually specified.

Because no specific definition of the term management indicator is acceptable, we should turn to Dunn, who offers the most inclusive description. An indicator, writes Dunn, is "a directly observable characteristic substituted for indirectly observable characteristics and used as operational definitions of variables."[5] As such, it measures input, process, output, and outcome variables.

A Short History of Management Indicators

In 1977, Victor Preisser (then Commissioner of the Iowa Department of Social Services) made a notable contribution to management indicators by asking managers in the department to select key items of information for their programs in order to better understand how the department was functioning. Indicators were developed and expanded into two sets: overall operations and field operations.

Utah, under the guidance of Anthony W. Mitchell, refined the indicator approach and continued the development of indicators. In 1981, the *New England Journal of Human Services* published a penetrating article by Mitchell entitled, "Dare to Compare."[6] The article stressed comparisons among indicators derived from similar programs and urged the federal government, in cooperation with state and local managers, to take the lead in designing management indicators for human service programs. Mitchell argues that:

> Managers would have more objective assessments of their agencies' major strengths and weaknesses compared to those of similar agencies and this information would, in turn, enhance rational decision making on priorities and resource allocations.[7]

Indicators are viewed by Mitchell as multipurpose tools to shape organizations by focusing on the variability and similarity of programs operated by different agencies.

On an operational level, several organizations, including the Urban Institute; Peat, Marwick, Mitchell, and Co.; the Financial Accounting Standards Board; United Way of America; the National Association of State Units on Aging; and Booz, Allen, and Hamilton have attempted to define and to develop management indicators. Several studies performed by these organizations were tied to the disbursement of federal funds by the Department of Health and Human Services. The National Institute of Mental Health developed indicators to compare federally funded comprehensive mental health centers along three program elements; accessibility, financial viability, and efficiency-productivity. Kamis-Gould added more rigorous procedures to developing indicators in this area by proposing a set of mental health performance indicators to be used in monitoring contracted services for the State of New Jersey.[8]

Hall proposed a framework for identifying fiscal problems and presented a set of indicators to monitor the financial condition of not-for-profit human service agencies using information from financial reports.[9] Hall's effort was directed toward planning and development activities. Indicators highlighted aspects of a declining revenue base, dependence on unstable revenue sources, increasing unit costs, and inadequacies in fiscal policy and management.

Rockart presented five approaches to assessing the information needs of chief executive officers from the private sector: the "By-Product Technique," the "Null Approach," the "Key Indicator System," the "Total Study Process," and his own creation, the "Critical Success Factors" approach.[10] All five approaches utilize indicators to measure important phenomena that occur in the operation of organizations, in varying forms, in varying degrees of inclusiveness, and in varying amounts.

Rockart's work and the works of other organizational theorists, consultants, and managers were used by Elkin and Molitor to develop a system of management indicators based on a general systems perspective and three recognized management concerns (effectiveness, efficiency, and adequacy of finances).[11] The interdisciplinary nature of Elkin and Molitor's study implicitly called for a greater awarness of research traditions and a breakdown in barriers among theoreticians, consultants, and managers. It was an attempt to apply certain private sector productivity concepts to the public sector.

In reviewing the literature, the authors came across four types of studies on management indicators. By far the most popular topic was the development of indicators for specific programs, including Aid to Families with Dependent Children (AFDC), substitute care, day care, and mental health programs. Development of indicators for measuring unit costs and the financial condition of human service agencies was the second most frequent type of study. Variants of studies on financial conditions include specialized studies on staffing and accounting. Indicators representing financial conditions represent inputs to management decisions concerning cost reduction programs and financial operations, in particular. We have already mentioned the third type of studies, endeavors that sought to develop and to explain management indicators for a wide range of organizational activities. Benton et al.[12] and Elkin and Molitor[13] proposed sets of indicators to be used in a number of different ways depending on the context, resources, skill, and ingenuity of persons using the system. Finally, the fourth type examined the uses and consequences of management indicators. Recently, Bowers and Bowers wrote a document that focuses on indicator usage by managers in human service agencies.[14]

The reader has been provided with a glimpse of the management indicator landscape and the areas in this field in which the literature has been growing. Additional information can be found in the references cited in the Bibliography. We now discuss experiences with management indicators in the New Zealand Department of Social Welfare.

The New Zealand Experience

Like central offices in most public agencies, the Head Office of the New Zealand Department of Social Welfare collects a large amount of data from its local offices. Prior to 1981, the primary use of these data was inclusion in the department's annual report, which was submitted to Parliament along with the agency's annual budget request.

In 1981, the department's newly created Social Programme Evaluation Unit was requested by the Director-General of Social Welfare to determine whether these data could be exploited, using the management indicator approach, to improve the performance of the department's fifty-three district offices.

Drawing from successful and unsuccessful experiences with management indicators in the United States and elsewhere, the Social Programme Evaluation Unit established three guidelines which, in retrospect, were critical to the initiative's success:

1. *"Ownership" for the system would be at the district manager level.* The responsibility for the design of the system (including the selection of the actual indicators to be used to monitor district office performance) would rest with district managers.

   In addition to ownership of the system by its primary users, this decision meant that important determinations as to data use were made by the producers of data.

2. *The indicators would utilize existing data wherever possible.* No new data were to be collected unless the district managers agreed that additional reporting requirements were essential. The practical effect of this decision was that no new data were collected to support the initial set of management indicators.

   Reliance on existing data meant that, in several instances, there was a need to develop "surrogate" measures for important areas of agency performance, relying on data less than ideally suited to the purpose for which they were used. A positive side effect was a heightened awareness at the district level of the importance of accurate and timely reporting.

3. *The number of indicators would be limited to approximately sixty for the entire agency.* In addition to this initial limitation, the system was subjected to a discipline whereby in order to add an indicator to the initial set, an indicator had to be dropped from the set.

   This constraint was designed to focus attention on key areas of performance and to keep the project from being killed by its own success (that is, the proliferation of indicators which appeared to have brought down other management indicator systems).

Perhaps the best way to illuminate the utility of this approach to management indicators is to provide one example of how indicators were used to improve agency performance. The example relates to substitute care (that is, the residential care of children and young persons outside of their homes by the Department of Social Welfare, whether in foster homes, group homes, or in government-run institutions).

The two indicators were: the frequency of reports to each of the department's district offices about problems related to children and young persons, and the incidence of children and young persons in substitute care per 1,000 in the communities served by the district offices.

These data were arrayed on a scattergram. District office experiences varied considerably. From this array, the following "outliers" (that is, district offices with prototypical experiences) were identified:

An office with a high rate of referrals and a high incidence of substitute care.

An office with a high rate of referrals and a low incidence of substitute care.

An office with a low rate of referrals and a high incidence of substitute care.

An office with a low rate of referrals and a low incidence of substitute care.

In-depth, on-site reviews of the way each office interpreted the department's policy with regard to the appropriateness of removing children and young persons from their homes was conducted by the Social Programme Evaluation Unit.

The on-site reviews revealed substantial variations in the way presumably "uniform" national substitute care policy was being implemented. These variations confirmed the validity of management indicators as a tool for monitoring local office performance, and led to the identification of exemplary performance ("best practices"), which were shared with other district offices. The review also triggered a national initiative designed to reduce inappropriate removal of children and young persons from their homes.

The Human Service Management Indicator Project

The Human Service Management Indicator Project was designed to develop a tool by which the managers of local human service agencies in the United States could monitor agency performance and identify areas for cost-effective improvement. This project was conducted by Urban Systems Research & Engineering, Inc., with sponsorship from the U.S. Office of Human Development Services (HDS) under the Small Business Innovation Research (SBIR) program. The project began in the fall of 1983 and was completed in early 1985.

The first task of this project was to define areas of organizational activity that could be addressed by managers of local human service agencies. This work was intended to help managers face critical areas of their organizational activity most susceptible to managerial action. Every effort was made to provide the fewest indicators possible, yet support the development of a comprehensive assessment of agency operations.

From available indicators, a set of priority areas for agency performance was selected, including generic measures such as community and organizational demographics, finance, personnel, and intake. The set of indicators also included candidate measures for specific program areas that were typically administered by local departments of social services. The five service programs were: Child Abuse and Neglect, Substitute Care, Child Day Care, AFDC, and Food Stamps. A detailed list of selected indicators is presented in table 11–1.

Candidate indicators were then selected for each priority area of organizational performance. From over 500 potential indicators identified in the literature, seventy-five were selected because they represented significant organizational performance areas, were factors over which managers had some control, and included areas where the data were likely to be easily available. Nearly 200 individual data elements were required to capture the initial set of indicators.

Table 11–1
Selected Management Indicators

Demographics
    Population of Jurisdiction
    Per Capita Income
    Unemployment Rate

Finance
    Local Revenues
    Personnel Costs & Fringe Benefits and Purchase of Service
    Objects of Expenditure

Space Utilization

Personnel
    Turnover
    Full Time Equivalent (FTE) in Particular Programs
    Mix of Staff (Administrative, Clerical, Program)
    Absenteeism
    Vacancies
    Use of Volunteers
    Utilization of Clerical Staff

Intake
    Waiting Time for Appointments
    Time to Complete Applications
    Workload and Productivity

Child Abuse and Neglect Investigation
    Number of Referrals to Department
    Abused and Neglected Children Sent to Substitute Care
    Disposition of Investigations

Substitute Care
    Substitute Care Caseload
    Length of Continuous Time in Care

Child Day Care
    Costs of Care
    Reasons for Care
    Percentage of Children in Day Care Centers

AFDC
    AFDC Approvals
    AFDC Participation
    AFDC Cases Referred for Fraud Investigation

Food Stamps
    Food Stamp Staffing
    Food Stamp Cases Referred for Fraud Investigation

Not surprisingly, the availability and quality of data varied among agencies as well as among programs within agencies. As a result, a variety of data collection methods were often needed for a single data element. In some instances, data were found in the desired format, while in other cases special sampling extrapolations were required. When data were not available or excessive effort was needed to secure information, indicators were eliminated. As a result of continuing work, areas of higher concern were substituted. The absolute number of indicators (approximately fifty) was held constant.

An important decision of the management indicator process is that an agency should be able to compare its performance with other agencies of similar character. At a minimum, there should be reasonable comparability of functions, organization size, and structure. The first four agencies included in the project were local human service organizations with comprehensive responsibility for most social service and income maintenance functions. The staff size was between 100 and 350 full-time personnel, and there were four or five levels in the organizational structure. The agencies participating in Phase I were Baltimore County, Maryland; Alexandria, Virginia; Wake County, North Carolina; and Jefferson County, Colorado. Four additional agencies, similar in character to the initial four jurisdictions, were added to the data base. The four new agencies were Monroe County, New York; San Joaquin County, California; Ramsey County, Minnesota; and Prince William County, Virginia.

Computer graphics were a central part of the project. Initial discussions were carried out with persons with extensive familiarity with computer graphics software. Based on these discussions and the expertise of project staff, it was concluded that selected use of graphics can have a powerful effect on the use of data. The contrast between data presented in the traditional format and with computer graphics is demonstrated in figures 11–1 and 11–2.

Reflections on Data Collection, Processing, and Analysis in Human Service Agencies

The management indicator approach is part of larger issues of organizational analysis and evaluation: the purpose and role of data in the everyday life of organizational action. The management indicator project was profoundly affected by processes of data collection, handling, and analysis in human service organizations. At the same time, the project was an attempt to address some of the problems facing human service organizations as they try to find ways to use data for learning about processes and for improving operations.

Two issues germane to data collection, processing, and analysis emerged from the project: the manner in which data exist in human services agencies and certain attitudes of agency personnel with respect to data collection, processing, and analysis. Finally, we discuss the ways in which this project addressed issues related to collecting and using data in organizational settings.

DEPARTMENT OF SOCIAL SERVICES
FINANCIAL DATA STATISTICS
MONTH OF FEBRUARY, 1984

REPORT JABPR1
PAGE 1
RUN DATE 03/01/84

LINE CODE (1)	CASE COUNT (2)	SSI CASE COUNT (3)	NON-SSI CASE COUNT (4)	N.H. CASE COUNT (5)	NON-SSI NH CASE COUNT (6)	ADULT COUNT (7)	CHILD COUNT (8)	TOTAL AMOUNT (9)	AVGE /CASE (10)	SSI AMOUNT (11)	SSI AVGE/ CASE (12)	N.H. AMOUNT (13)	N.H. AVGE/ CASE (14)	NON-SSI N.H. AMOUNT (15)	NON-SSI NH AVGE /CASE (16)	CHILD AVGE/ COUNT (17)
RQMNTS-																
ST ALW 10	695	351	340	4	4	674	0	257497.00	370.49	130532	371.88	573	143.25	573	143.25	.00
EX SHR 11	690	351	339	0	0	669	0	15824.00	22.93	8068	22.98	0	.00	0	.00	.00
ES PSN 12	0	0	0	0	0	0	0	.00	.00	0	.00	0	.00	0	.00	.00
MED ND 13	0	0	0	0	0	0	0	.00	.00	0	.00	0	.00	0	.00	.00
SP DTS 14	0	0	0	0	0	0	0	.00	.00	0	.00	0	.00	0	.00	.00
GD DOG 15	0	0	0	0	0	0	0	.00	.00	0	.00	0	.00	0	.00	.00
HME CR 16	70	31	39	0	0	70	0	17237.00	246.24	6865	221.45	0	.00	0	.00	.00
NH NDS 17	1,295	0	1	1,294	1,169	1,295	0	37556.24	29.00	0	.00	37527	29.00	33901	29.00	.00
CNSVR 18	3	0	0	3	3	3	0	137.11	45.70	0	.00	137	45.70	137	45.70	.00
AFC PA 19	1	0	1	0	0	1	0	113.00	113.00	0	.00	0	.00	0	.00	.00
TOTAL R1	1,986	351	341	1,294	1,169	1,965	0	328364.35	165.33	145465	414.43	38237	29.54	34611	29.60	.00
INCOME-																
NET ER 30	2	0	0	2	1	2	0	195.92	97.96	0	.00	195	97.96	194	194.68	.00
OASDI. 31	1,652	227	321	1,104	1,104	1,627	0	531673:65	321.83	51419	226.51	382287	346.27	382287	346.27	.00
RR BNF 32	73	0	4	69	69	72	0	29871.43	409.19	0	.00	28264	409.63	28264	409.63	.00
VA BNF 33	173	3	23	147	147	172	0	43109.33	283.86	232	77.56	45889	312.17	45889	312.17	.00
UNEMPL 34	0	0	0	0	0	0	0	.00	.00	0	.00	0	.00	0	.00	.00
WRKMNS 35	1	0	0	1	1	1	0	21.66	21.66	0	.00	21	21.66	21	21.66	.00
FR SHR 36	4	3	1	0	0	4	0	553.00	138.25	388	129.33	0	.00	0	.00	.00
CHLD C 37	0	0	0	0	0	0	0	.00	.00	0	.00	0	.00	0	.00	.00
CHLD V 38	0	0	0	0	0	0	0	.00	.00	0	.00	0	.00	0	.00	.00
RETRE 39	150	3	10	137	137	147	0	28093.97	187.29	300	100.15	26370	192.48	26370	192.48	.00
CSH CN 40	1	0	1	0	0	1	0	29.00	29.00	0	.00	0	.00	0	.00	.00
SP INC 41	0	0	0	0	0	0	0	.00	.00	0	.00	0	.00	0	.00	.00
VA AID 42	131	0	0	131	131	131	0	25046.27	191.19	0	.00	25046	191.19	25046	191.19	.00
SSI 43	495	370	0	125	0	474	0	61932.25	125.11	58827	158.99	3105	24.84	0	.00	.00
OTHER 44	87	8	11	68	66	83	0	10623.52	122.10	1089	136.19	8814	129.61	8716	132.07	.00
STPRNT 45	0	0	0	0	0	0	0	.00	.00	0	.00	0	.00	0	.00	.00
AL SPN 46	19	2	9	8	8	18	0	2052.99	108.05	256	128.37	1157	144.72	1157	144.72	.00
TOTAL I1	1,993	370	333	1,290	1,165	1,953	0	737412.52	370.00	112514	304.09	519362	402.60	516158	443.05	.00
PRE RR G0	728	346	312	70	3	728	0	70538.89	107.88	37806	109.26	370	5.28	87	29.00	.00
GRANT G1	795	349	319	127	4	795	0	80617.44	101.40	37757	108.18	628	4.94	116	29.00	.00
WTHHLD-																
FD STP 50	0	0	0	0	0	0	0	.00	.00	0	.00	0	.00	0	.00	.00
R RCVY 51	1	1	0	0	0	1	0	53.00	53.00	53	53.00	0	.00	0	.00	.00
S RCVY 52	0	0	0	0	0	0	0	.00	.00	0	.00	0	.00	0	.00	.00
PT PMT 53	0	0	0	0	0	0	0	.00	.00	0	.00	0	.00	0	.00	.00
OTHER 54	0	0	0	0	0	0	0	.00	.00	0	.00	0	.00	0	.00	.00
TOTAL W1	1	1	0	0	0	1	0	53.00	53.00	53	53.00	0	.00	0	.00	.00
LT 10 60	0	0	0	0	0	0	0	.00	.00	0	.00	0	.00	0	.00	.00
RF PMT RP	5	3	2	0	0	5	0	703.96	140.79	661	220.65	0	.00	0	.00	.00
WRRNT W2	790	346	317	127	4	790	0	79867.00	101.09	37046	107.06	628	4.94	116	29.00	.00

RECAP OF INDIVIDUAL COUNTS-

	ADULTS	CHILDREN	TOTAL	N.H. ADULTS
ZERO GRANT AMOUNT-G1	1170	0	1170	1167
ZERO WARRANT AMNT-W2	0	0	0	0
REFUSED PAYMENT -RP	5	0	5	0
CHECK ISSUED -W2	790	0	790	127
TOTAL FINANCIALLY ELIGIBLE	1965	0	1965	1294
MEDICAL ONLY	41	0	41	0
TOTAL ACTIVE ON FILE	2006	0	2006 *I	1294

AVGE ADULTS/CASE= 1.00 AVGE CHLDRN/CASE= .00

RECAP OF CASE COUNTS-

	FINANCIAL & MEDICAL	FINANCIAL ONLY	MEDICAL ONLY	TOTAL
ZERO GRANT AMOUNT-G1	1170	0	41	1211
ZERO WARRANT AMNT-W2	0	0	0	0
REFUSED PAYMENT -RP	5	0	0	5
CHECK ISSUED -W2	790	0	0	790
TOTAL ACTIVE ON FILE	1965	0	41	2006 *C

Figure 11–1. Data Presented in the Usual Way

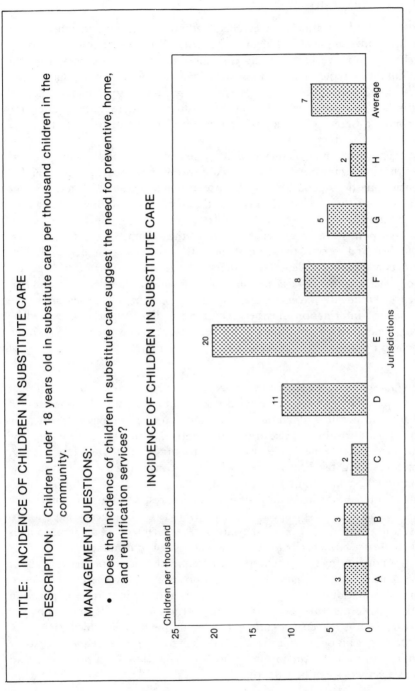

Figure 11–2. Data Presented in a Manner Conducive to Their Use

Current Status of Agency Data

Of particular frustration to researchers and human service personnel are the amount and complexity of data in agencies. Without question, the overwhelming initiative for new and ongoing data collection comes from the accountability requirements of outside organizations. Eligibility data, recertification data, issuance data, intake data, case data, historic data, change-in-status data, and fraud data are some of the diverse data that are required and that have different time and space schedules, forms of presentation, and collection procedures.

Agency personnel, as they obligingly generate facts and numbers, rarely have the time or the opportunity to ask of themselves or of the accountability agencies questions about the significance of the data, the ultimate use of the data, and whether the data are in forms that render the information meaningful and useful.

Two points are important here. First, the volume of the data is overwhelming, and second, the logic of the data is not easy to understand. This presents a serious problem that is the challenge and despair of most people who gather and reduce large amounts of data with substantial effort and persistence. Frequently, agency personnel are unsure of when they are active pursuers of information or when they are mindless puppets controlled by strings manipulated by others. The benefits of using the data are often obscured by the costs of collection and processing.

Data Gatekeepers. In almost every agency, someone acted as a kind of *data gatekeeper*. The gatekeeper assumed responsibility because of an interest in research or because of an interest in computer technology. Whether by appointment by someone else or by self initiative, the data gatekeeper was the conduit of much of the data that flowed into, out of, and around the agency. Sometimes the gatekeeper was responsible for converting the daily avalanche of information into figures and recording them on reporting forms. Gatekeepers often have dual and conflicting pressures. On the one hand, they have knowledge and perspectives of operations of the agency superior to most staff. On the other hand, they are not just recipients of data but sources and, at times, bottlenecks for the flow and use of information.

It is noteworthy that gatekeepers are frequently passive or unaware about their centrality and potentially powerful position with respect to organizational information that they occupy. There is another important implication to the gatekeeper role. Since it is often informal and role definitions are unclear, each gatekeeper is different. The unique way in which each gatekeeper shapes his or her role presents a dilemma. Given the frequent turnover in staff positions and the instability in data collection, data processing and analysis activities can be jeopardized.

Multiple Sources of Data. Similar data are collected through many approaches and sources. For example, data on the number of children in day care due to reasons of protective services may be obtained through day-care personnel, protective services personnel, the finance office, and social service personnel with responsibility for both protective service and day-care programs. The number of personnel devoted to a particular program can be extracted from the personnel office, from the finance staff responsible for the cost allocation plan, from the agency director's staff, and from the individual program director. What is interesting, but perhaps not surprising, is that such data are seldom strictly comparable and consistent. This is fine if the particular method of collecting the data is grounded in reality; however, this is seldom the case.

Procedures and Technology for Collecting Data. Data processing is generally a painstaking process. Although computer technologies have facilitated recording, storing, and retrieving information, the majority of workers do not have the necessary skills or time to record, store, and extract data. The rapid rise of personal computers will no doubt facilitate these processes; however, most workers are currently unable to obtain desired information in a timely manner, even when data are automated. In fact, both central and personal computers can be disrupting and can complicate the process of using data for managerial decision making. This is primarily due to the fragmented nature of data processing operations in local agencies.

Much "Noise" and Little Use of Data. Overabundance of data, multiple sources of data, redundancy in data collection, roles of gatekeepers, and complexity of data collection procedures and technologies have created situations in many agencies where there is more confusion or "noise" than useful data. Stacks of printouts sit on desks, shelves, and other less obvious places. Reports are not reviewed when they arrive, and there is little separating what is useful and what is not. As the data have become abundant, they have become confusing. Managers lack time or simply find it too difficult to try to identify good signals from the mass of numbers.

When data become noise, there is no valuable information. Not only does undifferentiated data add to the noise, but the resulting delays in getting data into the hands of the responsible managers or workers as a result of data overload cause useful data to be overlooked. Like anything that involves the use of current information, the indicator process is fragile and must be modified over time. As a result, without considerable and constant discipline, information is not sorted and is not used. Meanings are constantly changing within an individual agency and across agencies and governmental levels. There is no way to ensure that the meaning of the indicators will endure. Language, at time, clouds the purpose of data collection. As a result, the preparation of definitions and operational terms becomes a burden. This is especially true in trying to make interagency or intraagency comparisons over time. The longer it takes to get an individual's attention, the more likely it is that the data will become less valid and less valuable for informing action in a timely way.

Attitudes about Data Collection Activities

Several important recurring attitudes about data collection and information use characterize local agencies. Each attitude has a significant effect on the agencies' willingness and ability to develop a viable intelligence system that managers can use. One of the most startling is the local workers' attitude about the quality of data they produce for state and federal agencies. Simply put, they do not have confidence in the data that they send out of their agencies.

Frontal attacks on the validity and reliability of the data occur frequently. It is not unusual to hear a local program manager suggest caution against placing too much confidence in data forwarded to other levels of government. This is not because agencies deliberately lie, rather it is a result of excessive demands for producing data in addition to the range of services that must be provided to clients. This pressure, combined with a natural defensiveness and reluctance to supply data that may compromise local agencies' priorities, can create severe tendencies to distort or half-heartedly report data. On more than one occasion, researchers were told to select "the best of the worst data."

While the majority of agency workers acknowledge the need for "real-world" data about human service agencies and programs, agency staff are aware of the distorting effects of data and repeatedly indicated that certain data do not reflect what they feel to be the true characteristics of organizations and programs.

The actual time required to respond to a child abuse case is an example. States are now placing heavy pressures on local agencies to respond within twenty-four hours to certain kinds of child abuse cases. Most agencies report to the state that they respond within the required period. However, they know full well that what the term "respond" means is a nebulous piece of data to record. Is it a telephone call? A visit? A specific action that reduces the immediate risk to the child? A clear definition of what constitutes "respond" is not applied. In the pressure to work within state guidelines, the reporting is often made to ensure compliance with state standards rather than to tell the real story from an effective service delivery standard.

For practical purposes, the child is probably given the best possible service no matter how the data are recorded. However, the real cost is the local agencies' lack of confidence in the data they produce. Because of the demands to produce required data, they view data collection as a burden and forego opportunities to collect data that allow them to track the important nuances of services.

Role of Management Indicators in Agency Collection, Processing, and Analysis

In what ways do the management indicator projects address issues related to collecting and using data in organization settings? This section suggests how the management indicator approach is designed to address problems of data collection, processing, and analysis in human service agencies.

Issue: An Overabundance and Complexity of Data Renders Most Data Useless in Their Present Form. Management indicators, insofar as possible, utilize existing data or data that can be collected during a two-day period. If indicators are too numerous, the process confuses rather than simplifies the problem. During the course of the project, indicators that were simply too difficult to retrieve were discarded and information that took an inordinate effort to retrieve was eliminated. Strictly limiting the number of indicators suppressed an inevitable tendency to add new and interesting indicators.

Issue: Create Indicators That Are Comparable across Agencies and That Sensitively Reflect Agencies' Practices. During a conference with participating agencies, efforts were made to direct indicators to the managers' everyday worlds. At this meeting two competing project goals surfaced: to develop indicators that were comparable across agencies of similar size and organizational architecture and to develop indicators that captured the reality of each local agency.

As a result, indicators that were least comparable (for example, certain administrative budget categories and ways of defining standards for client treatment) were eliminated. In some cases, only subsets of agencies were compared. For example, many agencies assigned clerical workers to specific program areas. In these agencies, accounting for clerical services was not difficult. In other agencies, however, a common clerical pool was used for all programs. Comparison of these two types of clerical services was inappropriate among all agencies. This was resolved by presenting separate comparisons for agencies that used a pool and those that attached clerical support to individual programs.

Significant differences in practice were identified, subgroups were developed, and comparisons were made among agencies that have reasonably similar practices. This led to one of the major questions remaining with the management indicator approach: Is there enough similarity among medium-sized service agencies to make comparison across agencies meaningful?

Issue: Increase the Probability That Different Kinds of Managers Will Use the Data. The presentation of the indicators as ratios or relationships should appeal to managers with different preferences for data collection, processing, analysis, and problem-solving methods. Indicators should be welcomed by those with an intuitive preference for problem solving (including a linking of broad themes), that is, those who prefer generalizations, focusing on relationships, and often have disdain for detailed printouts and masses of individual data items.

The potential appeal of the indicators to intuitive types (see Keirsey & Bates[15]) is that indicators are presented in the form of ratios, use graphics, and involve a limited number of specific data elements. Indicators actually enhance the problem-solving capacity of intuitive types because they are grounded in data and do not rely on cognition and hunches—the usual sources of material for intuitive problem-solving activities.

On the other hand, indicators offer some appealing features to the intuitives' opposites: the sensing types. Sensing types are comfortable with the trees and show little concern for the forest (relationships, themes, issues). Their tendency to be fascinated with the here and now limits the possibility of using data for planning, goal-setting, and problem-solving activities. Indicators move sensing types away from the specifics of data to the broader picture while still remaining firmly grounded in the data.

A number of specific strategies were used to ensure that managers would use the data. Considerable emphasis was given to the participation of local human service managers in the development of indicators. The workshop of local project participants mentioned above was a significant part of that strategy.

Using ratios and graphics increased the clarity and appeal of the indicators. Managers could quickly see how their agency's performance on a particular indicator related to other agencies' performance, and how their current performance compared to their past performance. The use of ratios also gave indicators strong practical orientation and fostered the questioning of common-sense observations and expected patterns of quantitative data. Ratios helped reorder traditional thinking about organizational phenomena and introduced nontraditional measures. They sought to increase understanding of relationships of data without further manipulation and became powerful diagnostic measures in themselves. An indicator showing an average of fifty cases per caseworker presented a stronger image than 500 cases and ten workers. The relationships of ratios to graphic presentations was significant. Ratios were arranged and presented in tabular forms or as bar graphs, line graphs, or pie charts, thereby creating fewer ambiguities.

Finally, the management indicators' projects placed strong emphasis on feedback and review of findings. Since many of the managers seemed to have difficulty sustaining a sense of curiosity about the data—to dig behind the ratios to discover reasons and implications for particular relationships—project staff spent a half day at each site with the agency director and key staff reviewing the indicators and suggesting ways to use the results of the study. This feedback increased the local providers' confidence in using the data.

Conclusion

Management indicators are most effectively used in conjunction with other management tools. The acceptance of management indicators is growing. Indicators have been incorporated into basic textbooks in the disciplines of business and public policy. Both theoreticians and practitioners have come to regard indicators as useful analytic aids. On balance, a carefully selected set of management indicators can serve as a useful tool for improving the performance of human service organizations. This approach is preferable to data systems that generate more data than managers need or can absorb. In this instance, less is more.

Notes

1. Gary Bowers and Margaret Bowers, *Considerations for Improving the Use of Data in Human Service Organizations* (Washington, DC: U.S. Department of Health and Human Services, 1982), p. 4–1.

2. Robert Elkin and Mark Molitor, *Management Indicators in Non Profit Organizations* (Washington, DC: Peat, Marwick, Mitchell and Co., 1984), p. 1.

3. Edna Kamis-Gould, *Performance Indicators in Mental Healt and a Proposed Set for the Division of Mental Health and Hospitals* (Trenton, NJ: Bureau of Evaluation, New Jersey State Division of Mental Health, 1982).

4. E.A. Suchman, *Evaluative Research* (New York: Russell Sage Foundation, 1967).

5. William Dunn, *Public Policy Analysis* (Englewood Cliffs, NJ: Prentice-Hall, 1982), p. 332.

6. Anthony W. Mitchell, "Dare to Compare," *New England Journal of Human Services,* Winter (1981), p. 23–29.

7. *Ibid., p. 24.*

8. *Kamis-Gould, Performance Indicators in Mental Health.*

9. Mary D. Hall, "Financial Condition: A Measure of Human Service Organizational Performance," *New England Journal of Human Services,* Winter (1982), p. 25–33.

10. John F. Rockart, "Chief Executives Define Their Own Data Needs," *Harvard Business Review,* March/April (1979), p. 81–93.

11. Robert Elkin and Mark Molitor, *Toward a Model for Selecting Management Indicators in Nonprofit Organizations* (Baltimore, MD: University of Maryland, 1983).

12. Bill Benton et al., *Management Indicators* (New Zealand: New Zealand Department of Social Services, 1981).

13. Elkin and Molitor, *Management Indicators in Nonprofit Organizations.*

14. Bowers and Bowers, *Considerations for Improving the Use of Data.*

15. David Keirsay and M. Bates, *Please Understand Me: Character Temperament Types* Del Mar, CA: Prometheus Nemesis, 1978).

Bibliography

Administrator's Guide to Social Service Client Outcome Monitoring. 1981. Washington, DC: The Urban Institute and the American Welfare Association.

Anthony, Robert. 1965. *Planning and Control Systems: A Framework for Analysis.* Boston, MA: Harvard University.

Anthony, Robert and Dearden, John. 1980. *Management Control Systems.* Homewood, IL: Richard D. Irwin.

Argyris, Chris and Schon, Donald A. 1974. *Theory and Practice: Increasing Professional Effectiveness.* San Francisco, CA: Jossey-Bass.

Auditor's Guide to Performance Auditing. 1979. Washington, DC: Peat, Marwick, and Mitchell and the Assistance Group.

Azarnoff, Roysand and Seliger, Jerome S. 1982. *Delivery of Human Services.* Englewood Cliffs, NJ: Prentice-Hall.

Bale, Ronald L., Macauley, Walter W. and Stover, W. Robert. 1980. "Office Supplies: A Way to Increase Productivity." *Modern Office Procedures,* January, 126–133.

Balk, Walter L. 1978. "Toward A Government Productivity Ethic." *Public Administration Review,* January/February, 46–50.

Benton, Bill, et al. 1981. *Management Indicators.* New Zealand Department of Social Services.

Bowers, Gary and Bowers, Margaret. 1982. *Considerations for Improving the Use of Data in Human Service Organizations.* Washington, DC: U.S. Department of Health and Human Services, Office of Human Development Services.

Campbell, Alan K. 1976. "Approaches to Defining, Measuring and Achieving Equity in the Public Sector." *Public Administration Review 36:5,* September/October, 554–556.

Chackerian, Richard. 1977. "Environments for Self Management Organizations." *Public Administration Review 37:2,* March/April, 193–194.

Chase, Gordan. 1979. "Implementing A Human Services Program: How Hard Will It Be?" *Public Policy 27:4,* Fall, 386–435.

Cunningham, J. Barton. 1977. "Approaches to the Evaluation of Organizational Effectiveness." *Academy of Management Review,* July, 463–474.

De Jong, Fred J. 1982. *Human Services Information Systems: A Selected Bibliography—1970 to Present.* Washington, DC: National Association of State Units on Aging.

Department of Health, Education, and Welfare. 1979. *Generic Performance Auditing Programs for Area Agencies on Aging.* Washington, DC: Peat, Marwick, and Mitchell and the Assistance Group.

Dillon, Don. 1982. "Office Automation and Professional Productivity—What's the Connection?" Washington, DC: Coopers and Lybrand.

Dunn, William. 1982. *Public Policy Analysis.* Englewood Cliffs, NJ: Prentice-Hall.

Elkin, Robert. 1980. *A Human Service Manager's Guide to Developing Unit Costs.* Falls Church, VA: Institute for Information Studies.

Elkin, Robert and Molitor, Mark. 1984. *Management Indicators in Nonprofit Organizations.* Washington, DC: Peat, Marwick, Mitchell, and Co.

Etzioni, Amitai. 1975. "Alternative Conceptions of Accountability." *Public Administration Review 35:*3, May/June, 279–287.

Fosler, R. Scott. 1978. "State and Local Government Productivity in the Private Sector." *Public Administration Review 38:*1, January/February, 22–28.

Garn, Harvey, Flax, Michael J., Springer, Michael, and Taylor, Jeremy B. 1976. *Models for Indicator Development: A Framework for Policy Analysis.* Washington, DC: The Urban Institute.

Georyo Polores, Basil S., and Tannebaum, Arnold S. 1957. "The Study of Organizational Effectiveness." *American Sociological Review 22,* 534–540.

The Guide to Comprehensive Service Systems Development: An Area Agency Perspective, 1981. Silver Spring, MD: The Assistance Group for Human Resource Development.

Hall, Mary D. 1982. "Financial Condition: A Measure of Human Service Organizational Performance." *New England Journal of Human Services,* Winter, 25–33.

Hasenfeld, Meheskd and English, Richard. 1974. *Human Service Organizations: A Book of Readings.* Ann Arbor: University of Michigan Press.

Hatry, Harry P. 1972. "Issues in Productivity Measurement for Local Governments." *Public Administration Review 32:*6, November/December, 776–784.

Hatry, Harry P., Clarren, N. Sumner, van Houten, Therese, Woodward, Jane P., and Don Vito, Pasqual A. 1979. *Efficiency Measures for Local Government Services—Some Initial Suggestions.* Washington, DC: The Urban Institute.

Holzer, Marc. 1976. "Public Productivity: Defining a Managerial Framework." In Mark Holzer (ed.), *Productivity in Public Organizations,* pp. 3–22. Port Washington, NY: Kenickat Press.

Kamis-Gould, Edna. 1982. *Performance Indicators in Mental Health and a Proposed Set for Division of Mental Health and Hospitals.* Trenton, NJ: Bureau of Research and Evaluation, New Jersey State Division of Mental Health.

Katz, Daniel and Kahn, Robert. 1978. *The Social Psychology of Organizations.* (2nd ed.). New York: John Wiley.

Keirsey, David and Bates, M. 1979. *Please Understand Me: Character Temperament Types.* Del Mar, CA: Prometheus Nemesis.

Lucey, Patrick J. 1972. "Wisconsin's Productivity Policy." *Public Administration Review 32:*6, November/December, 795–799.

Mark, Jerome A. 1979. "Meanings and Measures of Productivity." *Public Administration Review 32:*6, November/December, 747–753.

Millar, R. and Millar, A. 1981. *Developing Client Outcome Monitoring Systems: A Guide for State and Local Social Service Agencies.* Washington, DC: The Urban Institute.

Miller, Edward W. "Labor Productivity in Large and Small Enterprises." *American Journal of Small Business V:* 2, October/December, 1980.

Mitchell, Anthony W. 1981. "Dare to Compare." *New England Journal of Human Services,* Winter, 23–29.

Mintzberg, Henry. 1975. "The Manager's Job: Folklore and Fact." *Harvard Business Review,* July/August, 49–61.

Mortensern, Charles. 1975. *Association Evaluation: Guidelines for Measuring Organizational Performance.* Washington, DC: American Society of Association Executives.

Newland, Chester A. 1976. Policy/Program Objectives and Federal Management: "The Search for Government Effectiveness." *Public Administration Review 36:* 1, January/February, 20–28.

Oberlander, De Wayne L., Lidoff, Lorraine, and Leanse, Joyce. 1979. *Senior Center Standards Self Assessment Workbook.* Washington, DC: National Council on Aging.

Quin, Robert E. 1978. "Productivity and the Process of Organizational Improvements: Why We Cannot Talk to Each Other." *Public Administration Review 38:* 1, January/February, 41–45.

Ratio Analysis in Voluntary Health and Welfare Organizations. Washington, DC: Peat, Marwick, Mitchell, and Company.

Rockart, John F. 1979. "Chief Executives Define Their Own Data Needs." *Harvard Business Review,* March/April, 81–93.

Ryan, Raymond. 1978. "The Impact of Three Years of Experience and a New Governor on the State of Washington's Productivity Program." *Public Administration Review 38:*1, January/February, 12–15.

Said, Kamal E. and Hughey, J. Keith. 1977. "Managerial Problems of the Small Firm." *Journal of Small Business Management, 15:*1, January, 37–42.

Suchman, E.A. 1967. *Evaluative Research.* New York: Russell Sage Foundation.

Touche Ross and Co. 1977. *Association Operating Ratio Report.* Washington, DC: American Society of Association Executives.

Van de Ven, Andrew H. 1976. "A Framework for Organizational Assessment." *Academy of Management Review,* January, 1976.

Washnis, George J. (Ed.). 1980. *Productivity Improvement Handbook for State and Local Governments.* New York: John Wiley.

Yessian, Mark E. 1978. "Delivering Services in a Rapidly Changing Public Sector." *American Behavioral Scientist 21:*6, July/August, 829–859.

12

A Role for Evaluators in Helping New Programs Succeed[1]

Wayne D. Gray

rmy training programs face many of the same problems as programs in education and industry. Programs developed in response to real needs fail to be implemented, and most of those that are implemented are modified and used quite differently than intended by the program's developer.

The U.S. Army Research Institute for Behavioral and Social Sciences (ARI) has had a continuing interest in the implementation and use of army training programs. We have recently developed a threefold approach to implementation:

> Initiate case studies of the problems that training programs face and must overcome if they are to be successfully implemented and used.
>
> Provide guidance that army sponsors can use to plan the implementation of new training programs (T. Gray, C. Roberts-Gray & W. Gray, 1983).
>
> Develop a framework for monitoring and evaluating the implementation of training programs (W.D. Gray, 1984). Such a framework starts before a program is fielded and continues, ideally, until the program either fails or, if successful, becomes obsolete.

In this chapter I present an overview of a framework for implementation monitoring and the important role of *evaluator as monitor*. The monitor examines the adequacy of implementation plans and looks at the effect of their execution upon the organization, individual, and new program. Immediate feedback is provided to adjust the implementation effort to better help the new program succeed. This is a more activist role than most evaluators assume.

The validation of the framework for implementation monitoring lies in its utility. I see three related uses. First, the framework may be used to guide monitoring efforts. At present, those anticipating problems in implementing an innovation are faced with a grab bag of rules-of-thumb and warnings.

Little systematic guidance is provided. The present framework should be of use to all workers in the field.

Second, the framework may be used in a retrospective analysis of implementation problems. In this way it provides a common basis to organize implementation studies and facilitate comparison across studies.

Third, the framework may be used to compare and contrast theories of implementation. This can occur in either the retrospective or monitoring modes. The factors suggested by different theories can be fed into appropriate parts of the framework. The data gathered can be used to determine which theories were more useful and suggest factors omitted by current theories.

Impetus

The impetus for much of ARI's work on implementation was the devastating failure of the army's *REALTRAIN* program for tactical team training. REALTRAIN's effectiveness was unchallenged. Studies by ARI (for example, Banks, Hardy, Scott, Kress & Word, 1977) leave no doubt that when used appropriately REALTRAIN was an astonishingly effective program for tactical team training. Yet, after the program developers withdrew, REAL-TRAIN died a quick and unnoted death (Roberts-Gray, Clovis, T. Gray, Muller, & Cunningham, 1981). Scott (1983) writes that after delivery of instructor training and equipment,

> REALTRAIN was plunged into a highly complex training environment rife with competing demands for time, personnel, and resources. Company and higher level commanders tended to indicate that they had considerable difficulty in meeting the REALTRAIN support requirements, especially the requirements for exercise controllers . . . additional equipment was required. Although many commanders did not see the additional equipment requirements per se as a major problem, the time and effort required to request, obtain, issue, install, organize, and account for the equipment was often seen as a more serious deterrent to the routine use of REALTRAIN. (p. 13–14).

REALTRAIN died because it did not "fit" the existing training environment. If the implementation process had been more extensively planned and monitored, the gap between available resources and REALTRAIN's support requirements would have become an important issue early on. Alternatives did exist. For example, the program could have been changed to minimize support requirements, additional resources could have been provided to local commanders, and streamlined procedures to "request, obtain . . . and account for the equipment" could have been instituted.

The impetus for ARI's continued interest in implementation lies in the army's increasing investment in technology-based training programs. In some of these programs, lasers replace bullets; in others computer simulations replace expensive and hazardous weapon systems. Large-scale use of computer-based training is becoming the norm in the army school system (T. Gray, 1985). Interactive videodisc technology is beginning to leave the research and development stage. Looking to the late '80s and early '90s, ARI and others have begun research on applying artificial intelligence and cognitive science to training (W.D. Gray, Pliske, & Psotka, forthcoming). Despite (or because of) the glitter of high technology, we expect none of these programs to be welcomed with open arms. All such programs require new roles for army trainers and place new demands upon the training support system. Attention to implementation issues must continue. Implementation monitoring is vital.

The Framework

An overview of the framework for implementation monitoring is presented in figure 12–1. There are three parts to the framework. Certain practical and theoretical background knowledge of both the innovation and organization

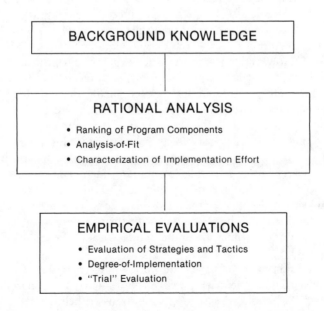

Figure 12–1. Overview of Implementation Monitoring

is needed. If the monitoring team does not have expertise in the areas listed, then they must have ready access to such expertise. (Note that expertise in program evaluation is assumed.)

The rational analyses result in a separation of the program into (more or less) independent components that are rank ordered, an analysis-of-fit between the program and its intended environment, and an analysis of the strategies and tactics needed to overcome potential "misfits." The term "rational" in rational analyses is meant to contrast with "empirical" in empirical evaluations. The analyses are conducted by a team that possesses the relevant background knowledge. Active data collection or statistical analysis is minimal.

The rational analyses require the evaluators to be team players. The evaluators' special subject matter expertise is not required at this point. Instead, the evaluators *may* have to provide the analytic framework within which the rational analyses are conducted. The evaluators *will* have to ensure that the results of the rational analyses provide what is needed for the empirical evaluations.

The empirical evaluations examine three issues: how well implementation plans (strategies and tactics) are working, how much of the program is currently implemented, and how effective the program is at its current level of implementation. Data are collected as they become available. Data analysis is ongoing, but although statistical analyses may be performed, preliminary conclusions typically are made and fed back into the system before enough data exist for statistical techniques to produce reliable results.

The evaluators' role is dominant in the empirical evaluations. Here their subject matter expertise in research design, data collection, and analyses is most needed. However, it is important for evaluators to realize that they are team members involved in implementation monitoring, and to temper their concern about premature analyses by recognizing the monitoring requirement for near-immediate feedback and mid-course corrections.

The distinctions among the three parts of the framework may become clearer by analogy to laboratory experimentation. In this analogy the background knowledge is the experimenter's knowledge of the problem area, previous research, tools available (computers, memory drums, and so on), subject population, and level of funding. The rational analysis corresponds to the process of deciding upon an experimental design that will test the hypothesis and that can be conducted with the tools and subjects available. Finally, the empirical evaluation is analogous to data collection and statistical analysis.

Not shown in figure 12–1 are the various interconnections and feedback loops both within and between parts of the framework. All parts, subparts, interconnections, and feedback loops are discussed below.

Background Knowledge

Both practical and theoretical knowledge are required to conduct implementation monitoring. For the innovation, practical knowledge of both the procedures involved in using it and the resources needed to support it is required. Practical knowledge of the implementing organization is also required. One or more in-house informants are needed who possess a detailed knowledge of current procedures, resource capabilities and limitations, staff morale and education, key players within the organization, and general organizational climate. Implementation monitoring, therefore, must be largely an in-house affair (or the monitoring team must work closely with in-house personnel).

In accord with Chen and Rossi's (1983) call for a theory-driven approach to evaluation, two types of theoretical knowledge are required by the framework. The first is an implementation theory. An adequate theory of implementation should provide a comprehensive analytic framework for considering potential implementation problems (for both adaptive and programmed implementation). It should recognize that not all problems have solutions but provide a clear and prescriptive mapping to solution strategies for those that do. At present, no one theory completely fits these criteria, but the ones proposed by C. Roberts-Gray (C. Roberts-Gray & T. Gray, 1983; T. Gray, 1981; C. Roberts-Gray, 1983) and Scheirer (1981; Scheirer & Rezmovic, 1983) are a good beginning.

Second, a theory that covers the domain of the new program (for example, classroom instruction, criminal justice reform, adult literacy, and so on) must be found. Such a theory provides a somewhat objective way of deciding what features of the new program are most important to its effectiveness and what features are merely nice to have. Any theory selected must be appropriate to the innovation and user environment. (This may require using different theories to characterize different innovations even within the same institution and subject domain. For example, for army instruction, one theory may be appropriate for characterizing tactical field training, another for "schoolhouse" training, a third for "simulator" training, a fourth for computer-based instruction, and yet another for the army's "educational" programs.)

In sum, four types of background knowledge (in addition to knowledge of evaluation theories and procedures) are required to do implementation monitoring: practical knowledge of the innovation, practical knowledge of the implementing organization, knowledge of domain-relevant theories, and knowledge of implementation theories. This knowledge requirement necessitates a talented team with cross-disciplinary expertise that is part of or works closely with, the implementing organization.

Rational Analyses

The program evaluator begins implementation monitoring by conducting three rational analyses (see figure 12–1): a ranking of program components, an analysis-of-fit, and a characterization of the implementation effort in terms of strategies and tactics. These analyses provide the basis, or design, for the three empirical evaluations. In addition, they provide for a rational (as opposed to empirical) evaluation of both the innovation and implementation planning.

> It is not usually clear whether the recorded failures of programs are due to the fact that the programs were built on poor conceptual foundations . . . or because treatments were set at such low dosage levels that they could not conceivably affect any outcomes . . . or because programs were poorly implemented. Note that the emphasis in the above statements is on deficiencies in the theoretical underpinnings of the treatment or of the treatment delivery systems. (Chen & Rossi, 1983, p. 184)

Ranking the components of the program provides a basis for deciding which components are most important to the program's effectiveness. The goal is to separate the "must have" components from the "nice to have" ones. When resources are limited, this ranking allows implementation and evaluation efforts to focus on the most important aspects of the new program.

Ranking is a two-step process. First, the new program must be separated into (more or less) independent components. In the monitoring framework this separation is based upon background knowledge of the new program with the domain theory providing the organizing framework. For cases where this background knowledge is insufficient, then a more formal procedure such as that discussed by Emshoff, Mayer, Gottschalk, Blakely and Roitman (1984) is required. An example of a theory-based component analysis is provided in table 12–1. The example shows the result of using the "feedback" part of a theory of tactical training to identify feedback components of an army program. (More information on this training program can be found in W.D. Gray, 1983.)

Second, each component should be ranked as, at a minimum, "must have" or "nice to have." (Generally, finer rankings convey more information; however, for most new programs fairly gross rankings should suffice.) This separation into and ranking of components provides input to both the analysis-of-fit and the evaluation of degree-of-implementation. Note that the ranking of program components does not consider the resources each component may require. Resources become an issue in the analysis-of-fit.

Table 12–1
Theory-based Component Analysis: Feedback Procedures for an Army Tactical Training Program

III. Practice
    B. FEEDBACK
        1. Concerning tactical proficiency
           a. Malfunctioning equipment: replaced or repaired during exercise (Note: this is to ensure feedback from the laser devices which simulate weapons effects).
           b. During exercise: no feedback provided to individuals or groups concerning tactical profiency (Note: controller stays as unobtrusive as possible to encourage realism).
           c. After exercise—After Action Review conducted (Note: "socratic" procedure meant to encourage participation of all trainees).
               (1) Feedback on *collective* performance is emphasized.
               (2) Feedback on *individual* performance minimized.
               (3) Frequency of After Action Review and timing (for example, immediately after each exercise, once a day, and so on).

        2. To control trainee attention to task
           a. On-the-spot corrections to enforce rules-of-engagement
           b. Control of the After Action Review process (to focus discussion on relevant training objectives, and minimize "who-shot-whom" discussions).

Analysis of Fit

The purpose of an *Analysis-of-Fit* is to identify areas where the routine use of the innovation will require changes in the user's operational environment, that is, places in which the innovation currently "misfits" the organization. The evaluators' first step is to cross the ranked program components with relevant parts of an implementation theory to form a matrix of potential implementation problems. After the matrix is generated, expert opinion (for both the organization and resource needs of the innovation) is required to decide whether any given cell of the matrix "makes sense."

As an example, consider several items from a matrix that was generated by crossing the theory-based component analyses provided in table 12–1 with some of Scheirer's (1981) implementation hypotheses. Her hypothesis that it is important for "central administrators [to] strongly and actively support the program" (p. 69) does not seem to apply at this level of analysis. Presumably, central administrators support or do not support the program as a whole, not those subcomponents involved in providing feedback to students. On the other hand, the hypothesis that supervisors need to "receive adequate training to understand the philosophy and behaviors specific to the innovation" (p. 70), makes sense to apply. Again, with reference to table 12–1, the issue of malfunctioning equipment requiring repair or replacement on-the-spot is different than the issue of prevailing attitudes toward tactical training. Likewise, having the controllers *not* provide feedback on tactical proficiency during the exercise involves a different philosophy concerning the value of realism and the place for feedback than had previously been accepted. Hence, both these cells are meaningful and should be kept.

As shown by the above examples, making judgments concerning the meaningfulness of any given cell requires expert familiarity with the implementing organization and the resource requirements of the innovation. Also, these two expertises are required to assess whether the meaningful cells represent a match, important misfit, or trivial misfit of the innovation to the organization. If information is lacking concerning the importance of the misfit, then a separate data collection effort may be required. Those cells in which the mismatch is deemed important and for which the components are ranked as "must have" represent *potential implementation problems* (PIPs) that must be solved to implement the new program.

Characterization of the Implementation Effort

The implementation effort can be characterized in terms of strategies and tactics. A *strategy* is what must be done to overcome a PIP, whereas a *tactic* is one way of accomplishing the strategy. For example, if computer-based instruction (CBI) is being implemented and one PIP is instructors' fear of computers, then one strategy to solve this PIP would be to hire instructors who know and love computers. Another strategy would be to educate the current instructors on the advantages of CBI. If the latter strategy is chosen, then one tactic might be to enroll all instructors in CBI courses. An alternative tactic might be to provide instructions with basic reference materials and actively involve them in the development of new courseware. Hence, a strategy is "what to do" while a tactic is "how to do it."

The monitor team may be asked to either develop implementation plans or to clarify (evaluate) existing ones. In either case the activities are about the same (see figure 12–2); however, the order of the steps will vary. In developing plans, the monitors can follow the steps listed in figure 12–2. In contrast, clarifying existing plans may require a top-down, bottom-up analysis. Starting at the bottom (of figure 12–2) with an analysis of the implementation efforts (tactics) and at the top with PIPs, the monitor will have to determine what problems the tactics may potentially resolve. Having an implementation theory that maps problems onto solution strategies is helpful.

For example, one PIP in implementing an army tactical training program might be the redefinition of the controller's role in an exercise as an observer and data collector as opposed to providing on-the-spot feedback and advice

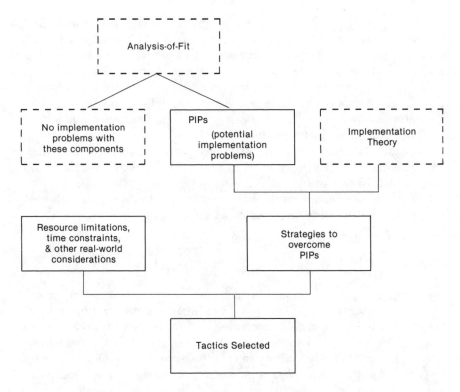

Figure 12–2. Characterization of Implementation Effort

concerning tactical performance. As part of the implementation, the following efforts are planned: (1) the value of exercise realism is stressed in train-the-trainer programs; (2) program manuals emphasize the importance of the controller's remaining "tactical" during the exercise and collecting information to use in the After Action Review; (3) local training regulations are revised to eliminate the requirement that controllers wear white hats and belts when conducting an exercise; (4) special manuals are prepared and targeted at battalion and higher commanders, explaining the philosophy of the new program. All four efforts are examples of tactics taken to resolve the PIP. Tactics 1, 2, and 4 are examples of an education strategy with the goal of educating the controllers and their commanders on the new way of doing things. Tactic 3 is a power strategy (C. Roberts-Gray & T. Gray, 1983) with the goals of eliminating regulations inconsistent with the new program.

Clarifying what is being done and why has two functions. First, clarification is prerequisite to evaluating strategies and tactics, and this evaluation provides a reading of the success of the implementation effort in resolving PIPs. For example, to resolve the PIP of role change for controllers, implementation theory (C. Roberts-Gray & T. Gray, 1983) suggest two strategies: the use of power and education. To determine if the use of power was successful, the strategy of power must be tied to a particular tactic: change of certain regulations. Likewise, the strategy of education must be tied to certain tactics: train-the-trainer programs, manuals, and officer education. As discussed later, evaluations of strategies, tactics, and PIPs are interrelated, and the relationship of a given tactic to strategy to PIP must be determined for the evaluation to provide useful results.

Second, a rational analysis of the implementation effort will more than likely pinpoint PIPs that are not being addressed and tactics that serve no purpose, that is, that would not resolve any PIP. Such a clarification represents a rational evaluation of the implementation effort and should be fed back to the implementing organization as soon as possible.

Empirical Evaluations

The three empirical evaluations (see figure 12–1) are the heart of implementation monitoring, and it is here that the evaluators' skills are most needed. Not discussed here are details concerning how to conduct the various evaluations. The tools to do such evaluations already exist in the evaluator's toolbox. Put another way, the implementation monitoring framework assists the evaluators in deciding *what* questions to ask and *why*. *How* these questions are asked is left to the discretion and inclination of the evaluator.

Evaluating Degree-of-Implementation

Typically, assessing degree-of-implementation is viewed as important to interpreting summative evaluation data (for example, Fullan & Pomfret, 1977; Leinhardt, 1980). Hall and Loucks (1977) offer guidelines concerning how such an evaluation might be conducted.

The emphasis of the current framework is different. First, the ranking of program components determines the relative importance of various aspects of the new program (discussed above). Second, the evaluation is started during the implementation process, and long before any complete implementation is expected. Once started, the evaluation is continually updated until all implementation efforts have stopped. Third, measurement of degree-of-implementation falls into two different categories, fidelity and sufficiency. For *fidelity* the task is to assess what aspects of the innovation have been implemented, which have been dropped, and which have been altered. *Sufficiency* focuses on those parts that were *altered* to assess whether the alterations fulfull the function of the omitted part and therefore will support the goals of the innovation.

The evaluators must expect that for many programs, alterations by the user are a fact of life (Berman, 1978); however, alterations per se should not be assumed to be innately bad or good. An alteration is not bad just because it differs from the developer's ideal. It is not good just because it represents an adaptation of the innovation to the local way of doing things. Rather, all alterations must be measured by the more objective standard of sufficiency: Based upon the domain theory, does the alteration fulfill the function of the omitted part? Will it support the goals of the innovation?

For example, many training programs include procedures to provide feedback to the trainees. However, if the exact procedures specified by the program are not followed, feedback may still be provided by other procedures. We could find a case where excellent feedback is being provided, but the procedures called for by the training program are not followed. That is, the function is being filled, but the procedures are not followed.

Reanalysis of Fit

The various measures of degree-of-implementation provide input to the *reanalysis-of-fit*. The reanalysis identifies implementation problems that are still unresolved and permits the implementation effort to focus on finding strategies and developing tactics to resolve them. Strategies and tactics that focus on already implemented components can be dropped from the implementation effort.

Trial Evaluation

The *trial evaluation* fills the gap between formative and summative evaluation. A double meaning is intended. It is an evaluation of program effectiveness during the trial period of implementation (C. Roberts-Gray & T. Gray, 1983), and it is a trial summative evaluation. The trial evaluation is expected to be constantly revised or redone during the implementation period. Because of this, it is not evaluating a fixed target, that is, the program itself changes (the hope is that more becomes implemented) during the course of the evaluation. The interpretation of trial evaluation results must be weighted by considering what program components are implemented currently. The more "must have" components that are implemented, the more the trial evaluation data can be interpreted as a true summative evaluation.

Where formative evaluation provides an assessment of program effectiveness under ideal conditions, trial evaluation assesses the effectiveness of the program as implemented currently. The gap between current and expected effectiveness can act as an argument for continued attention to the implementation effort. Although the same gap might be found in comparing a summative evaluation with a formative one, by the time the summative evaluation is conducted most implementation efforts have stopped. Intuitively it seems much easier to keep the implementation effort going than to restart it once stopped.

Finally, in many cases the summative evaluation can be built upon the design, methodology, and instruments used in the trial evaluation. If techniques such as time-series analyses are used, then even the data collected in the trial evaluation may be included in the summative evaluation.

Strategies and Goals

An early reading on how well a program is being implemented can be gained from evaluating the achievement of strategic goals. If the theory-driven selection of strategies pinpointed certain strategic goals as necessary to resolve certain PIPs, then achievement of these goals logically precedes full use of the innovation. A close monitoring of strategic goals may allow the monitor to recommend changes in implementation tactics before the organization's initial burst of enthusiasm and money allocated for implementation are spent.

If the initial evaluation of degree-of-implementation has been completed, then the only strategic goals evaluated are those pertaining to components not yet implemented. In the example given earlier, if evaluation of degree-of-implementation reveals that controllers are not interrupting tactical field exercises to give feedback to trainees, then the PIP identified above has been resolved, and evaluation of the strategies proposed to resolve the PIP would not be conducted.

In contrast, if a component is not implemented but the relevant strategic goals are achieved, then additional strategies must be selected and tactics chosen. However, if a component is not implemented and the strategic goals have not been achieved, then an evaluation of tactics is conducted.

In evaluating tactics the basic question is whether the tactic was well executed or not. For example, to educate controllers on the virtues of uobtrusive behavior a training manual might be produced (a tactic). The monitors can ask whether the manual actually presents arguments in favor of unobtrusive behavior, whether the reading level and format is appropriate for the intended audience, whether controllers actually received the manuals, and whether the controllers have read the manuals.

If the tactics were well executed, but the strategic goal was not achieved, then there is a need to develop and execute a new set of tactics to achieve that strategic goal. In contrast, if the tactics were *not* well executed, then revision or reexecution is required.

The evaluation of tactics may be empirical or rational. For example, in writing training pamphlets, the "nice to know" information is often confused with the "must know" information. In this example, the monitor team may first have to determine what is "must know" and what is "nice to know."

Then they would perform a critical reading of the pamphlet to determine if the "must know" information is adequately represented. For other tactics the monitor may have to perform a miniprogram evaluation. For example, for new army training programs, it is common to send a mobile team to each post to train the trainers. In this case, the monitor might want to assess whether course graduates can indeed train others.

Implementation monitoring is an iterative process. By the time the evaluation of strategies and tactics is completed, an update of the degree-of-implementation evaluation or a reanalysis-of-fit will have been started. Either action will restart the cycle and eventually lead to a re-evaluation of strategies and tactics.

Summary

At first glance, the role of implementation monitor conflicts with the typical professional stance of program evaluators. Evaluators are expected to dispassionately pursue their assignments and not become advocates for the programs they are evaluating. In contrast, monitors are expected to openly advocate the new program and to do everything in their power to ensure its success. I do not believe that this is a true conflict.

There is nothing wrong with using the tools and training of the program evaluator to work toward a program's success. The conflict occurs when these tools are abused so that data is slanted or distorted for partisan purposes. I argue that such abuse is not likely to occur in the course of implementation monitoring.

In implementation monitoring, working openly for a program's success means using the evaluator's tools of trade to overcome PIPs. To somehow abuse these tools to "conclude" that a PIP has been overcome when in fact it has not, is to condemn a favored program to a premature demise.

By becoming the new program's advocates, the monitors may find themselves in the position of providing the program's developer and/or the implementing organization with bad news. The developers may have to be told that for the program to succeed major revisions are needed or that postfield support (such as the train-the-trainer programs) will be required. The implementing organization may have to change its norms, policies, or allocation of resources more than they had expected. Such recommendations are not greeted with joy and will require that the monitor back them up with hard data, which are based upon a valid theory of implementation.

The framework discussed in this chapter provides a systematic procedure for ensuring that implementation planning is complete and is well executed. The framework defines certain types of background knowledge as important prerequisites to implementation monitoring. This background knowledge is needed to conduct three rational analyses: a ranking of program components, an analysis-of-fit between the innovation and organization, and a characterization of the implementation effort in terms of the strategies and tactics required to resolve areas of misfit (PIPs). Although important in themselves, these rational analyses also define the questions asked in the three empirical evaluations.

Evaluation of the degree-of-implementation looks at the fidelity of the implementation to the developer's ideal and assesses the sufficiency of any adaptations. The trial evaluation assesses how well the innovation is working at its current level of implementation. It provides an impetus to continued implementation efforts as well as feeding into the summative evaluation when implementation efforts cease. Evaluation of strategies and tactics provide both an early reading on the effectiveness of the implementation effort and the feedback needed to increase the degree-of-implementation.

To conclude, the framework for implementation monitoring defines a new role for evaluators in implementing new programs in organizations. An optimal use of the framework would be to improve the use of new programs by implementation monitoring. A sufficient use of the framework is to raise the awareness in organizations (and among evaluators) of the issues involved in implementing new programs.

Note

1. I want to thank Drs. Joseph Psotka, Zita Simutis, and James Banks for providing the time and encouragement to complete the "framework." Also thanks are due to Drs. C. Roberts-Gray and M.A. Scheirer for the many discussions (arguments) that contributed to my thinking about this topic.

The thoughts expressed in this chapter are my own and do not represent Department of the Army policy.

References

Banks, Jr., J.H., Hardy, G.D., Scott, T.D., Kress, G., and L.E. Word. October 1977. *REALTRAIN validation for rifle squads: Mission accomplishment* (ARI Research Report 1192). Alexandria, Va.: Army Research Institute. NTIS #AD A0433515.*

Berman, P. 1978. "The study of macro- and micro-implementation." *Public Policy* 26:157–184.

Chen, H. and Rossi, P.H. 1983. "Evaluating with sense: The theory-driven approach." *Evaluation Review* 7:283–302.

Emshoff, J.G., Mayer, J., Gottschalk, R., Blakely, C., and Roitman, D. October 1984. "Innovation in public sector organizations: Measuring fidelity of implementation and program effectiveness." In W.D. Gray (Chair), *Implementation:*

A key to high organizational performance. Panel conducted at the November, 1984 meeting of the Evaluation Research Society, San Francisco, California.

Fullan, M. and Pomfret, A. 1977. "Research on curriculum and instruction implementation." *Review of Educational Research* 47:335–397.

Gray, T. 1981. "Implementing innovations: A systems approach to integrating what is known." *Journal of Technology Transfer* 6:19–32.

Gray, T., Roberts-Gray, C., and Gray, W.D. September 1983. *A guide to implementation of training products* (ARI Research Report 1350. Alexandria, Va: Army Research Institue. NTIS #AD A143669.*

Gray, W.D. 1983. "Engagement simulation: A method of tactical team training: *Training and Development Journal* 37(7):29–34.

Gray, W.D. October 1984. *Implementation monitoring: A role for evaluators in helping innovations succeed* (ARI Technical Report 656). Alexandria, Va.: Army Research Institute.*

Gray, W.D., Pliske, D., and Psotka, J. Forthcoming. *Smart technology for training: Promise and current status* (ARI Research Product). Alexandria, Va: Army Research Institute.*

Gray, W.D. (Ed.) In press 1985. *Army computer-based training: Snapshots from 1985* (ARI Technical Report). Alexandria, Va: Army Research Institute.*

Hall, G.E. and Loucks, S.F. 1977. "A developmental model for determining whether the treatment is actually implemented." *American Educational Research Journal* 14:263–276.

Leinhardt, G. 1980. "Modeling and measuring educational treatment in evaluation." *Review and Educational Research* 50:393–420.

Roberts-Gray, C. September 1983. *On closing the implementation gap: Symposium proceedings* (ARI Research Report 1344). Alexandria, Va: Army Research Institute.*

Robets-Gray, C., Clovis, E.R., Gray, T., Muller, T.H. and Cunningham, R.F. May 1981. *Field survey of current practices and problems in army unit training, with implications for fielding and training with the MILES: Volume I-Report* (ARI Technical Report 524). Alexandria, Va: Army Research Institute. NTIS #AD A128479.*

Roberts-Gray, C. and Gray, T. 1983. "Implementing innovations: A model to bridge the gap between diffusion and utilization." *Knowledge: Creation, Diffusion, Utilization* 5:213–232.

Scheirer, M.A. 1981. *Program implementation: The organizational context.* Beverly Hills, Cal.: Sage.

Scheirer, M.A. and Rezmovic, E.L. 1983. "Measuring the degree of program implementation: A methodologial review. *Evaluation Review* 7.

Scott, T. September 1983. "Implementing innovations in the Army: A case study." In C. Roberts-Gray (Ed.), *On closing the implementation gap: Symposium proceedings, pp. 9–17.* (ARI Research Report 1344). Alexandria, Va: Army Research Institute.*

---

*These documents can be ordered from the National Technical Information Service (NTIS). For information write: National Technical Information Service: Department of Commerce, 5285 Port Royal Road, Springfield, VA; or call (703) 487-4650.

13
Managing for Improved Performance: Evaluating the Civil Service Reform Act

Anne H. Hastings
Larry S. Beyna

The Civil Service Reform Act (CSRA) of 1978, which created the Senior Executive Service (SES) and substantially reformed the federal personnel management system, was widely applauded by its supporters as the best hope for improving public management and, in turn, government performance. In particular, it looked at the time to be a promising vehicle for increasing the attention of top executives to performance management and for actually providing some financial incentives for effective managerial performance. Because of its promise, the leadership of the Department of Health and Human Services (HHS) in the Offices of Personnel, Planning and Evaluation, and Management and Budget joined forces in 1979 to examine the effects of CSRA on the management of departmental operations. Five years later, in the fall of 1984, the evaluation was completed.

The principal conclusion of the study, which consisted of an initial evaluability assessment followed by a full-scale, three-year evaluation, was that in the short term the program had been a success, but its long-term prospects were less certain. The machinery of civil service reform had been successfully installed and was operating smoothly in the department. HHS had demonstrated that the law was indeed workable. Moreover, the program was showing some signs of healthy maturation. For instance, some of the department's senior managers had been experimenting with CSRA tools and found them useful for surfacing performance problems, rewarding performance achievements, and managing their human resources—all things a good personnel management system should do. And the changes had generated intense, but seemingly healthy, debates about performance throughout the department—something else that was expected from a successful performance management system.

At the same time, there were clear signals that the long-term health of the reform effort was in jeopardy. Large numbers of SES members expressed discontent with the new system and its operation in the department. A certain amount of discontent was certainly to be expected, but we found little evidence that top management had, even five years into the life of the program, developed mechanisms for diagnosing and addressing these challenges to the system and quieting the criticism. In addition, even the operating division[1] (OPDIV) and agency heads who used the system most actively agreed that poor performance was not really being addressed as aggressively as it should be. Thus, as we concluded our investigation, we left with the sense that the CSRA did represent a viable solution to a problem, but a problem that few acknowledged and fewer still seemed willing to address.

In this chapter, we first review the intentions of the law and the initial obstacles to its implementation. Next, we focus in some depth on our approach to assessing its successes and failures, and the findings of our evaluation of its operation in HHS. We conclude with a few general observations about the pitfalls involved in evaluating a reform effort early in its implementation.

The Logic of CSRA

When Alan K. Campbell, then chairman of the U.S. Civil Service Commission, testified before Congress in March 1978 in support of civil service reform, he declared that the federal civil service was in the midst of a crisis, a crisis brought about by the accumulation of laws, regulations, and policies that had grown up over the preceding 100 years, and that threatened the ability of federal managers to perform their duties effectively. Mr. Campbell reported to Congress:

> Managers in charge of government programs claim that personnel management procedures seriously impede their efforts to be good managers. Employees believe they are not adequately protected from partisan pressures, will not get much recognition if they do good work, and cannot get a fair shake if they register legitimate complaints.[2]

A year earlier, President Carter had established the Federal Personnel Management Project to investigate these complaints and to propose remedies. Members of the project reported that the complaints were, in fact, legitimate. Their examination revealed, for instance, that excessive centralization of personnel authorities had taken from line managers the authority to carry out many types of personnel decisions necessary to accomplish program and organizational objectives. The system restrained federal managers from expeditiously hiring the best qualified people, curbed their efforts to hold subordinate managers accountable for program performance, precluded them from recognizing and rewarding exceptional performance, and inhibited their ability to discipline or to remove employees whose performance was inadequate. At the same time, civil servants were equally justified, according to the project, in their concerns about the protection of employee rights and application of the merit concept.

The central purpose of the reform package that Congress passed in 1978 was to address simultaneously the concerns of both managers and employees. That is, the act was designed both to provide managers the tools essential to the effective accomplishment of the missions of the federal government and to establish a sound public merit system that would ensure fair treatment of individuals in that system. The merit principles established in Title I of the act make clear that career civil servants are to be recruited, hired, advanced, and retained only on the basis of individual ability and performance and without regard to political affiliation. In addition, they also establish that employees who do not adequately perform and who cannot or will not improve must be removed.

The act addressed the complaints of managers by shifting the locus of personnel authority to the agency level, by clarifying and streamlining personnel procedures, and by introducing some important new management tools designed to increase managerial flexibility. For instance, the act: (1) delegated the authority to fill positions and to carry out other personnel functions to top agency managers; (2) established new procedures for removals and demotions based on unacceptable performance; (3) provided for a new system of appraising employee performance to be used as the basis for rewarding good performance and punishing poor performance; (4) instituted the SES to give agencies more control over the selection, assignment, advancement, and management of the senior career and noncareer managers in the agency; and (5) provided agency heads with a system for allocating financial incentive awards for outstanding performance to career members of the SES.

Thus, the problem addressed by the reform package was how to enhance managerial control over the federal work force while also protecting the rights of personnel. The solution was to design a comprehensive reform package that clarified the merit principles on which the civil service system is based and provided agency heads with greater authority over personnel matters and a new set of personnel management tools. The ultimate goal was to improve the management and functioning of the programs and agencies operated by the federal government.

Obstacles to Successful Program Implementation [3]

In the fall of 1979, HHS began evaluating the implementation of the CSRA in that agency. The principal purpose of the multiyear evaluation effort was to ascertain, on an ongoing basis, the extent to which the new personnel management tools and increased flexibility were contributing to improvements in the management and performance of the department. From the outset the study was viewed as a diagnostic tool that would help those responsible for the reform effort in HHS to judge whether the program was realizing its potential.

Early in the evaluation effort, it became apparent that the program, although conceptually sound, was, as one analyst put it, "uniquely vulnerable and perhaps perpetually fragile."[4] Although the initial evaluability assessment for the study disclosed an unusual amount of agreement among decisionmakers inside and outside of HHS with both CSRA's goals and its strategy for achieving those goals, there was also general agreement on the problems and pitfalls that threatened its success as an intervention to improve government performance. Although the list was long, three problems contributed the most to the law's vulnerability.

1. From the outset, SES members greeted the changes with skepticism.
2. Although CSRA provided sound managerial tools, it could not create good management.
3. Improvements in performance, in all likelihood, would require more than just a reformed personnel management system.

The next sections address each of these problems in turn.

SES Members Were Skeptical

The skepticism with which SES members greeted the reforms had its roots in a number of concerns. Fear of political abuse headed the list. There was little doubt that membership in the SES brought with it risks previously unknown to these managers. Although it was inevitable that mechanisms increasing the flexibility of agency heads to reassign executives and dismiss those deemed incompetent would threaten the security of SES members, the fears were compounded by the epithets hurled at federal bureaucrats during passage of the legislation. As the 1980 presidential campaign neared, it became obvious that the competency of the career service would once again be a principal campaign issue.

Interviews conducted early in the study documented that most senior managers appeared willing to accept the risks of membership in the SES if they could see visible evidence that the benefits of the new system would also be realized. The benefits included performance awards for up to 50 percent of the SES population, a revised compensation system with six salary levels, sabbaticals, and the authority to accept presidential appointments while maintaining reinstatement rights. Unfortunately the number of performance awards was reduced by Congress soon after the inauguration of the SES and then reduced even further by the Office of Personnel Management (OPM).

Moreover, a pay cap was imposed that effectively negated the benefits of the new compensation system. These actions bred resentment and disillusionment in the SES so that even as the new reforms were being implemented, predictions were growing that none of the other benefits would materialize as promised—predictions that subsequent events proved true. The skepticism of most members of the SES and the anger of a sizable subset, apparent even as the evaluability assessment for this study was being conducted in the fall of 1979, constituted a significant, though potentially reversible, threat to the success of the reform.

CSRA Provides Tools But Does Not Guarantee Their Use

CSRA, even if properly implemented and managed, cannot create good management. The law attempted to improve the tools available to agency managers and to increase managerial flexibility, but the motivation and know-how to put the new personnel management system to good use to improve government performance rested with the political leadership of the agency.

Although it was the responsibility of the Assistant Secretary for Personnel Administration to install the new system (an enormous task in itself), the ultimate success of the reform depended on the use of the new system by those in the best position to improve agency performance, that is, the top leadership. For instance, performance appraisal could only be successful if leaders established organizational objectives, defined the measures against which performance would be measured, fostered an environment where objectives were taken seriously, legitimized the performance appraisal process and the role of Performance Review Boards (PRBs) in that process and then used the appraisals as a basis for rewarding high performance and punishing poor performance.[5]

It was apparent from the outset, then, that the success of CSRA in improving the performance of HHS depended not only on whether the Assistant Secretary for Personnel Administration could implement the provisions of the law as intended, but also on the priority the leadership of the agency gave improved performance, and their involvement in and use of the system as a means of reaching that goal. Yet nothing in the law could ensure the attention at top management to civil service reform and government performance. In fact, there were enormous constraints that worked against that attention. For example, as former Secretary of the Treasury, Michael Blumenthal, remarked in a *Fortune* interview:

> You learn very quickly that you do not go down in history as a good or bad Secretary in terms of how well you ran the place, whether you're a good administrator or not. You're perceived to be a good Secretary in terms of whether the policies for which you are responsible are adjudged successful

or not: what happens to the economy, to the budget, to inflation, and to the dollar . . . and what the bankers and the financial community think of you. Those are the things that determine whether you are a successful Secretary.[6]

CSRA May Not Be Enough

CSRA represented a major—indeed, some would argue unprecedented—overhaul of the federal personnel management system with the intent of improving the management and performance of federal programs. If one considers the changes it introduced into federal personnel management, its potential impact appears enormous. If, on the other hand, one looks at the reforms from the perspective of the problem they intended to address, that is, government performance, the remedy appears almost inconsequential. The list of potential causes of inefficient or ineffective government programs is probably unending, but must, at a minimum, include inadequate resources, a poor program design, and the absence of an effective technology for addressing the problem the program is intended to attack. None of these potential causes of poor government performance is even addressed by CSRA.

Moreover, even if it is true that an important cause of poor government performance is poor management, civil service reform can only affect one component of management: personnel administration. When federal managers complain that they are captives of a cumbersome internal management system that they cannot control, they are in all likelihood referring not just to the personnel management system but also to the financial management system, the procurement system, the information systems, and the administrative services system.[7] From this perspective, even a comprehensive redesign of personnel administration may be only a relatively meager step toward improved managerial control.

Thus, a third factor that threatened the success of civil service reform was, ironically, its promise. Too often, well-designed programs flounder because the expectations held for them are too great. In an evaluation-conscious government, establishing ambitious objectives for a program may assist in getting the measure through Congress but will almost certainly guarantee the program's perpetual vulnerability.

Monitoring the Program's Effectiveness

As we reflected on the vulnerability of CSRA during the early stages of this project, the first question we posed was: Should the expectations for CSRA be drastically lowered so as to simply evaluate whether or not HHS was successful in implementing the reform irrespective of its effects on performance? The response of the department was no. As a member of the initial evaluability assessment team explained, the reform was "based on the best thinking that could be marshalled, and the final product [was] as true to that thinking as the political process is ever likely to allow."[8] Although vulnerable, the reform effort deserved a chance to prove itself.

What was clear during that period was that it was too much to expect CSRA to have resulted in demonstrable improvements in HHS performance by the end of the evaluation effort, just five years into the life of the program. Even if the reform had not had to face the problems reviewed, it was reasonable to expect the first five years to be consumed by the effort to install and administratively fine-tune the system. Real improvements could only be expected after the program had a chance to mature, that is, after departmental managers had been given the time to become familiar with the opportunities the new system could offer for improving management and to understand its potential for surfacing performance problems, for linking individual and organizational objectives, and for providing mechanisms for holding managers accountable for the organization's mission.

Thus, for purposes of evaluating the reform effort, two phases of implementation were distinguished: an introductory phase and a mature phase. In the introductory phase, the department's top management team and SES members at all levels would begin working with the provisions of the act. This period was expected to be at once exciting, noisy, and troublesome. Because the act implied new roles (encouraging and rewarding performance), new values (organizational and program performance is important), and new behaviors (risk taking, performance planning), we expected many of those whose behavior was to change to challenge the system, to be defensive or hostile. We expected others to be excited and energized by the system. This early phase would, we anticipated, generate a great deal of "noise" in the system, making progress easy to underestimate.

By the end of the five-year period, however, we expected to see clear signs that the program was beginning to mature. We established four major tests that would allow us to judge whether CSRA was on track after five years, tests that together would constitute a reasonable measure of the health of the reform effort. The four are:

1. Has CSRA been successfully installed and is it operating smoothly?
2. Is top management experimenting with the CSRA tools and increased flexibility to improve agency performance and have the SES managers below them adopted the principles and techniques of performance management in their own programs and organizational units?
3. Is top management use of the tools perceived as legitimate by the SES population?
4. Is there evidence of positive, supportive attitudes toward the SES among its membership?

Next, we had to determine how we would know if the four tests had been met. As we anticipated, the most important requirement for successfully conducting the tests was a flexible method. Like a physician who, before making a final diagnosis, couples some scientific tests with a great deal of observation and questioning of the patient, as well as some random poking of "where it hurts," we, too, brought to this job an eclectic set of diagnostic instruments, some of which were clearly less "scientific," although no less useful, than others.

Following the initial evaluability assessment, we conducted an annual survey of the SES membership for three consecutive years (1982–84); conducted two-year case studies in eleven HHS program offices; and interviewed SES members, their superiors, and personnel officials throughout the HHS. In the final year we built a database of information on each of the SES members that included, among other things, performance ratings, number of performance awards, and initiation date. We were able to use this information to refute some of the myths about the operation of the performance management system that we had heard from the SES membership and to suggest ways the Assistant Secretary for Personnel Administration might construct a management information system to assist him in managing the problem. Throughout the three-year period, we continued to design and to redesign informal tests that would allow us to "check out" our hunches as they were developed. This approach meant that our conclusions were always being challenged and subsequently modified, but we believe that in the end it left us on firmer ground.

In the next sections we provide a rationale for the four tests that we established and summarize our findings with respect to each.

CSRA Has Been Successfully Installed

Before any improvements in performance could be expected, the new personnel machinery had to be installed and refined with several successful cycles completed. This alone was no easy task to complete, especially in a department as large, as diverse, and as organizationally fragmented as HHS. The performance appraisal system had to be designed and implemented, and thousands had to be trained in its use; performance plans had to be developed and appraisals conducted, which involved multiple negotiations between every superior and every subordinate in the department; the conversion from the old supergrade system to the SES had to be implemented, a process that required consultation and communication with over 600 senior managers; Performance Review Boards (PRBs) and Executive Resources Boards (ERBs) had to be appointed and their roles and responsibilities delineated;[9] an executive development program had to be created and refined; new recordkeeping systems had to be designed; procedures for awarding performance rewards had to be established and rewards allocated; and the list goes on.

In fact, the department has successfully installed virtually all of the required machinery, and it does operate smoothly. Each of the organizational units of the department has in place a performance management system, and there is nearly universal compliance with the requirement that all SES members have an annual performance plan and are appraised annually against the objectives and standards in that plan. Moreover, the department has aggressively sponsored the bonus and rank award programs. The maximum number of bonuses has been granted each year, and the department has continually nominated a full complement of rank award nominees.

This is not to say that either the installation or the operation have been troublefree. For instance, in the first several years there were many complaints about the increased paperwork burden, and paperwork is still an issue in some agencies, although we have noticed a pronounced decline in these complaints in the last two years. Yet our evidence demonstrates convincingly that for the most part the new procedures and processes were operating smoothly—a positive sign that the system is indeed workable. In our judgment, HHS should be given high marks for its success in installing and "debugging" the machinery of civil service reform.

Use of CSRA Tools Was Sporadic and Not Necessarily Directed to Performance Problems

Earlier we made the point that although it was the responsibility of the Assistant Secretary for Personnel Administration to install the new system, the ultimate success of the reform depended on whether and how the system was used by the management team that directs the work of the agency, for example, the Secretary and the Assistant Secretary for Health, and the Director of the National Institute of Health.[10] Not only is it these managers who maintain control over many of the tools introduced by CSRA (bonuses, reassignments, appointments to PRBs and ERBs, SES merit recruitment, and so on), but it is also they who set the objectives, the standards, and the tone of the agency. The quality of their leadership is critical to attaining CSRA objectives.

We expected that in the early stages of the program, as it was being installed, use would be "reactive"—that is, top managers would use the system only as required by law. But gradually, when the system began to function more smoothly, we anticipated that top management use would become more "proactive" as debates about the linkage of individual and organizational objectives ensued, performance problems surfaced, and managerial opportunities for improving performance appeared—opportunities which, if recognized and acted upon, would lead to improvements in performance. If, on the other hand, these opportunities either did not surface because the management system was not working properly or went unrecognized, the promise of performance improvements would not be realized even though the system itself might continue to operate.

Based on the reports we were receiving from the SES membership, we were initially doubtful that top management was paying any attention to the reform and were, therefore, surprised to find that half of the top managers with whom we spoke were very supportive of the concepts and operation of the new personnel management system, had been experimenting with different designs of their systems to find the one most appropriate for them, and had been using not only the performance appraisal and bonus provisions of CSRA, but other tools as well in pursuing their own managerial agendas. To test that use, we put top managers through several exercises to help us understand how purposeful their use of the bonus system was, and we discovered that each of them could clearly articulate their managerial philosophy for allocating bonuses, could explain who the winners and nonwinners were in their agency, could assess the information on bonus distributions in their agency or OPDIV in terms of both individual and organizational problems. Certainly these were positive signs that the program was beginning to mature in at least some organizations within HHS.

Even below the top managerial level, within the SES, we found signs that some positive use was occurring and that when it was being used, there were positive results. In some cases, CSRA tools were being applied to resolve minor, yet potentially troublesome personnel problems; in other cases, the use had dramatic effects for an entire organizational unit. Moreover, we were encouraged that use was not confined to any particular type of organization or any particular type of managerial style. Admittedly, it was sporadic and somewhat idiosyncratic, but it was occurring, nonetheless.

These positive signs must, however, be balanced against other less encouraging evidence. Although half of the top management team found the tools useful, the other half was best described as "disinterested" in the mechanisms. For these managers, CSRA had not improved their ability to manage—indeed, from their perspectives, it was all but irrelevant to the management of their organizations. And even those managers who were using the tools offered no firm evidence that performance had been improving as a result. In fact, they all agreed that the management of poor performance had *not* improved as a result of CSRA, although they stressed that this was as much a management failure as a lack of tools to address performance problems. As they admitted, the tools that were available were simply not being used, although the reasons why were complicated and included: (1) the time and energy involved; (2) the lack of incentives at the top level to do anything about poor performers; (3) a tradition and organizational climate in which demotion or dismissal were unacceptable except in the most extreme cases; and (4) a lack of courage on the part of most managers to take on a case of poor performance, either individual or organizational.

Two of our three top management "nonusers," both of whom manage organizations with very few SES members, argued that poor performance was not a problem among the SES membership in their organizations and that they were pleased with the organizational performance of the units under them. The third did claim to have serious performance problems not only with particular SES members, but also with particular organizational units. But, at the same time, this manager did not feel that those problems had as yet been adequately addressed, nor had a strategy for solving them been fully developed and implemented. Perhaps most disturbing was the fact that the three managers who were not using the system did not seem to have an alternative system in place for addressing performance problems as they arose. Nor did they acknowledge that performance was a serious problem, except in the case of a few isolated individuals who may have been performing poorly. Thus, few acknowledged that poor performance was a problem in their organizations, and fewer still expressed any interest in addressing it.

Below the top management level, the evidence regarding use of CSRA tools was equally contradictory. Although there was within HHS a group of senior executives who had adopted the tools of performance management, considered them useful, and staunchly defended their utility, the group was not large by any reckoning. Only one-fifth of the SES managers surveyed in 1984 both used the performance appraisal system and found it helpful in influencing staff performance; less than one-sixth used it and considered it helpful in influencing organizational performance. The numbers were even lower still if one looked at the members of the SES in scientific organizations. These SES members viewed themselves as scientists first and managers second. Even after several years' experience with the system, most of them continued to treat it as a burdensome distraction from the well-established peer review system that had been working long before CSRA was passed.

The results of our second test, then, were mixed. After five years, some top managers were actively experimenting with and refining the tools of CSRA in an effort to improve their own managerial effectiveness and the performance of their organizations—evidence that the reform effect was maturing as expected. Just as many, however, found the same tools either unnecessary or irrelevant to their managerial effectiveness. Below the top leadership group, the proportion of senior managers who aggressively used CSRA tools to correct performance problems was smaller still. In fact, among SES managers and those who supervised them, we could find relatively few who acknowledge that performance is a problem in their organizations and fewer still who expressed an interest in addressing it.

Challenge to the System's Legitimacy Were Not Addressed

The designers of CSRA attempted to strike a balance between, on the one hand, the need for safeguards against political abuse of the career civil service and, on the other, the need for a reformed personnel management system that would increase the responsiveness of career managers to agency leadership. The foundation of this balance resides in the merit principles acticulated in Title I of the act, which established that the basis for personnel decisions must be ability and performance. Thus, an individual cannot be dismissed because of political preferences, but can be dismissed for performance reasons. And the law mandates a series of specific safeguards to protect SES members, such as the 120-day moratorium on involuntary reassignments following changes in political supervision. On balance, however, these protections pale somewhat in comparison to the greatly strengthened managerial controls the SES makes available to the political leadership, for example, by providing a basis for dismissal of those who fail to perform competently, by instituting a system that provides financial rewards to the few rather than the many, by mandating that individual executives be held accountable for the failure of their programs.

Although we argued that CSRA could not be expected to lead to improved performance unless these personnel management tools were aggressively used by top management, we also argued that their use would have to be perceived as legitimate by the SES membership if performance improvements were to be realized. We fully expected that a new system designed specifically to enhance managerial control over the SES and to encourage the removal of poor performers would, unless it were being totally ignored by the whole department, result in a certain amount of anxiety, discontent, and challenges to its legitimacy. If the system was to have any hope for success, it would have to get people's attention. But over time we expected the noise to diminish as top management brought the concerns and complaints to the surface and addressed them. Thus, legitimacy would evolve gradually, but if not firmly established after five years, there should at least be visible signs that progress had been made and that substantially more SES members accepted the fundamental concepts and principles on which the reform was based and believed that the system treated them fairly.

In part, our expectations were met. The reform did elicit the attention of the SES. Few, if any, of the hundreds of SES members with whom we spoke and who returned our questionnaires did not have well thought-out reactions to and concerns about the concepts and operation of the new system and its implications for them. Wherever we went, we heard people discussing performance, what it meant, how it should be measured, who should get rewarded, and how poor performance should be handled. This kind of debate was, we believe, not only necessary, but healthy to the reform effort. In addition to these debates, we also heard lots of questions: Why did this person get a bonus when I did not? Why is our organization not getting its fair share of bonuses? What happens in the PRB? Who really decides on bonuses?—again, all questions that a healthy incentive system should be expected to engender.

There were, however, few signs that these initial challenges were being effectively addressed. The early signs of discontent did not diminish during the period of our evaluation—in fact, they may have even increased. In the survey of the SES membership fielded in early 1984, we discovered that only about half of the SES membership fully accepted the principles and assumptions that underlie the performance appraisal system (PAS), the bonus system, and the Performance Review Boards. Although most reported appropriate use of the PAS by their supervisors and felt they had been fairly treated in the appraisal process, considerably fewer felt that appraisal had worked fairly across all SES members in their agencies, and many felt the costs of the system had far outweighed the benefits. Just over one-third believed they had been treated fairly by the financial incentive system (bonus and rank awards), while fewer than one-fifth believed the system had treated all SES members fairly. Many SES members perceived the operation of biases in the awarding of bonuses from year to year, although our examination of the distribution of bonuses over a four-year period failed to substantiate most of these concerns. A full third reported they had *no* idea what they personally needed to do just to be *considered* for a bonus. A majority of SES members felt that the PRBs had not been effective in ensuring the fairness of the performance appraisal system and bonus system; and that they (SES members) had not benefitted from PRB reviews of performance plans and ratings. Finally, and most discouraging, even five years after its introduction, very few SES members saw the PAS and the bonus system, and the SES as a whole, as having had a positive impact on their own and their colleagues' individual job performance.

Our concern was that the level of discontent had remained remarkably consistent over time. And even though the root of much of the discontent was a misunderstanding of how the system operated—and thus could have been avoided—so little had been done to address the challenges. We left HHS feeling that increased communication between the SES community and both department and OPDIV leadership was needed to clarify misunderstandings and to relieve anxieties. Maturation of the system depended on the institution of a mechanism for amplifying, rather than muffling, the "noise" in the system so that it could be heard, addressed, and ultimately eliminated.

The SES Was not Maturing into an Elite Cadre of Professional Managers

The designers of the SES recognized its potential for fostering a commitment to one's organization and to excellence in management and attempted to create a system not only for enhancing control over executives but also for motivating them to strive for exemplary performance in carrying out organizational missions. The thinking was that over time the SES would develop into a respected and prestigious cadre of professional public managers and that SES members would begin to manifest those special feelings of esprit that have for so long been fostered in other public career services like the Forest Service, the Public Health Service Commissioned Corps, the Foreign Service, and the Marine Corps. The designers understood that if successful, the SES would then constitute a vehicle for fostering among its members, through a process of enculturation, a commitment to excellence in public management, which could, in theory, "unleash the motivation and tap the enthusiasm of its membership to an extent that made attainment of the ultimate objectives . . . possible."[11]

Initial indications were that the SES would have a difficult time establishing itself in the eyes of either the external world or the SES membership itself. Created in the midst of President Carter's "Bash the Bureaucrat" campaign, a period of criticism of public managers that may have actually intensified during the 1980 election, and greeted by its membership with skepticism and in some cases hostility, the fledgling system seemed threatened from the outset. Early in our evaluation, we surmised that if after five years the apathetic and/or hostile attitudes had taken root, there would be little likelihood that this second strategy would succeed in attaining its objective of improving executive performance.

There was, by the conclusion of our study, ample evidence to demonstrate that the initial skepticism, apathy, and hostility toward the SES had not been reversed. As an example, in our 1983 interviews with four of the five ERB chairpersons, seventeen PRB members, and sixteen rank-and-file SES members, only five of the thirty-seven interviewed answered the following question positively: "Do you feel that you are part of an elite cadre of managers in the department by virtue of your membership in the SES?" The following quote from one SES member was typical:

> You've got to be kidding! I would have this sense if the SES were hard to join; they grandfathered too many people in. SES has no meaning outside the job. You have a range of folks from extremely talented to extremely incompetent. It's not like a stamp of "CHOICE" on a beef carcass.

Much of the negativism we documented since the inception of the SES could be boiled down to one principal explanation: SES members felt that although they, in good faith, had accepted the risks of membership in the new system, the benefits never materialized. The reductions in the proportion of an agency's membership that could receive a bonus in any given year, coupled with the pay caps, bred deep resentment among the SES membership. In addition, there were other sources of frustration. Sabbaticals never became a reality. Individual development plans were negotiated regularly only for members of the SES candidate development program. Only three HHS SES members had, over the five-year period, accepted presidential appointments.

Finally, there was no formal mechanism in place by which SES members could request reassignments. In sum, the risks of membership were very real; the benefits were not.

Moreover, despite the intentions of those who designed the reform, there was little "new blood" in the ranks of the SES because so many supergrades were grandfathered in and because relatively few new members were added. When they were, they tended to be recruited from inside the department. And, finally, a sizable proportion of the HHS membership—those in scientific organizations—did not think of themselves as managers and reacted negatively to many components of the system. Developing a positive identification with the SES among scientists proved to be a nearly impossible task.

Conclusion

Like most attempts to convert sound theory into workable solutions to real problems, the reform effort in HHS has met with perhaps as many failures as successes. As we consider what we have learned about management, about performance, and about evaluation from this study, three lessons seem most salient. First, it is easy to blame a management system for the shortcomings of those who manage it. When we saw that CSRA had been successfully installed in HHS but could find no evidence of performance improvements in the department, it was easy to conclude that the law had not worked. Yet we continued to be impressed with the design of the act, which so delicately defines the balance between top management control of personnel, on the one hand, and the protection of employee rights on the other and still leaves plenty of room for agency management to mold its system to its needs. We have found little to suggest that when coupled with strong leadership and a commitment to excellent performance, civil service reform could not work. But the evidence we have collected also convinces us that no management system, no matter how well designed or how well installed, can create good management or force performance onto the managerial agenda. Management systems are nothing but tools and, as with tools, the quality of the product is more dependent on the skill of the craftsman than the precision of the implement.

A second lesson of our evaluation is the importance of allowing a program the opportunity to mature before assessing its potential. This study, although begun as the act was being implemented, was designed not to judge the results of the intervention in its early years, but rather to provide feedback to its managers as it was being implemented—that is, to suggest ways the program could be kept "on track." The dilemma of the evaluator is how to resist the temptation to judge too soon. Too often, interest in a program is at its peak right after passage; if one waits too long, one often discovers that nobody cares any longer how the program is faring because new issues, new problems, and new programs have taken over the agenda.

Finally, one of the hardest lessons for the evaluator is to decide exactly what can be expected from a program and when. Evaluability assessment has gone a long way to address this problem by encouraging evaluators to work with decisionmakers soon after a program is in place in order to determine what outcomes can be expected. Where disagreement exists, evaluability assessment stresses the need for early clarification with program managers. In the case of the evaluation of civil service reform, which proceeded in an almost textbooklike manner, one obstacle was never successfully overcome: although installation of the system depended on the efforts of the Assistant Secretary of Personnel Administration, the program's ultimate success required the attention and dedication of the top management team in the department—a group of political leaders who, since the start of this evaluation, have been completely replaced by new people, in some cases more times than once. Moreover, it is a leadership group that must fight the temptation to neglect internal management issues in order to attend more closely to policy initiatives for which credit can be claimed. As one senior manager explained to us, "There are just not many bennies in searching out and correcting poor performance."

Notes

1. HHS is divided organizationally into five Operating Divisions, commonly referred to as OPDIVs. These are: the Public Health Service, the Social Security Administration, the Health Care Financing Administration, the Office of Human Development Services, and the Office of Community Services.

2. Testimony of Alan K. Campbell, Chairman, U.S. Civil Service Commission, before the Committee on Post Office and Civil Service, U.S. House of Representatives (March 14, 1978).

3. In developing the conceptual framework for this and the next section of this chapter, the authors borrowed some of the ideas developed by the original evaluability assessment team for this study. These ideas were summarized in an article by Bruce Buchanan, entitled, "The Senior Executive Service: How We Can Tell If It Works." The article was published in the May/June 1981 issue of *Public Admininstration Review,* pp. 349–358. We gratefully acknowledge the contribution of this developmental work.

4. Ibid., p. 355.

5. Performance Review Boards in HHS are charged with (1) reviewing performance plans early in the appraisal period, (2) reviewing the initial appraisal of a senior executive's performance, (3) recommending performance awards for deserving executives, and (4) recommending final performance ratings.

6. "Candid Reflections of a Businessman in Washington," *Fortune,* January 29, 1979.

7. See, for instance, *Revitalizing Federal Management: Managers and Their Overburdened Systems*. A report by a Panel of the National Academy of Public Administration (Washington, D.C.: National Academy of Public Administration, November 1983), p. 3.

8. Buchanan, "The Senior Executive Service: How We Can Tell If It Works," p. 355.

9. ERPs provide advice to top management on aspects of executive resources management and policymaking. Specifically, they are charged with conducting the SES merit staffing process by reviewing the qualifications of each candidate and making written recommendations to the appointing authority. In HHS, they may also be involved in a variety of other activities, such as approving qualification standards for SES positions, recommending pay rates, and recommending disciplinary action.

10. According to our definition, the top management team in HHS includes those agency or OPDIV heads to whom the ten PRBs report.

11. Buchanan, "The Senior Executive Service; How We Can Tell If It Works," p. 356.

Part V
Stimulating Improvements in the Performance of Programs and Organizations

The topic of part V is how managers and evaluators can stimulate improvements in the performance of agencies and programs. This task is the third element of performance oriented management.

Michael Knapp and Marian Stearns write that the current public policy environment requires a reformulation of the evaluator's task. In the past, evaluators looked for program or policy impacts. Their agendas and methodologies were strongly influenced by federal program requirements and resources. In today's interdependent environment, evaluators must attend to efforts to improve *collective* performance.

Citing the case of state educational reform, Knapp and Stearns argue that policymaking responsibility has now developed to the states. State educational reforms seek broad and multiple changes in schools. Rarely is there a unified "program" to evaluate because state policymakers pass reform packages to affect an entire system, rather than a single problem. The authors suggest that evaluators should direct their efforts toward examining whether the system itself is moving in the direction policymakers desire. This is a new focus for evaluation, one that requires a reconceptualization both of methodology and the audience for evaluation.

The climate of public and policymaker opinion depends on the information collected about the problems the reforms address. If evaluators can show how reform energies are mobilized and turned into solutions and then find ways to communicate their findings to appropriate audiences in a timely fashion, evaluators can help build and sustain the reform movement that is at the heart of education improvement efforts. Knapp and Stearns describe the central elements of an emerging evaluation strategy that evaluators can use in the new policy environment.

Liese Sherwood-Fabre examines two recent federal reforms and identifies characteristics that facilitate efforts to change large systems. Based on her review of planned changes in bail reform and in the U.S. civil service, she identifies several factors present in successful reform efforts.

Two factors are important during the development of reforms. Successful change is helped when there is broad support for the proposal and when change agents take into consideration the needs and concerns of special interest groups.

During implementation, the change agent's goal is to get the new reform institutionalized. Successful implementation is facilitated when there is a monitoring body responsible for ensuring the change is being implemented and when personnel rewards and organizational structures are compatible with the change.

Sherwood-Fabre's conceptual framework can be used by evaluators with an interest in encouraging and monitoring organizational or system change.

Alan Balutis describes the central features of the Reagan administration's "Reform '88," a governmentwide movement to improve the administrative management of federal agencies. To illustrate the potential of Reform '88, Balutis discusses the comprehensive efforts to improve the management of the U.S. Department of Commerce. The management reform's goal in Commerce was to create a unified, integrated department with a clearly established mission and programs and structures to support that mission. Using a management-by-objectives system linked to the department's budget and performance appraisal systems, Commerce was able to save more than $15 million in administrative overhead costs within two years. Savings were allocated to operating programs within the department.

Balutis identifies the factors that are helping the department achieve its goals: the reforms were initiated and supported by the top level of the department. The department's top management team had substantial experience in the areas targeted for reform. Political appointees to the department were educated about the reform before they had the opportunity to be "captured" by their jobs or by interest groups affected by the proposed changes. The same management team oversaw the reform efforts from formulation through implementation. The department looked to well-run organizations outside of government for ideas about how to improve performance. Finally, the reforms concentrated on improving administrative practices and avoided wherever possible making changes in the structure of the organization.

Balutis closes his chapter by discussing the problems associated with attempting to reform federal management practices, with specific reference to the barriers facing Reform '88.

Anabel Crane describes how the Health Resources and Services Administration uses "Program Review," both as a method of organizational renewal and as an evaluation tool. Program Review is intended to provide a national overview of a program, concentrating on program design, the appropriateness of the resources used, the impacts of the program, and possible changes. The ultimate goal of the review is to help managers define what they can realistically do to improve program performance.

The program review technique requires selecting significant program issues that can benefit from a review, and bringing together top-level practitioners and other experts for, typically, a three-day conference. Participants are guided through a structured discussion of the program issues, and the conference concludes with recommendations and implementation plans for change.

Crane identifies criteria for selecting and for rejecting programs suitable for review. She provides examples of several programs whose reviews led to specific changes.

The program review is best used for broad overviews of programs where new ideas are sought rather than for detailed examinations of technical issues. Program reviews are most effective when top-level managers are interested in and participate in the process, when there is focused and sustained oversight of the review, and when the review conference is well planned and conducted.

In addition to providing managers with action ideas for improving programs, the review process encourages organizational and professional renewal, team building, networking, and shared knowledge. Program review also offers evaluators the opportunity to present their findings on significant issues to a broader range of decisionmakers and in a more timely fashion than is normally possible.

14

Improving System-Wide Performance: Evaluation Research and the State Education Reform Movement

Michael S. Knapp
Marian S. Stearns

Discussions of organizational performance and ways to improve it frequently take a discrete organization—a government agency, a service delivery unit, a firm—as the locus of the problem and hence the level at which solutions are sought. This way of construing the problem ignores or downplays systematic causes of organizational failure and system-wide efforts to stimulate improvement. But a society characterized by growing interdependence of organizational units can ill afford to ignore efforts to improve the *collective* performance of organizations.

Systematic information, whether from evaluation research or other sources, can play a central role in system-wide improvement processes. But current evaluation research techniques, conceptual frameworks, and arrangements for sponsoring evaluation are not up to the task. System-wide improvement poses to the evaluation research community a major challenge that it can—and must—meet, if the profession is to make a contribution to problem solving at a higher level than the individual organization.

The challenge is nowhere more clearly seen than in current efforts by state governments to reform public attention. Across the nation, states are taking vigorous and unprecedented action to improve the quality of instruction for public school students, typically by enacting far-reaching legislative packages that change simultaneously many aspects of school and school district operations. State initiatives are a response to profound shifts in federal policies and funding, which coincide with renewed public interest in the quality of education. In the view of many analysts, these efforts represent the beginning of a long period in which the states are the principal arena in which policymakers address the nation's concerns about public education.

Neither the producers of evaluation research nor the consumers are well prepared to answer, or even ask, the kinds of questions that system-wide reform efforts raise. The evaluation research profession has burgeoned over the last two decades, primarily in response to the call for evaluations of federal interventions in education and other areas. Studies were mounted, often on a grand scale, to track the implementation or to determine the effects of a program or policy that aimed at a specific target population (for example, the disadvantaged), a particular kind of practice (for example, innovative teaching approaches), or a particular grade level or curricular area (for example, preschool grades, career education). Current state reform efforts are more ambitious by an order of magnitude. The omnibus bills that state legislatures have passed in the last few years contain numerous provisions that potentially affect many, if not most, facets of local educational systems. To capture and to assess the changes these reforms may accomplish, a different framework of ideas and research methods needs to be developed that is national in scope, responsive to the nature of reform initiatives, and respectful of the diversity among state needs and priorities.

The State Education Reform Movement

A series of events have converged in the last few years to present states with an opportunity to enact major legislation aimed at reforming public education. Most states have risen to the challenge by passing sweeping legislative bills that mandate more instructional time, competency testing, merit pay for teachers, reduced class sizes, and the like. Furthermore, these initiatives are not only occurring in the states like California and Florida, which have strong traditions of active legislative effort in educational matters, but also in states like Mississippi and Arkansas that are not usually in the vanguard of educational reform.

The forces driving these reforms are strong and promise to be long term. Initially, by virtue of repeated funding and staff cutbacks, a philosophy of a reduced federal role in education, and explicit legislative design (for example, in the Education Consolidation and Improvement Act of 1981), the federal government has placed the matter at the states' doorsteps. At the same time that the federal presence has receded, public concern over educational quality has grown, fueled by media attention to test score decline, international competition, and a lag in productivity. State political debate has increasingly reflected the public's appetite for renewed attention to issues of education; as a result, governors and legislatures have become as heavily involved as state education agencies. Now, with the deepest parts of recent recession behind them, most states are in a political and economic position to move forward. Renewed activism among state governments, the private sector, and state-level interest groups has added impetus to the reform movement. Finally, a spate of national reports has helped build consensus behind a diagnosis of what is wrong with public education and helped outline our approach toward righting it.

The targets of reform are broad and elusive. Where earlier reform movements aimed at the needs and rights of special populations or the equitable distribution of resources among school districts, the current wave of reform has a more ambitious agenda. Overall educational quality is the rubric for a series of related concerns that have been rising to consciousness for over a decade. Higher standards, increased learning (and teaching) time, stricter discipline, improved instructional staff quality, and enhanced teacher compensation are among the areas of perceived deficiency for which legislative remedies have been sought. Accordingly, reform packages have been assembled in the form of omnibus bills rather than discrete, relatively focused programs that were the outcome of reform in the 1960s and early 1970s. A case in point, the recent Hart-Hughes Educational Reform Act of 1983 (S.B. 813) in California strings together finance provisions, personnel policies, staff development initiatives, graduation standards, curricular requirements, and testing provisions, among others. A major education bill passed by the Florida legislature, which aimed at improving school finance reform, teacher salaries, teacher training, mathematics and science education, and computer literacy, is another such example.

The Challenge for Evaluation Research

The need for information about these reform initiatives is beginning to emerge as the initial reform fervor dies down and people ask, "What are these reforms accomplishing?" Because of the nature of the reforms, the information necessary to answer that question cannot be easily or straightforwardly assembled. Within any given state, new kinds of information are called for. A short list of the tasks facing evaluators includes:

Developing appropriate indicators of cumulative system change.

Making intelligent short-term estimates of long-term reform trends.

Understanding how multiple, simultaneous reform measures interact and collectively contribute to educational improvement.

Developing comprehensive, yet inexpensive, information bases (for example, that rely on nontraditional data sources) and imaginative ways of analyzing these.

Determining how state-wide policy changes interact with varying local conditions.

Sorting among the numerous reform provisions to determine effective ones.

At the same time that the effects of reforms within individual states are being described and documented, there is a need to derive comparative lessons across states to help guide further policy developments in any particular state—or for that matter, development of policies at the federal level intended to support state reforms. In the remainder of this chapter, we will concentrate on the challenge of evaluating reforms within an individual state, but we note that this task can be informed by the experiences of other states.

Current frameworks and techniques for conducting evaluation and policy research are not well suited to address the above-listed tasks. The working tool kit of most evaluators and policy researchers has been shaped to date by models of federal program evaluation. Federal "interventions" in state and local education institutions predisposed policymakers and researchers to ask certain kinds of questions (Was the program implemented? How did it affect specified outcomes?) and employ certain research designs (for example, experimental designs, discrepancy studies of compliance, implementation case studies). These approaches assumed that (1) the focus of evaluation was a discrete "program" (or "policy" or "civil rights mandate"); (2) the program could be seen and identified at the state and local levels (if for no other reason than to satisfy accountability demands); and (3) clear cause-effects relationships could be traced between the program and one or a few outcomes at a time. Also, the scope of application was nationwide: despite variation in the way each federal program or policy was interpreted, it nonetheless applied to all states or program sites. Finally, most approaches to date require extensive and expensive primary data collection.

State reform initiatives alter these premises in the following ways:

Broad, multiple targets. Reform packages such as California's S.B. 813 seek to alter simultaneously many aspects of schools and school district operations.

Significant increases in funding for education. Most state reform packages now in place or contemplated include large increases in base funding for education.

Limited resources for assessing reforms. Due to tight financial situations in most states, the analytic resources remain quite limited; federal sources of support for this kind of activity have all but dried up.

Lack of programmatic connections. Though varying across states, each of these reform efforts combine under a single authorization many kinds of reform elements. The educational reform is no longer a "program," but a set of minimally related policies that will cause various forms of action at the local level.

The high profile of reform. The movement to improve public education takes place at center stage in the public policy arena, where the results of initiatives (as perceived by many audiences) have great visibility. High expectations of fast payoffs are thus inevitable.

Because the thing to be evaluated has changed so dramatically, existing techniques and approaches are frequently inappropriate. It becomes virtually impossible, for example, to conduct "controlled" studies of program effects. Conventional implementation studies (for example, to determine degree of compliance with program goals or legislative intention) are less meaningful. Furthermore, most attempts to document "program implementation" would inevitably meet frustration because the "program" does not exist (or, put another way, is too many things or is too loosely specified to be readily visible). In fact, many goal-referenced evaluation modes can only be applied with difficulty to the situation because the overriding "goal" of omnibus reform packages is so global (improved educational quality) or so diffuse (the aggregate of stated or implied goals for each component of the package). Finally, the lack of resources for conducting policy research necessitates more cost-effective and efficient designs. In short, a new approach must be developed.

Elements of an Approach to Evaluating State Reform

The challenge to the evaluation research community has several dimensions. First, we need to reconstruct the evaluation problem. That includes framing questions more appropriately, developing a framework that better conceptualizes a reform initiative and its effects, and adapting or inventing methods that can capture these effects. Second, we need to identify appropriate audiences and clients for evaluation of reform initiatives. In the wider arena in which such evaluations must happen, conventional notions of the evaluator serving the "program decisionmakers" do not apply as well as they have in the past, if they apply at all. Alternative vehicles will need to be found that bring evaluative insights to the audiences that matter.

Reconstructing the Evaluation Problem. Three bodies of research help to conceptualize state reform initiatives and their effects, which in turn helps to frame evaluation questions and to adapt or invent research methods.

Cumulative effects of government policies. Studies of the "cumulative effects" of government initiatives on agencies at lower levels offer a framework for thinking about the way multiple policies affect the activities of local institutions (for example, Kimbrough & Hill, 1981; Knapp et al., 1983; Moore et al., 1983).

Local response to regulation. Research on organizational responses to change in the regulatory environment has helped to identify how local institutions notice, interpret, and act in response to laws, provisions, and regulations (for example, Sproull, 1981).

Teaching policy. Recent work on the nature of connections between teaching or teachers and policies at higher governmental levels has helped delineate the linkages in the policy process that have most to do with general educational quality as it occurs at the classroom level (for example, Sykes, 1983; Kirst, 1983).

Drawing from this work, we can suggest the outline for an approach.

Study the Local System—Not the Program. State reform initiatives aim at many aspects of the local educational system simultaneously. If there are effects that contribute meaningfully to educational improvements, they will derive from many small changes that cumulatively shift the climate for education, the perceived opportunities, and the tenor of the curriculum. These shifts will be best detected by "taking the pulse" of the local educational system in ways that capture more than conventional indicators such as student test scores. This means identifying appropriate indicators such as student test scores. In turn this means identifying appropriate indicators of system functioning, somewhat analogous to "social indicators" research, only at an institutional, rather than a societal, level of analysis. It also means keeping a watchful eye for unanticipated measurement effects; social indicators can and often do lead to change in the behavior that is counted without contributing to improvement in organization functioning.

Focus on Attention, Incentives, Morale. The many pieces of the reform agenda compete with a buzzing universe at the school and district levels for the attention of educators. Collectively, the reforms will have their greatest impact if they: (1) capture the attention of a critical mass of educators (and their relevant local constituencies); (2) provide positive incentives for committing further energy to education (by current staff, as well as by new recruits); and (3) generate hope for, and supportive imagery of, schools among students, educators, and the public. Accordingly, evaluation research must document what is (and is not) noticed at the local level, and determine the effects reform initiatives have on local motivation and morale (at the administrative, teacher, and student levels). In such reform movements the whole is greater, and far more important, than the parts. Those aspects of the local scene that reflect the whole—such as the commitment educators feel to reform goals—are consequently the most appropriate indicators of reform effects.

Watch for State–Local Interactions and Adjustments of Policies over Time.
State reforms will not be treated by local educators as static commandments,
but rather as a set of resources and constraints that provide opportunities for
local problem solving. Over time, the meaning of regulations will be clarified
and altered as they are reinterpreted by local institutions or amended by state
administering agencies, or both. Whether or not a particular reform provision is implemented at the local level, it may stimulate new solutions to the
problem addressed by that piece of the reform package.

*Differentiate Early from Mature Responses and Direct Research Attention
Accordingly.* The initial response of schools and districts to the kinds of
reforms now being initiated will combine confusion (while educators decide
which reforms to emphasize and debate the meaning of particular reforms)
with inaction (while districts reorganize to accommodate reforms or get used
to the idea or simply begin to notice that things have changed). The surface of
things may change, but the deeper shift in habits and expectations will take
longer. At first, the effects of reforms will appear at the "input" side of the
equation: changed teacher retention rates, increased hours spent in class or
doing homework, different course choices, and so on. Consequently, evaluation research should concentrate at first on these aspects of reform; little
should be expected in the short term from educational outcomes such as student achievement measures that may require the combined effect of various
reforms over time. As the years go by, evaluation research attention can
gradually be redirected toward outcomes such as student learning.

Identifying Appropriate Audiences and Clients. Reconstructing the problem
is only half the battle. Evaluation researchers need also to identify whom they
serve and who will sponsor their work. The state reform movement in education redefines the roles of audience and client, and their relationship with
evaluators. Ultimately, the public and its representatives are the most important audience for evaluation findings; their role in promoting and sustaining
reforms cannot be overestimated. But so broad an audience demands a different kind of relationship with evaluators, who need to learn both how to
listen to their concerns and to communicate results to them. The appropriate
communication modes are not generally developed as yet. Experiments will
need to be tried such as the inclusion of journalists and media representatives
as members of the interdisciplinary evaluation team investigating education
reform. Although this suggestion may be anathema to many evaluators who
have struggled to establish "scientific" credibility for their profession, it illustrates the extent of the challenge systemwide improvement efforts pose. If
evaluation wishes to play an important role in such efforts, political or public
credibility is equally important.

But "the public and its representatives" is too broad and amorphous a
group to constitute the immediate client for evaluation of reforms. Some-

one—or some group—needs to sponsor evaluative activity, and someone or some groups (not necessarily the sponsors) need to engage in the constructive, educative dialogue that directs evaluation to particular concerns of actors in the policy community, who will determine the funding, implementation, and details of reform initiatives. Evaluators must find key members of the "policy shaping community" (as conceptualized by Cronbach and Associates, 1980) who are both prominent and relatively neutral. Many apparently logical choices such as the chief state school officer or education committees of the legislature are often inappropriate because they are too closely associated with defined positions vis-a-vis reform initiatives. As clients, they would tend not to see the problem from various perspectives, to ask the appropriate (and critical) questions, or ultimately to lend the findings the public credibility they need to be influential. Where does one find the right clients?

Some solutions are beginning to emerge as demonstrated by two examples from one state. One solution is to find (or help to create) intermediary groups with broad, nonpartisan membership that have the credibility and the resources to encourage evaluation research in the public interest. An example is the California Roundtable, a consortium of 250 chief executive officers from leading firms in the state, who pool resources and support investigations on issues of importance to state development. (Among the roundtable's efforts have been studies contributing to the enactment of California's current reform initiative.) Another solution is to engage the concern of private foundations; many have taken an interest in educational reform efforts and some have put substantial resources behind efforts to evaluate them, for example, the Hewlett Foundation's support of the Center for Policy Analysis on California Education (PACE) operated by Berkeley and Stanford universities. Groups such as these are beginning to appear in other states as well.

From Evaluation to Improvement

If the approach we have been describing is implemented and appropriate sponsors found, there is a high likelihood that evaluation will make a contribution to system-wide improvement of public education. Even if state education reforms are poorly measured, the information available is likely to keep attention on education and to focus political debate on areas of attempted change.

A number of states have taken tentative steps toward the approach we are advocating. Once again taking California as an example, the state education agency has developed an evaluation strategy that relies heavily on multiple indicators of progress (or lack of it) at several levels. Not only are student performance scores on a state-developed standardized test included in the set of indicators, but also such measures as the number of academic courses offered, the enrollments in these courses, the amount of homework assigned, and the number of written essays required. The evaluation philosophy guiding this approach emphasizes accountability of the units at the bottom of the system (students, and schools) to the top (legislature and state education agency), but also includes feedback by means of interdistrict comparisons as well as a school and district self-assessment process.

Experiments such as this may have both positive outcomes and significant risks. By taking a stand on what is to be counted to indicate educational improvement, state educational leaders have made their priorities and directions for change explicit. They have wisely emphasized multiple indicators of success, and at least some of these are on the input side of the equation. But there are many missing pieces in this evaluation strategy. For one thing, there are no measures of local morale or even local attention to reform initiatives—though obviously more difficult to tap, these areas of reform impact would yield a broader assessment of the reform initiative as a whole. In addition, as we noted earlier, the choice of indicators may encourage changes in educational practice that represent no improvement whatsoever. Measuring the amount of homework assigned, for example, may lead to more burden for students without enlightenment, or worse, to inflated counts by administrators wishing their units to look good (with no real change at all in homework assignments). Finally, the fact that the state educational agency both sponsors and conduct the evaluation may hurt the credibility of evaluation results in future policy debates.

But for all the apparent or potential shortcomings, such experiments must be tried, and tried soon, if evaluators are to play a useful role in system-wide reform of public education. The climate of opinion among the public at large and within the policy community that supports reform, is heavily dependent on information gathered about the problems to which reforms are addressed. Taxpayers are expecting some signs that increases in educational funding are leading to improvement. If evaluation researchers do not develop means of capturing the many things that reform initiatives may accomplish, others will step forward with less accurate or systematic representations of reform effects. To the extent that evaluation research can illustrate the way reform energies are mobilized can find ways to communicate this to the appropriate audiences, and can do so before too many legislative sessions pass, it stands a reasonable chance of helping to sustain the local reform energies that are at the heart of the educational improvement process. Even if the success of these evaluations is limited, the social importance of the reform goals makes the effort worth it. And if evaluation research does meet this challenge, both the systems studied and evaluation's role in them will be strengthened.

References

Cronbach, Lee J. and Associates. *Toward Reform of Program Evaluation* (San Francisco: Jossey-Bass, 1980).

Kimbrough, Jackie and Hill, Paul. *The Aggregate Effects of Federal Education Programs* (Santa Monica, CA: Rand, 1981).

Kirst, Michael. "Teaching Policy and Federal Categorical Programs." In L.S. Shulman and G. Sykes (Eds.), *Handbook of Teaching and Policy* (New York: Longmans, 1983).

Knapp, Michael S. et al. *Cumulative Effects of Federal Education Policies on Districts and Schools* (Menlo Park, CA: SRI International, 1983).

Moore, Mary T. et al. *The Interactions of Federal and Related State Education Programs* (Washington, D.C.: The Educational Policy Research Institute of Educational Testing Service, 1983).

Sproull, Lee. "Response to Regulation: An Organizational Process Framework," *Administration and Society* 12 (4) (February 1981):pp. 447–470.

Sykes, Gary. "Public Policy and the Problem of Teacher Quality: The Need for Screens and Magnets." In L.S. Shulman and G. Sykes (Eds.), *Handbook of Teaching and Policy* (New York: Longmans, 1983).

15
Achieving Federal Reform

Liese Sherwood-Fabre

Change is basic to a successful organization.[1] Organizations that fail to adapt to pressure both from within and without will eventually fail altogether (Aldrich, 1979). For government organizations, change often appears as legislated reform. Congress provides legislation to achieve new goals, and government agencies and their managers must carry them out. The evaluator can play an important role in achieving reform by providing information to policymakers and managers alike. He or she can help sift through the interpretations and perceptions of different interest groups and provide a basic understanding of what was intended and can actually be accomplished by the reform. Evaluators can also examine the reform's implementation and identify where specific changes are or are not occurring. Such information is valuable in indicating where the reform is working well and what still needs to be changed for all goals to be met.

In this chapter I highlight factors in the development and implementation of a reform that affect its success, drawing upon my experiences in two different reform evaluations. These evaluations provide insight for the reformer and the evaluator alike.[2] For the reformer, it indicates which factors he or she should consider when drafting and implementing reform. For the evaluator, it anticipates some of the factors that must be examined when evaluating a particular reform.

The two evaluations included here considered two very different reforms. One evaluated the results of civil service reform in the Department of Health and Human Services. The other examined the impact of pretrial service agencies on judicial decision making in federal courts. Because a comprehensive evaluation of any reform requires both an examination of its development and its implementation, and since what occurs in the development may affect the implementation, I review the factors in their chronological order.

An Overview of the Two Reforms

In civil service reform, Congress sought to change personnel practices by restructuring the system. Criticism of civil service from several sources—

including President Carter—created a concern that led to a new system that included a greater emphasis on individual performance and the development of a new organization for top management: the Senior Executive Service. A major provision of this new system was a yearly performance plan that held government workers responsible for organizational activities and goals. Supervisors assessed employees at the end of the year using this plan and used these ratings to determine salary increases and monetary bonuses. Congress designed the new system to increase public confidence in the federal government by making federal employees responsible for their programs.

In bail reform, Congress directed changes at judicial decision making. The Bail Reform Act of 1966 identified new factors (in particular, a defendant's "community ties") to be considered in determining pretrial release conditions. The Speedy Trial Act of 1974 provided a further attempt at changing decision making by providing judges with systematic information for these factors. Bail reform sought to increase the equity of the pretrial release system by decreasing court dependence on a defendant's monetary resources and ability to post bail.

Developing the Reform

Pressures for change occur both inside and outside organizations (Aldrich, 1979). These forces create strains in existing structures to which the organization must adjust or fail. Because such changes in the federal government often require congressional attention, those who desire change must make Congress recognize that a problem exists and that they, the reformers, have a solution. At the same time, those proposing change must recognize the concerns of various interest groups and gain their support. These groups become involved in reforms that they feel will affect their members or their power. Reformers must placate or co-opt such groups if they are to develop the interest and support needed for their cause.[3]

The reform's development is important to the evaluator because the pressures appearing at this time affect the shape of the final reform. Different groups seek different goals for the proposed reform. If evaluators are to understand what exactly the reform was expected to do and how, these different pressures must be included in their analysis. This information provides understanding of the context within which the reform occurred and helps identify realistic objectives to examine during implementation.

The Initial Pressure for Change

A major prerequisite for reform involves a perceived need for change. Reformers may use various techniques for creating attention to the needed change: personal contacts, political power and visibility, or sheer numbers. Whatever the method, the reformers place pressures on Congress to *do* something. Congress seeks to relieve pressure by offering legislation to address the problem and to satisfy concerns. In civil service and bail reform, Congress considered changing the current situation because *someone* perceived a problem and brought it to their attention.

With civil service reform, administrative pressure played a major role in developing concern. President Carter began a campaign against a government overburdened by inefficient and ineffective bureaucrats. His criticisms led to increased concern over the effectiveness and efficiency of federal programs, to which Congress responded by proposing private-sector personnel strategies for federal employees.

For bail reform, a social movement helped to influence the proposed legislation. Government studies, social activists, and a broad concern for defendant rights all influenced congressional consideration of current pretrial release practices. The liberal climate of the 1960s and early 1970s pressured Congress to examine the federal pretrial release system. This examination showed major inequities in pretrial release decisions. From such pressures, Congress proposed changes in a system that had existed virtually untouched since the 1700s.

Having convinced a significant portion of Congress that a problem exists, the next step is to form the legislation to solve it. It is usually at this point that interest groups become aware of proposed reforms and seek to protect their own position, and thus it is here that reformers take steps to include or coopt interest group activities.

The Influence of Interest Groups

Interest groups seek to influence the reform's final form in a way that benefits their members or enhances their power. They appear at congressional hearings or meet with legislators to change proposed legislation. These groups can work either for or against a particular reform, depending on how they perceive its possible impact. Reformers must focus either on gaining support from these groups or on co-opting their opposition—usually by altering some provision in the proposed legislation that affects the group. Once they feel that they have protected their interests, these groups may then actually help lobby for the reform or at least remove their opposition to it.

The reform, as finally passed, usually contains compromises and provisions influenced by different groups and not envisioned in the original draft of the legislation. These changes, however, provide a flexibility with several possible advantages. Federal reforms affect an entire nation that is far from homogeneous. A more flexible reform allows for geographical and cultural variations when those in different regions begin to implement it. A second advantage of flexibility is the possibility of co-opting interest groups while maintaining the option of carrying out the original reform. Feeling they have obtained legislation that protects their position, interest groups may fail to follow through on the reform's implementation. Where legislation provides options in implementation, those creating the actual changes can do as they desire as long as the interest groups are not monitoring implementation.

For example, the probation officers' lobby influenced the provisions of legislation proposed to extend the pretrial services agencies to all federal districts. They sought to change the statute's language to include an option for the different federal court districts to provide pretrial services within the probation office—desired by the probation lobby—or under an independent agency—desired by the Administrative Office of the U.S. Courts. This option was not available in the original legislation. At the same time, the revised legislation provided for the Administrative Office to evaluate pretrial activities in the different districts and create an independent agency if the probation office was not performing pretrial duties adequately. Thus, while the probation lobby was satisfied, the Administrative Office still had the power to implement the reform as they originally desired.

The Final Reform

The final reform legislation reflects Congress' attempt to relieve the pressure from as many of the groups that become involved as possible. After the legislation passes, the responsibility for change shifts from Congress to those mandated to implement the changes. For the evaluator, focus shifts from the stated reform goals to the actual methods used to achieve these goals. Here, new factors come into play that affect the reform's implementation. It becomes apparent at this point whether the legislation adequately provided for the changes needed.

Implementing the Reform

In the best of all possible worlds, once a reform has been legislated, implementation easily follows because those involved recognize and understand the need for change. In such cases, the implementers have internalized reform goals. Unfortunately, this is rarely the case. For example, the evaluation in the Department of Health and Human Services (HHS) showed that many top managers questioned whether their agencies truly needed the improvement sought by the civil service reform. They viewed their agencies as performing well *before* the reform (Hastings, Beyna, & LeBlanc, 1984).

Because groups often exist that reject or resist change, legislation must include incentives that will ensure compliance with the new law. These measures may involve coercive techniques to force others to comply, rewards for compliance, or incentives to create organizational changes that incorporate reform goals.

One possible outcome of such measures may be internalizing reform goals once behavior is forced to change. Attribution theory suggests that people interpret their beliefs according to their behavior: "I act as if I believe in this reform, therefore I must believe in the reform." Changing the behavior of those implementing the reform, then, can lead to their re-interpreting behavior and eventually identifying with the reform itself.

Compliance measures, on the other hand, can also affect change even without internalization because reforms often involve several types of goals. They typically include immediate structural changes (in activities, decision making, and so on) which reformers hypothesize will lead to less specific, but more far-reaching, ultimate changes (Berk, Berstein, & Nagel, 1980). Achieving the immediate structural change, then, may actually achieve some, if not all, of the ultimate goals.

The evaluator can prove to be very helpful during implementation by examining how these compliance measures are working, particularly for immediate goals. In a formative evaluation, such as that conducted for civil service reform, this information can be used to redirect or to enhance these measures. In a more summative evaluation, like the one that examined the pretrial service agencies, the information becomes important in helping to manage or to improve the changes that have already occurred, or for possible expansion of the reform to other areas or agencies.

The Monitoring Body

The monitoring body provides an example of a coercive compliance mechanism. It seeks to force change by ensuring structural changes occur as required. Looking over the implementor's shoulder and reviewing completed forms are two examples of monitoring that occurred during implementation of bail and civil service reform.

The immediate goal of the pretrial services agencies was to help judges comply with the Bail Reform Act of 1966 by supplying needed information. The pretrial officer collected the information from the defendants, summarized it, and provided judges with a recommendation for release. With all this information in front of them, the judges had no excuse for considering only the defendant's current and past criminal activity, as they had done in the past. The pretrial officer gave them verified information on all of the characteristics identified in the Bail Reform Act. The legislation creating the pretrial service agencies did not include any further changes judges were to make when forming pretrial release decisions. These agencies were simply to ensure that a past law (the Bail Reform Act) could function as intended.

The agencies' monitoring involved both formal and informal pressures to increase compliance. The formal pressures were to guarantee that the judges had the information required. The pretrial officers collected and summarized information on each defendant and persisted in providing this information to judges. Some pretrial agencies went so far as to obtain a court injunction requiring their presence at all bail hearings. Informal pressures, on the other hand, focused judges' attention on the *use* of the information. The pretrial officers' presence in the courtroom and their recommendations reminded judges that they *should* be considering the defendant's community ties in setting release conditions and use the information the pretrial officers provided.

The civil service reform also had its own monitoring body—the Office of Personnel Management (OPM). Although OPM representatives did not stand over each supervisor and manager to ensure that they completed their subordinates' performance appraisals, they did review information provided by each department to determine that a performance appraisal system was operating and that managers and employees were developing and reviewing performance plans.

Evaluators may also act as a monitoring mechanism. Evaluators will often observe agencies and organizations involved in a reform to ensure that it is actually implemented. They may also request that those involved complete special forms or they may examine documents that would indicate compliance. Such observations can create an effective monitoring system during implementation. For example, the Administrative Office of the U.S. Courts required the individual pretrial agencies to complete and return forms containing defendant information. The office used this information primarily to track the impact of the reform on release rates. This had the added effect, however, of ensuring that pretrial officers interviewed defendants and prepared the information for the judges.

Reward Structures

Rewards provide a positive, less coercive incentive for compliance. Although money is the best known and most often used reward, others include special privileges, public recognition, and promotions. In a formative evaluation, the evaluator can examine which rewards are working and provide that information early in the implementation so the reward structure can be changed.

Civil service reform achieved a minimal compliance with the new personnel performance process by linking monetary bonuses and awards directly to it. This link proved effective in making virtually all career managers develop and review yearly performance plans. Even HHS scientists who criticized the system and noted that it was not as good as their own peer review system still completed their performance plans and reviews. Without these plans, they would not have been eligible for a bonus.

Rewards, however, have their limits. Those involved must view the reward process as fair and legitimate, or their ability to identify with the reform is weakened. For example, although the career managers did develop their performance plans, most were dissatisfied with the system. Many viewed the process for awarding bonuses as unfair and arbitrary. An analysis of the bonuses conducted by evaluators, however, indicated that this was not the case. In a formative evaluation, such dissatisfaction can be detected early and misinformation corrected to enhance compliance.

Organizational Structure and Character

Organizations develop a culture and philosophy around their activities. Their members have a set of beliefs related to organizational goals and the methods to achieve them. When an existing organization must redirect its activities toward new goals, its members often try to redefine these new activities according to past organizational philosophy. Such "redirection" can end with no change occurring (Selznick, 1957). Because reforms often require a redirection of current goals or changes in how the organization should achieve them, reformers and evaluators should carefully examine the organization assigned to the reform and should consider whether a redirection has occurred or is likely to occur.

Such redirection, however, is much less likely to appear when a new organization is formed specifically to implement the reform. In the case of the pretrial services agencies, for example, Congress experimented with the organizational placement of pretrial functions. In five districts the probation office assigned pretrial duties to some of its officers. Five other districts created a new organization specifically for pretrial activities. Analysis of the release rates indicated that the rates were higher in the districts with the new pretrial agency than those in districts where pretrial activities were within the probation office. The evaluation also indicated that those in the probation offices with pretrial duties tended to redefine pretrial work according to probation standards, resulting in a more conservative attitude toward defendants.

The use of a new organization also proved helpful for one agency within HHS during civil service reform. In this agency, the director created a new personnel division to implement the performance appraisal system. The result was greater comparable use of the system within that agency.

A new organization provides a body without history. No entrenched cultures exist to redefine new procedures and processes according to old standards. Reformers and evaluators must carefully consider *where* a reform will be implemented and by whom. A new organization provides the most positive structure for change. Where a new organization is not possible, a conscious effort must occur to break with current organizational patterns. Legislators, for example, left the existing court system virtually untouched when they passed the Bail Reform Act of 1966. Judges were simply to change the way they made their decisions. It was not until the pretrial services agencies appeared and redefined pretrial hearing procedures by including new information and forms that judges showed a marked change in the factors they considered in setting pretrial release conditions. Had the earlier reform included a more definite break in court procedures and processes, there might have been a more significant change in pretrial release decisions without the pretrial services agencies.

For the evaluators examining a reform, it is important to identify where changes are expected to occur within the organization and ascertain whether they are occurring as desired. Where they are not, he or she should analyze the organizational character to determine whether this factor is resulting in some redirection of reform goals.

Conclusion

Federal reforms require careful attention if they are to achieve fruition. When a strain appears and captures someone's attention, that person must be in a position to bring the problem to a legislator's attention. This often requires a dedicated person or group because they must compete with other people or groups who are selling their own cause. Legislators will address the problems that create the greatest pressure and for which viable solutions are available.

During the drafting of the reform its implementation must also be considered. The immediate and ultimate goals must be carefully considered to ensure that all mechanisms needed to achieve them are available. Reforms must also include provisions for ensuring compliance. Reformers should consider the relationship of the immediate changes and the ultimate goals and examine whether interest groups have changed the original legislation and created "loopholes" in the reform.

Once the reform is implemented, reformers must continue their efforts to ensure compliance. Where compliance appears not to be occurring—as with the Bail Reform Act of 1966—reformers should examine alternative measures to increase compliance. The evaluator is a valuable asset to the reform during implementation. He or she can objectively analyze the actual legislation and compliance measures. From such analysis, he or she can offer solutions to problems that will enhance the likelihood the reform will succeed.

Notes

1. Portions of the research presented here were supported by Grant Number 82–IJ–CX–0052 from the National Institute of Justice, U.S. Department of Justice. Points

of view or opinions stated in this chapter are those of the author and do not necessarily represent the official position of policies of the U.S. Department of Justice.

2. The term "reformer" is used rather broadly in this chapter to represent the group involved in developing and overseeing change. The participants in this group can change depending on where the strain occurs and who becomes the first to recognize it. The group can also expand or contract, depending on the involvement of various interest groups, etc.

3. "Co-opt" here refers to removing the interest group's power and making them ineffective in opposing reform.

References

Abramson, M., B. Buchanan, M. Pagano, R. Schmidt, M. Strosberg, and J. Wholey. 1982. "Developing an Evaluation Design for the Senior Executive Service," *Review of Public Personnel Administration, 2.*

Aldrich, H. 1979. *Organizations and Environments.* Englewood Cliffs, NJ: Prentice-Hall.

Berk, R., P. Berstein, and I. Nagel, 1980, "Evaluating Criminal Justice Legislation." pp. 611–628 in *Handbook of Criminal Justice Evaluation.*

Hastings, A., L. Beyna, and L. LeBlanc, 1984, "Better Management Through Personnel System Reform: Has the Civil Service Reform Act Helped?" Department of Health and Human Services.

Selznick, P. 1957. *Leadership in Administration: A Sociological Interpretation.* New York: Harper & Row.

Sherwood-Fabre, L., 1984, *An Experiment in Bail Reform: Evaluating Pretrial Release Service Agencies in Federal District Courts.* Unpublished doctoral dissertation.

16
Improving Governmental Management Systems

Alan P. Balutis

S ubstantial effort is now being devoted to reform of the federal government. As a candidate, Ronald Reagan spoke often of his intention to initiate a major reform of the executive branch if he was elected.

No doubt these promises struck a responsive chord in the electorate. To many citizens the growth of the federal structure seems out of hand. Appalled by huge annual increases in the federal budget, they view the executive bureaucracy as a modern leviathan—too big to control and too cumbersome to be effective. Rarely in the past have the agencies of government fallen to such low esteem. They carefully are being criticized not only by their traditional enemies—political conservatives—but also by those who previously have been their strongest supporters—moderates and liberals. The deficiencies of "big government" and the federal bureaucracy are noted daily in the newspapers, on radio and television, and in the halls of the Congress.

As president, Reagan has instituted a major reform effort, dubbed "Reform '88." Reform '88 encompasses a set of initiatives on the part of the current administration aimed at bringing about lasting reforms in the management and administrative processes that drive the bureaucratic behemoth.

Reform '88 is actually an umbrella concept—a name chosen to highlight the president's commitment to large-scale reform of the management systems of the federal government. A number of short-range initiatives designed to get the project off the ground made up Phase I. Phase II involves fundamental changes in four broad areas: administrative systems, the budget process, resource management, and a management information system that integrates the entire effort. Out of these four broad areas, nine specific projects have been identified:

> *Budget automation*—expand application of automated data processing (ADP) technology to the various systems that drive the budget process, from formulation through final congressional appropriations actions.

The views expressed in this chapter are solely the author's and should not be attributed to the Office of Management and Organization of the Department of Commerce.

Standard financial data base—develop a standard, governmentwide financial data base for use at the department head or governmentwide level.

Approved accounting systems—bring all agencies' accounting systems up to the General Accounting Office (GAO) standards.

Payroll/personnel—develop standard systems with a high degree of automation in these two areas for use by all civilian agencies.

Streamlining administrative payments centers—install a centrally developed payment system for operation at multiple locations, using more automated processes to increase productivity and efficiency.

Credit management—intensify automation and use techniques utilized by private industry.

Cash management—same as credit management.

Electronic telecommunications—establish a full-scale, general-purpose telecommunications network between the Executive Office of the President and the agencies and among the agencies themselves.

Automation—upgrade and standardize the government's ADP hardware and software.

The Department of Commerce has a major role in a number of these projects and in other associated initiatives. The secretary serves on the Cabinet Council on Management and Administration (CCMA), and the Assistant Secretary for Administration has been asked to take the lead in several major projects. Moreover, the department's former Deputy Secretary (Joseph R. Wright), Deputy Director of the Office of Management and Budget (OMB), has been "the prime moving force" for Reform '88.[1] The former Assistant Secretary for Administration (Arlene Triplett) became the Associate Director for Management at OMB.

Despite the outburst of reform activity, the relationship between institutional and procedural reform and the policy output of the bureaucracy remains almost wholly unresearched. Indeed, a review of the current state of knowledge concerning governmental reforms and their effects is an unrewarding task, for knowledge of this kind is impressively slight.[2]

The purpose of this chapter, then, is to examine the recent Reform '88 initiatives in the Department of Commerce (DOC) in an attempt to ascertain what happened, why, and with what effect. Through an examination of one of the self-proclaimed "major successes" to occur in the Reagan administration, this study attempts to shed light on the administrative and policy origins, the problems and pitfalls, the traumatic effects, and the consequences—

intended and accidental, functional and dysfunctional—of the administrative reform effort. In so doing it presents a description of Reform '88 initiatives in DOC, an examination of the rationale for the changes, and a partial assessment of their first years of implementation.

What Happened?

The goal of the department under the administration of Secretary Malcolm Baldrige is to foster the vitality of American business and industry and to create a business climate that will allow the full potential of our economy to flourish. But early in his term as secretary, he made clear his view that this goal could not be accomplished without good management. Put most succinctly, his position was: "If we're going to serve business, we have to operate like a business."

Commerce had historically functioned as a holding company, a loosely run confederation of twelve major operating components that existed as relatively autonomous fiefdoms. In fact, Commerce had often been called the "attic of government" in recognition of that fact. A former Secretary, Juanita Kreps, made a familiar observation: that there is a great similarity between Commerce and Noah's ark. The difference between them, she said, was that Commerce had just *one* of everything.

A detailed review of the department was initiated: organization, policies, programs, systems, and operational approaches. As a result of this review, a number of major changes were made in Commerce.

Structuring the Department for the 1980s.

A first priority was creating a unified and integrated department—one with a clearly established mission and an operating structure focused to support that mission.

The department's economic policy analysis resources, formerly under a separate assistant secretary, were consolidated with the data collection and analysis functions of the Bureaus of Census and Economic Analysis to form a strong economic affairs operation. The department is now in a stronger position to represent business and industry at the federal level and to support them with economic analyses and data.

The International Trade Administration (ITA) was reorganized to strengthen its international trade and business promotion capabilities. Its trade development activities were refocused from a functional (that is, program oriented) structure to an industry structure. Industry analysis functions were transferred from the Bureau of Industrial Economics to bolster ITA's existing industry expertise.

Several programs that did not support the department's objectives were reduced or eliminated. A review of the Maritime Administration, for example, indicated that as a transportation-oriented organization it did not fit with the primary mission of the department. As a result it was transferred to the Department of Transportation.

Correcting specific problems in a poorly organized conglomerate is one thing; coming up with the blueprints for a new organization and a new image to knit Commerce together into a vibrant, focused department is quite another. Previous attempts in this area were limited to tinkering with the department's image. Now it has been made clear what Commerce really should be doing, and the department is being organized to carry out those goals.

Managing for Results

Managing an organization as large and varied as the Department of Commerce and focusing its resources on the most important tasks require an effective planning and control system. Senior management officials must be in a position to provide guidance in the form of

Long-term goals and directions.

Key strategies and policies.

Objectives to be pursued over the next twelve to eighteen months.

Overall resource levels for the pursuit of long-term goals and the distribution of available resources for the accomplishment of short-term objectives.

Review of planned versus actual accomplishments.

A departmentwide Management-by-Objectives system has been established to provide senior officials with a mechanism for carrying out this guidance. The system provides for setting annual objectives to attain departmental goals, including resources required, milestones to be reached, and regular progress reviews. In addition, bureau-level subsystems are being established to ensure that bureau officials exercise equivalent planning, monitoring, and control over the programs for which they are responsible.

The MBO system is being linked to the department's budget system so that resource requirements are tied to the objectives for which they are needed and to the department's performance appraisal system and so that officials will be reviewed and rated on actions that further the goals of the department.

Creating a Streamlined Department

An important aspect of improved management involved reducing administrative and overhead costs. Funds that can be saved from administrative expenses can be applied to program operations, such as issuance of patents or development of economic data.

In March 1981 a departmental administrative study was initiated. Its goals were to identify ways to improve management and to achieve savings through centralization, consolidation, contraction with the private sector, and reduction or elimination of staff.

The study found that the number of administrative positions in the department totaled over 6,300 people. Each bureau seemed to have its own "shadow staff" duplicating units within the Office of the Secretary. With the assistance of bureau officials, this total was reduced by over 1,600 positions, or 26 percent, by the end of fiscal year (FY) 1983. Administrative overhead as a proportion of the department's total staff declined from 15 percent to just over 10 percent, with savings of over $15,000,000. A series of projects was initiated to bring about even further reductions. For example:

The department had five different automated payroll systems and five different automated personnel systems, costing about $5 million a year and requiring 160 people. These are being integrated into a departmental system scheduled for completion in April 1986. Consolidation of these systems into a single central system has saved almost $1 million a year and reduced staffing by forty.

Performance of administrative functions required for department grants was centralized. This reduced the number of grants administration positions by 50 percent, with savings of $1 million and provided more uniform administrative management.

Common administrative services—such as mail and messenger service, travel services, and so on—for all organizations in the main Commerce building and nearby locations were consolidated.

A consolidated departmental computer center was established by combining the Office of the Secretary, the ITA, and National Technical Information Service computer centers. This action will serve as the basis for a departmental Management Information Service Center to operate all consolidated adminstrative systems.

Administrative payments (for example, contracts, purchase orders, travel payments) for all of the department are being consolidated in one center, instead of twenty-three offices once scattered through the department. This not only provided increased control, but saved $1.5 million and eliminated ninety-three positions.

Monitoring Performance

Intense efforts are underway to improve our ability to monitor organizational and individual performance using up-to-date, accurate information to do so. The payroll and personnel systems consolidations and the integration of administrative payment centers are the first steps in such an endeavor. These consolidations provide standard output obligations and payment data to commerce operating units for integration in their accounting system.

A project is now underway as a model for building common financial information repositories across government. Commerce is taking data from its existing accounting systems and putting them into an accessible, controlled repository, using a "bridge" program concept. The "bridge" software extracts, standardizes, edits, and stores information in a departmental financial data base to be used to prepare management reports, to answer ad hoc queries, and to carry out special analyses.

Managing Public Funds

A number of steps have been taken to improve departmental financial management practices. For example, a Financial Assistance Review Board was established to review grants, loans, loan guarantees, and cooperative agreements prior to award. During the past year, the board reviewed approximately 2,000 financial assistance actions. This review process resulted in over $10 million in awards being disapproved or withdrawn.

Field Support

Fifty percent of the department's 35,000 employees work at over 700 sites worldwide—in all fifty states plus fifty-one foreign countries. In 1982 the department established a pilot program in Seattle to provide consolidated administrative support services for our field elements. Based on the success of that pilot Regional Administrative Support Center (RASC), three additional RASCs were established in Boulder, Colorado; Kansas City, Missouri; and Norfolk, Virginia. The services provided by these centers include:

Administrative Payments,

Personnel/Payroll Systems,

Real Property and Space Management,

Personal Property Management,

Publications,

Procurement,

Personnel,

Mail Management, and

Vehicle Fleet Management.

A RASC operations office was recently established in headquarters to provide day-to-day management coordination of these centers. A fifth RASC was created to provide support to the National Oceanic and Atmospheric Administration (NOAA) employees in the national capital region.

Why?

Why is there the record of accomplishment at the Department of Commerce? Let us examine the factors that contributed to the department's success.

First, even before the announcements about Reform '88, the secretary had emphasized "improved management." He added the objective of making Commerce the "best run department in government" to a list of major programmatic goals set in the agency's strategic planning system (an MBO-like system used to establish objectives, to allocate resources, and to evaluate performance). Thus, a key ingredient for any major undertaking—top-level support—was present from the very beginning.

Second, to improve the department's ability to draw from private-sector experiences, a list of well-managed or innovative U.S. corporations was prepared. Senior Commerce managers visited several of those firms and met with their managerial counterparts. Firms were selected in areas in which it was felt the department had critical needs (long-range planning, management information systems, and the like). The visits to firms like Xerox, Hewlett-Packard, Emerson Electric, and Intel Corporation yielded a number of innovative ideas.

Third, as was noted earlier, several characters key to the government-wide Reform '88 initiative came into major management positions at Commerce during the transition. Joseph Wright, a former Assistant Secretary for Administration at the Department of Agriculture (USDA), was named deputy secretary. Wright had also served in the Bureau of the Census—a major operating component of the Department of Commerce and, therefore, had some familiarity with Commerce and its programs and some preconceptions about how they should be organized and administered. Arlene Triplett was nominated to be Assistant Secretary for Administration. Several senior careerists were brought into top positions in the Office of the Assistant Secretary from the Department of Agriculture. These individuals had worked for Wright during his tenure at USDA.

These interrelationships were not merely coincidental. The members of Wright's management team were carefully selected. But their backgrounds facilitated a change in the structure of the department.

Fourth, as each new senior political appointee was brought into his or her position in the department, Wright explained his proposal to improve management, to consolidate systems, to reduce administrative overhead, and so on. Internal bureaucratic resistance was thereby muted as bureau heads were co-opted into the reform process before they fell victim to Washington's famous "policy whirlpools" or "cozy little triangles."[3]

Fifth, opposition from Commerce components was also reduced by a commitment to apply savings achieved through management reforms to program initiatives, such as processing patents or improving economic analyses. Thus, program managers were given some incentive for cooperating in a "hard look" at administrative overhead.

Sixth, many of the Commerce initiatives—forerunners of Reform '88 projects—could be considered "value neutral." Many of the previous management changes had floundered on the shoals of reorganization. Change in governmental procedures had been attempted through organizational realignments. This emphasis on reorganization as a tool for reform often seemed to reflect a managerial fascination with box-shifting and line-drawing on an organization chart. But more importantly, structural reforms are traumatic and involve congressional committees top administrators, program clients, and employees.[4] As W. Harrison Wellford has noted:

> Structural reforms are traumatic. Every major reorganization causes enormous confusion and bitterness. As a general rule, it should be a last resort after internal reforms have been tried and found wanting.[5]

But the Commerce changes—and most of Reform '88—have focused on "administrative" reforms. The initiatives have been in such areas as payroll/personnel systems, consolidation of administrative payment centers, closing of printing plants, and improved financial management information. Although change is still involved, such reforms are considerably less traumatic than organizational realignment of program components.

Seventh, as a general rule, secretaries have not been able to (and could not be expected to) master the details of the hundreds of programs conducted by the department. A major problem exists for any secretary in trying to manage a large organization with related programs dispersed among different organizational units. These programs also involve complex relationships with congressional committees and state and local governments. The dilemma of being responsible for programs and agencies that are subject to statutory restrictions beyond secretarial authority has been compounded by the relatively short tenure of departmental secretaries. Each change of secretary also normally involves a change of the deputy secretary, under secretaries, and all the politically appointed upper management of the department.[6] Commerce has not had to face this transient pattern because most of its senior team has remained in place. This continuity has proved consistency in the department's management directives and philosophies.

Finally, Commerce's senior employees were greatly influenced by the ideas presented in the best seller, *In Search of Excellence*.[7] In the summer of 1981, a xeroxed copy of a McKinsey & Company report on organizational characteristics and management practices in a group of excellent American companies was circulated to three or four senior aides to Arlene Triplett. The group was profoundly affected by the fifty-page paper and spent several evenings discussing it. The effect of the ideas presented are best revealed in the conceptualization and implementation of the department's RASCs.

Three senior career officials had been assigned to review the department's field structure. Between 1978 and 1981, there had been five major studies of Commerce's field organization. But nothing had come of them. After visiting two field sites in the spring of 1982, the three aides came back with a recommendation for a "do it, try it, fix it," approach to regionalization. They recommended the establishment of a pilot RASC in Seattle, Washington, to provide common administrative services to 3,500 employees from six Commerce bureaus at 217 sites in ten states. The Western Administrative Support Center (WASC) was to be built on an existing NOAA unit that provided a smaller range of services to a limited number of employees in eight states. The concept paper was prepared in late April and approved by the Assistant Secretary for Administration, the Deputy Administrator of NOAA, and the Deputy Secretary in June. The center opened on October 1, 1982.

An evaluation six months later indicated that, although improvements were needed, the WASC was providing quality services in an efficient manner.[8] With that, the department moved to establish similar centers elsewhere. The Mountain ASC opened on July 1, 1983, in Boulder, Colorado. The Central ASC in Kansas City, Missouri, began providing certain services at the same time and was fully open on October 1, 1983. An Eastern ASC in Norfolk, Virginia, opened in January 1984.

In less than two years, four centers with almost 700 employees were created to serve almost 16,000 employees in fifty states. Staffs were relocated, delegations to both program and administrative officials modified, office space obtained and renovated, and new procedures established. A special assistant to Triplett was charged with quickly implementing the centers. She was granted extraordinary powers (Peters and Waterman would term her a "czar") to cut across normal authorities and to put in place the new practices that would lead to regional servicing of Commerce employees. She took action for fifteen months—effective action—aided by a small implementation task force. Then the team was abolished.

The management philosophy underlying the establishment of the RASCs was one that stressed "better service to Commerce employees in the field." In any list of project goals, that *always* appeared first. Again, we followed the notion that,

> "Excellent companies succeed by maintaining an overpowering, straightforward, external focus on their customers, rather than the dominant internal focus that characterizes most of their less excellent competitors."[9]

Another lesson learned related to "simple form and lean staff." Staffing for the four centers was done on the basis of an in-depth workload analysis and the application of proposed productivity ratios (that is, one personnelist for every seventy-two employees served). These ratios equal or surpass the proposed governmentwide standards recently proposed by the CCMA and endorsed by the OMB.[10]

Other parallels could be made, but suffice it to say that even before its current popularity, the pathbreaking work by Thomas Peters and Robert Waterman had a major impact on Commerce's management.

So What?

The current motif in both popular and academic discussion about bureaucracy is that of reform. The administrative reform effort has resulted in a mass of newspaper and magazine articles, a welter of speeches, and numerous reports. Thus no one can say that the movement for governmental reorganization suffers from lack of information. The what, the what is wrong, and, to a certain extent, the what ought to be done, have been adequately covered to say the least.[11]

But the specific effects of particular organizational patterns, the consequences of restructuring efforts, have been largely ignored. Thus, recommendations for reform of executive agencies are likely to be troublesome for both the bureaucrat and the academician, for they reveal a gap in our knowledge. No one really knows whether proposed reforms will do what their sponsors say they will. No one has said much about the unintended consequences of these changes. No one really knows whether major changes in structure, procedures, or process will make an agency (or the executive branch) a better place in which to work, a more resourceful institution for the generation of imaginative political ideas, and so on. No one should expect executive officials to take quixotic risks for the sake of tenuous political theory. We need to know what happens when specific changes are introduced.

In order to anticipate intelligently how proposals for change may work in the future, it is necessary to evaluate how they have worked in the past. With these thoughts in mind, let us attempt to assess the effects of the management reforms within Commerce.

Reform '88 appears to be at a critical juncture. Certain efficiencies (that is, staff reductions and dollar savings) have been achieved and major systems initiatives are underway in such areas as payroll/personnel, administrative payments, and accounting. A number of major accomplishments were noted in a recent consultant's report.[12] But whether Reform '88 will achieve its goal of "bringing about lasting reforms in the management and administrative processes" that drive the federal government remains open. A number of problems normally encountered in any major governmental reform effort are apparent. Perhaps this chapter can offer its greatest contribution by raising the specter of those barriers.

First, there is a need to define Reform '88—what it is, what the goals are, where careerists fit into the effort, and so on. We are, after all, trying to change federal employees' lives; it remains to translate Reform '88 concepts into the sort of specific, appropriate, and individualized actions that managers are likely to take seriously. A troubling opinion today is that discussing Reform '88 is "good management" generalities. The attitude in many departments and even in Commerce itself might be categorized as one of the general acceptance and receptivity, along with a sense of expectation that Reform '88 will soon be more fully developed and defined.

The parable of the blind man and the elephant is often used in discussing certain aspects of public management. The image conveyed is of a number of sightless individuals with their hands on various portions of the elephant. One, with his hand on the tail, thinks he is holding a piece of rope. Another, with his hand on the side of the animal, thinks he is standing next to a large wall. A third, sitting on the elephant's back, believes he is on top of a hill. Still another, holding the trunk, pictures a large snake. The parable is meant to illustrate those aspects of management theory in which different individuals, while talking about the same thing, "see" very different things in it. Reform '88 needs some clearer definition if it is not to be seen as "all things for all people."

A problem in accomplishing any major organizational change is the posture of the key executives. If they are perceived as enthusiastic, as advocating and using the changes being made, a major hurdle is overcome in getting the changes accepted. The continuous effort of key executives—cabinet secretaries, deputy secretaries, and assistant secretaries for administration—will be essential because they are the major holders of power and authority in their organization. Furthermore, in their behavior they have to be models for the behavior they expect from other members of the organization.

People do not like to feel that they are in a state of always becoming, but never being. Reform '88 will have to deal with the problem of taking too long to install the system. People want to feel that they will, at some known future point, be able to use new systems and derive the benefits from them rather than always building those systems.

During the first term, not all the basic elements of Reform '88 have been installed. Real achievements have been scarce. A related problem may be an inadequate supply of change agents. The "management" side of the OMB is woefully understaffed, supplemented by detailees who do not bring either the expertise or continuity needed to such a substantial undertaking. As a result, the administration is trying to develop, market, and install a comprehensive governmentwide management reform program in an enterprise with 2.8 million civilian employees, over 22,000 facilities, 400,000 buildings, 700 million acres of land, 332 different accounting systems, 200 different payroll/personnel systems, and 18,700 computers—doing all that with a staff of less than fifty.

The parts of an effort like Reform '88 are so interrelated that to install one part without the supporting ones limits the likely effectiveness of the installed part. An effort to install MBO-like systems in departments can prosper only if the supporting planning, budgeting, monitoring, and appraisal systems are installed simultaneously or very soon thereafter. Since Reform '88 is working with such a small staff over an extended period, these mutually supporting mechanisms may not be put in place.

Reform '88 and its management initiatives need to be tied to the budget process. Such an effort is now underway through the so-called "management reviews." But the jury is out on how successful this union will be. Many would argue that all that has been achieved to date is a status of "separate and unequal." Moreover, there are the problems of linking management improvements to a process that is inherently negative, adversarial, and constantly in search of cost reductions. Although it is clear that the budget process contains planning and management features, the control orientation has been preponderant. This has meant the subordination of planning and management functions.

Finally, individuals who do not understand or are not knowledgeable about various aspects of Reform '88 obviously cannot contribute effectively. There are still many managers and employees who are not aware of the Reform '88 initiative or, if they are aware of it, are waiting for further direction.[13]

Conclusion

Our assessment of the impact and future of Reform '88 can only be viewed as preliminary. But it is my hope that this chapter may serve to stimulate more refined examinations of governmental reforms, their implementation, and effects. Such studies could contribute significantly to our understanding of the executive system.

Notes

1. John D.R. Cole, "Joe Wright on Reform '88," *The Bureaucrat 12*(Summer 1983):7.

2. In the months since this paper was presented at the Joint Evaluation Network/Evaluation Research Society Conference, there has been a great deal of activity. The Senate Subcommittee on Civil Service, Post Office, and General Services held two days of hearings on the subject of private and public sector management theories. The hearings represented a joint effort by the majority and minority of the subcommittee to understand how federal government management could be improved. Early in 1985 the president sent his first annual report to the Congress on efforts to improve the management of the federal government. See also the form on "Management Reform: High Stakes or Trivial Pursuit," *The Bureaucrat 13* (Winter 1984–85):7–41.

3. See Douglas Cater, *Power in Washington* (New York: Random House, 1964); Ernest S. Griffith, *Congress: Its Contemporary Role* (New York: New York University Press, 1961); and Dorothy Buckton James, *The Contemporary Presidency* (Indianapolis: Bobbs-Merrill, 1974).

4. See Alan P. Balutis, "Death by Reorganization," *The Bureaucrat 10* (Summer 1981):38–44.

5. W. Harrison Wellford, "Reflections and Insights on Reorganization," *The Bureaucrat 9* (Winter 1980–81):5.

6. See Hugh Heclo, *A Government of Strangers: Executive Politics in Washington* (Washington, D.C.: The Brookings Institution, 1977), especially pp. 103–105.

7. Thomas Peters and Robert Waterman, *In Search of Excellence,* (New York: Harper & Row, 1982).

8. "Evaluation of the Department of Commerce Western Administrative Support Center," prepared by the Policy and Systems Staff, U.S. Department of Commerce, April 1983.

9. Peters and Waterman.

10. See "Report of the Federal Field Structure Working Group," Cabinet Council on Management and Administration, August 1983.

11. See, for example, "Revitalizing Federal Management: Managers and Their Overburdened Systems" (Washington, D.C.: National Academy of Public Administration, 1983).

12. McManis Associates, Inc., "A Report on Management Reform Initiatives in the Federal Government," March 1984. See also the management report to the Congress cited above.

13. Allen Schick's explanations for the demise of Program Planning and Budgeting (PPB) are equally relevant to Reform '88. See "A Death in the Bureaucracy: The Demise of the Federal PPB," *Public Administration Review 33* (March/April 1973).

17

Program Review: A Way to Use Evaluation for Organizational Renewal

Anabel Burgh Crane

I t is important for leaders at all levels of public organizations to promote a sense of mission and enthusiasm for carrying out the work in an increasingly effective manner. One approach to organizational renewal that has been adopted by the Health Resources and Services Administration (HRSA) is program review.[1] It is intended to provide a national overview on (1) the design of the program, (2) the appropriateness of level and allocation of resources, (3) the extent to which the program has achieved the objectives for which it was established, and (4) the need for changes in design or administration. A program review include three major phases: planning and documentation, discussion and recommendations, and decisions and implementation planning. The ultimate purpose is to enable managers to define actions to deal with significant program issues.

In a program review, information from evaluations and other sources is used to improve decisions about selected programs and to improve performance. A program review involves synthesis of multiple sources of information about a program's nature, objectives, and outcomes, and may include gathering of new data. Evaluation findings are a major resource; in turn, proposals for new studies may be an outcome.

Program reviews relate closely to management reviews, but there are some distinct differences in scope and purpose. A *management review* emphasizes the efficiency of program operations such as the processes for selecting among applicants and awarding grants. A *program review,* by contrast, should include the results of any management reviews but should also take into account all *other* sources of information about the program.

Initial Steps in a Program Review

Although the design of a review should be tailored to meet the needs of particular managers, typical steps are as reflected in table 17–1. Phase I includes

Table 17-1
Major Steps in a Program Review: Health Resources and Services Administration, HHS

Phase I *Planning and Documentation*	Phase II *Discussion and Recommendations*	Phase III *Decisions for Implementation Planning*
Select program(s) to be reviewed	Conduct plenary session	Draft, refine and distribute summary report
Develop overall schedule; establish Steering Committee to guide entire process	Refine notes; gather materials to draft summary report of plenary session	Consider plenary session recommendations
Identify issues to be included		Establish Agency response to recommendations and inform participants
Draft and refine agenda; set location and dates for plenary session		Make plans for implementation; assign responsibility to specific organizational units for (a) implementation or (b) monitoring of progress
Develop list of people to attend plenary session; designate chairperson and other specific roles for attendees		
Plan and prepare background book		
Complete travel and other logistical arrangements; distribute final agenda and background book to plenary session participants		

planning all steps in the review and preparing for the plenary session during the second phase.

Once a program has been selected for review, a steering committee of senior officials is established to oversee all aspects of the review, and staff are identified to perform the day-to-day work.[2] (Criteria for selection of programs are discussed in a subsequent section.)

The staff's most significant early work is drafting and refining the issues that are to be the subject of the review. The list of issues establishes the scope of the review and forms the basis for all subsequent tasks.

Once the issues list is developed in reasonably final form, staff draft an agenda for the plenary session and outline the contents of background materials to be mailed to plenary session participants before the conference. Staff typically spends several weeks assembling background materials relating to the issues. Staff may obtain help from consultants or contractors, depending on the time available and the extent to which existing materials meet the needs. Types of data gathered normally include legislative, funding, and operational history (for example, numbers and types of projects/grantees, numbers and characteristics of patients/clients served, numbers of people trained), program accomplishments, and problems. Sources include evaluation reports, published literature, program management information, research reports, legislation, congressional testimony, reports from advisory councils, and budget justifications.

Concurrently with development of the background materials, the steering committee approves an agenda and selects people to be invited to the plenary session. The committee also identifies presenters to lead the discussion of particular topics and selects a chairperson. (Presenters are also participants.)

The Plenary Session

The main activity during phase II is the plenary session, usually a two- or three-day meeting. (The term "plenary session" is not meant to imply that all participants must function as a committee of the whole for the entire conference. As suggested in the Lessons Learned section below, the format should be adapted to meet the needs in each case.) Participants typically include line managers, other Department of Health and Human Services (HHS) line and staff officials, grantees, and others who are knowledgeable in the field but who are not directly connected with the program. University-based researchers and health practitioners may also be invited. Because the review is national in scope, participants should represent the principal geographic areas in which the program operates and the major variations in program design. Based on the issues developed earlier, participants discuss the philosophical and legislative base of the program and the national problem(s) it was designed to address; history and current operational status; completed, current, and planned evalutions; and effectiveness and impact.

Through an active exchange of views, the participants clarify issues and make recommendations for further action. Recommendations may be expressions of consensus based on a vote or they may be the opinions of one person or a small group of participants. The extent to which recommendations evolve for each major issue may be affected by the structure of the agenda and the roles assigned to individuals or subgroups. During the course of the conference, gaps in information and needs for particular types of evaluation studies are likely to be identified.

If the conference has been successful, nonagency participants and managers alike will leave with an expanded knowledge of the program. Agency people will have gained a clearer understanding of their own role in conducting the program and a sense of having contributed to an endeavor that will lead to positive changes.

Decisions and Implementation Planning

Phase III consists of documentation of the conference and agency responses to the conclusions and recommendations. Within two to three months following the plenary session, staff (possibly with help from a contractor) prepare a draft report that summarizes key points and places recommendations in context. (For a plenary session involving multiple topics, drafting of the report is a major undertaking. It is worth the effort to produce an informative product, however, especially if there are potential uses other than the review.) Based on participants' comments, staff prepares and distributes a final report. In the meantime, agency officials review the recommendations, particularly within the bureau with responsibility for the program. Program officials are free to accept or reject the recommendations. Once they have taken a position on each one, they may choose to send a letter to all participants stating the responses. The agency then institutes changes stemming from the recommendations and monitors the progress of implementation. Monitoring may be selective and may be carried out at different organizational levels, depending on manager preferences.

Criteria for Selecting or Rejecting Programs for Review

The operating definition of *program* for the purposes of review is "an organized set of resources and activities directed toward a common set of goals." Activities may be grouped for review by individual programs (for example,

Area Health Education Centers), by organizational unit (for example, Division of Nursing), by related programs (for example, primary care), or by agency mission (for example, expansion of access to health care in medically underserved areas and for special populations).

The selection of programs should take into account the following criteria, all or most of which should be met:

The recommended program or topic is a priority of the administrator and a bureau director rather than simply a special interest of the manager with direct responsibility.

Significant decisions which would benefit from a broad range of viewpoints need to be made about program scope or directions.

The program is well established, is staffed with knowledgeable and experienced professionals, and has sufficient history to form the basis of discussion.

Data are available for documenting the recent history.

Enough time is available to complete the full process before decisions are needed.

A secondary factor should guide the timing of a program review: the status of the program relative to the agency's budget, planning, and legislative cycles.

Conversely, a program probably should *not* be selected for review if any of the following apply:

It is about to be discontinued in the absence of legislation to authorize similar activities, or it is about to be transferred to another federal department.

It involves highly sensitive issues that tend to polarize views.

There is little information to form the basis of discussion, or most of the information is not open to more than one interpretation.

Most of the program issues are administrative or procedural.

Major relevant evaluations will not be completed for six months or more.

There is insufficient staff time for coordinating and conducting the work.

These criteria are also discussed in the Advantages and Disadvantages sections.

The Indian Health Service Mental Health Program Review

Beginning in 1981, program reviews of a wide variety of health programs have been conducted by HRSA and one of its predecessor agencies, the Health Resources Administration.[3] The Mental Health Program Review is a recent example of the current process and its outcomes.

The Mental Health Program, begun on a pilot basis in 1966, operates through the multitiered Indian Health Service (IHS) field structure. The Mental Health Programs branch, currently located in Albuquerque, New Mexico, provides national coordination and consultation with eight area and four program offices across the country. The mental health staffs at these twelve locations work with their counterparts at 123 service units, where services are delivered at the local level.

Mental health professionals train, supervise, and supplement the work of a larger number of Indian mental health paraprofessionals. The mental health teams provide a range of services that are mainly outpatient. Typical conditions presented by IHS patients are similar to those in the general population.

Planning began in April 1983, the plenary session occurred in January 1984, and IHS officials made decisions based on the recommendations in September.

The plenary session agenda and background materials were organized according to a common set of major issues concerning program management and the needs of Indian populations for preventive and curative services.

Approximately forty recommendations resulted from the plenary session; these varied widely in the nature of actions required and in the extent of support that was expressed. In this case, the participants decided not to seek consensus on most topics.[4]

At the request of the Director of the IHS, a small ad hoc group of participants developed a consolidated set of nine recommendations (which encompass the intent of most of the earlier ones) and suggested initial action steps. All except one of the nine recommendations have been adopted. Major program changes include the following:

Adoption of a broad mission statement for the mental health program emphasizing orientation to the individual community and to outpatient care and preventive services, and integration of mental health with all other IHS programs.

Development of appropriate involuntary commitment processes for the treatment of seriously mentally ill patients who need such treatment.

Development of a national plan to address more fully services for children and adolescents through a new time-limited task force with an emphasis on prevention of mental health problems.

Development of a plan for evaluation and research relating to Indian mental health needs.

The mission statement is a significant positive outcome of the review, as is the plan to strengthen services for children and adolescents. The three administrative actions listed below should also have major impact in integrating the behavioral health programs into the rest of the IHS system.

Plans for closer collaboration of all IHS behavioral health programs (which include alcoholism and medical school services).

Movement of the position of the National Director of Mental Health Programs from Albuquerque to the IHS headquarters in Rockville, Maryland.

Rapid development of a new data system for the mental health program, designed for integration with other IHS data systems.

Implementation of five recommendations had begun by October, and work on the other two (the task force on children and the evaluation and research plan) was expected to begin with the appointment of a new Director of Mental Health Programs.

Advantages of Program Review

Despite the cost and time required, the program review offers several advantages to federal managers. First, the process can serve as a source of organizational and professional renewal, especially for those who have a major role. More specifically, the process of identifying the issues and developing the background materials can increase the knowledge and sense of cohesiveness of the program staff.

A plenary session draws together experienced, knowledgeable people who are recognized as leaders in the subject area and who are committed to solving the problems toward which the program is directed. Focusing this array of talent on one set of issues for two or three days is rare and valuable. The process of group exchange yields ideas that are not likely to emerge if the same individuals were consulted separately or if a less diverse group were contacted. To this extent, the resulting changes in policy and/or administration can lead to significant improvements in the quality of public programs.

Additionally, a review can be a useful and timely learning experience for a new manager. Involvement in preparation of background materials (or just reading them) should broaden his or her knowledge of program history and current issues. In addition, preparations for and attendance at the plenary session present opportunities to meet new people and hear divergent views.

A plenary session offers a forum in which interested parties can express their concerns and perspectives to officials. Similarly, agency leaders have an opportunity to demonstrate their own interest in the program and the needs for which it was created.

The design of a program review is flexible: content, total elapsed time, format of the plenary session, participants and their roles, and the nature of agency responses can all be geared to the particular program under consideration.

Disadvantages of Program Review

The main disadvantage of the process is its labor-intensive nature. Moreover, the bulk of the work must be carried out by reasonably senior federal people because of the need for institutional memory, for contacts with people within and outside the federal government, and for broad knowledge of the subject matter. In addition, a substantial amount of support staff time is required.

If the subject matter is not suited to the review process, the results can be disappointing and resources can be wasted. A program review tends to provide a broad view rather than a deep or profound one. Consequently, this approach is best applied when program needs are served well by an idea-generation process.

Lessons Learned from the Program Reviews
Conducted to Date

Experience has shown the importance of "ownership" by the senior program officials; in the case of HRSA, these include the bureau director and the agency administrator. Without keen interest and participation on their parts, a review may not consider the most significant program issues, and the results may not be as relevant or timely as they might otherwise be. Similarly, these senior managers must be willing to consider recommendations for change. Otherwise, plenary session participants are likely to have a sense of frustration and the morale of agency staff may be lowered.

Second, if a manager believes a review has been imposed from a higher organizational level, some noncreative tension and inefficiency can result. It is important for managers who will be involved in conducting the review to be positive about it.

Third, focused planning and oversight of substantive content and logistics lead to notably better products than if oversight is sporadic or fragmented. Thus, it is important to assign responsibility for day-to-day management to a qualified person.

There are also several lessons concerning the plenary session itself:

A length of three (or fewer) days encourages attendance for the entire conference and permits people to travel and attend within a five-day work week.

It is highly desirable to create a retreatlike atmosphere at a location that will remove participants from the distractions of their regular responsibilities.

It is critical to have a chairperson who is skilled in moderating and facilitating the flow of the proceedings because this role is a demanding one that requires different skills from those needed by other participants.

All key people who are likely to be involved in implementing changes stemming from the review need to be included, or at least need to believe that their views are represented in a credible manner.

The conference should include people with perspectives and professional or occupational backgrounds that are broadly representative of the field.

The number of participants should be kept small enough to allow for full participation during meetings of the entire group. Consequently, a total not exceeding thirty may be advantageous.

It is desirable to consider having some concurrent sessions, depending on the subject matter and size of the group. If much of the time is allocated to subgroup meetings, it is possible to accommodate a significantly larger number than would be workable otherwise.

Program reviews, if appropriately designed, serve the current information needs of program managers by providing a forum for reassessing the definition of program mission, accomplishments, approaches, and organization in relation to major program issues. In fact, this tool has value only as it serves the needs of line managers.

Finally, one of the most important benefits of a program review is the intensive interaction between federal managers and the knowledgeable advisors at the conference, many of whom are not in regular contact with the agency. This interaction offers an opportunity to consider evaluation findings and other relevant information from a broader perspective than is possible in a typical evaluation study. As a result, this process should help to ensure that agency officials continue to ask the right questions.

Notes

1. HRSA includes four bureaus that provide direct health services to designated beneficiaries; fund primary care and public health education; support efforts to integrate health service delivery programs with public and private health financing programs, including health maintenance organizations; improve the use of health resources; and provide technical assistance for modernizing or replacing health facilities.

2. In HRSA, the steering committee typically includes the Associate Administrator for Planning, Evaluation, and Legislation; the director of the bureau in which the program to be reviewed is placed; the national program manager; the director of program development for the bureau (whose responsibilities parallel those of the associate administrator); and one or two other officials designated by the bureau director.

3. Among the programs that have been reviewed are the Health Careers Opportunity Program, Nursing Special Projects, National Health Service Corps, and Migrant Health.

4. Health Resources and Services Administration, *Summary Report: Indian Health Service Mental Health Program Review Plenary Session,* Rockville, Maryland, HRSA, May 1984.

Part VI
Credibly Communicating the Value
of the Organization's Activities

Communicating the value of an organization and its programs is an integral part of performance-oriented evaluation. Informing people outside the organization about the worth of a program can help secure allies and resources. Political and fiscal support is particularly important in the 1980s environment. Communicating the value of the organization's activities to people inside the organization is a tangible way to make the organization's members aware of their contributions to a program's success. It is also a way to help renew an organization's spirit.

Christopher Bellavita begins part VI with a review of the major barriers that prevent effective communication in a public policy environment. He then identifies five elements of an effective communication strategy: knowledge of the audience, knowledge of communication techniques, an intelligible message, timeliness, and a well-managed communication program.

Bellavita argues that communication in public policy is largely a political act, and that evaluators are reluctant to acknowledge their political role because of their traditional concern for objectivity. Bellavita outlines the elements of a model of communication that encourages evaluators to retain their tradition of objectivity while also recognizing their political role. The policy management model of communication views evaluators as people who use data to help programs and organizations do the most they can with the resources they have available.

Joseph Wholey provides two examples of evaluations that have been used to influence legislative and budget decisions. In chapter 19 he describes how an evaluation that demonstrated the effectiveness and value of the Job Corps was used to resist the Reagan administration's efforts to cut the program's funding.

The Job Corps evaluation demonstrated that the job training program effectively achieved its goals and returned more benefits to society than the program cost. The evaluation results were used by the *Washington Post* and by politically conservative legislators to oppose efforts to eliminate the Job Corps at a time when the budgets of other federally funded employment and training programs were being reduced.

In chapter 21, Wholey gives another example of how Congress used evaluations of the Women, Infants, and Children (WIC) nutrition program to block Reagan administration attempts to reduce WIC's budget and to merge the program into the Maternal and Child Health block grant.

The WIC program had been evaluated many times by state, local, and other agencies. Although none of the evaluations was methodologically flawless, the preponderance of the evidence indicated that WIC was successful in improving nutrition and in helping to reduce the percentage of low birthweight infants born to women eligible for the program. Other studies suggested WIC's cost effectiveness; one evaluation reported that every dollar spent by WIC saved $3 that would have been otherwise incurred providing hospital care to low birthweight infants.

Throughout the early 1980s, WIC evaluations were used by congressional decisionmakers, health and nutrition program staffs, the medical community, and advocacy groups to defend WIC in a harsh political and budget environment. Wholey's analysis illustrates that, while many factors influence legislative and budget decisions, evidence of program effectiveness can play a useful, constructive role in policymaking.

Jean Smith describes how the four steps of performance-oriented management—establishing realistic objectives, assessing performance, achieving high performance, and communicating the value of program activities—helped a prenatal demonstration program in Tennessee to expand, in spite of a reduction in federal funds. The program, "Toward Improving the Outcomes of Pregnancy" (TIOP), provided prenatal services through local health departments in seven areas in the state. The evaluation team first developed program objectives and performance indicators in consultation with prenatal program policymakers, managers, and staff. Existing data sources were used to provide evidence about program performance, and the evaluation was timed so that results would be available to influence state budget decisions.

The evaluation showed that TIOP reduced the proportion of low birthweight infants born to program participants when compared to infants born to a similar group of low income women. The evaluation was used in a successful lobbying effort to obtain state funds for an expanded statewide prenatal program. The evaluation served also as the basis for a conference at which program participants described particularly effective practices they had developed, and received public recognition for their contributions to the program's success. The evaluation team subsequently provided a plan for managing the expanded program that was incorporated into the state's prenatal plan.

Although Smith's case study describes the successful use of performance-oriented evaluation, she closes with a cautionary note that underscores the limitations of evaluation. Recent personnel and leadership changes and shifts in organizational priorities have reduced the momentum of the statewide prenatal program. The central lesson is that, in the absence of management continuity, the promise of performance-oriented evaluation may be difficult to fulfill.

18
Communicating Effectively about Performance Is a Purposive Activity

Christopher Bellavita

There are four steps that evaluators can take to help an organization or program become more performance oriented: (1) identify performance objectives, (2) assess performance in terms of those objectives, (3) identify ways to help improve performance, and (4) communicate the value of the organization or program.

Communicating evaluation results often takes a backseat to designing and carrying out evaluation studies.[1] It is difficult enough for evaluators to identify performance objectives from a set of partially defined—at times conflicting—policy goals; to figure out logistically and economically feasible ways to assess performance; and then to come up with realistic ideas for helping to improve the performance of programs and organizations. It is not surprising to discover that by the time data collection and analysis are completed, evaluators have been largely content to consider the communication part of their job finished when the final report comes out of the copier machine.

Increasingly, however, evaluators have become less confident about the power of the written word or statistics to convince an audience about the validity of their findings. Communicating findings to program or organizational stakeholders is as important a task as asking the right question is when designing the evaluation.

The argument I wish to make here is that evaluators have not been very effective communicating their findings because they have not invested much effort in trying. The central message of this chapter is that effective communication is a purposive, not an incidental, activity.

In this chapter I first review the findings of a study designed to identify how research organizations communicate in a public policy environment. I describe the major barriers to effective communication, and then summarize the elements of a strategy for effective policy communication. Finally, I discuss three models of policy communication and argue that performance-oriented evalutors need to recognize the political and organizational implications of policy communication.

I surveyed eighty-eight public, private, and nonprofit organizations across the country that conduct public policy-related research, from basic research (for example, a conceptual study of alternative models for the delivery of mental health services) to applied research (for example, a participant evaluation of a program to educate new state legislators about housing issues). I wanted to find out what these organizations did with the information they produced. I was trying to identify exemplary communication strategies that other researchers might use to communicate their findings.[2]

Six Barriers to Effective Communication

The research organizations I surveyed identified six barriers to the effective communication of policy information: the information to be communicated, the researchers who develop the information, the public policy process, the character of specific policy issues, the policymakers who might use the information, and the process that links information to the user.

Information

Information that is poorly presented is a barrier to communication. Material that is too long, complicated, full of esoteric jargon, or disorganized will not be well received. The form in which information is presented is as important as content. Communication is inhibited when information is of limited relevance to an audience; when the conclusions or policy implications of the information are missing, unclear, or incorrect; and when the quality of the research is poor.

Researchers

The researcher and the decisionmaker often do not live in the same world. One respondent to the survey wrote that researchers tend to be interested in problems, while decisionmakers are interested in solutions and possible solutions. The gap between the foci of the two worlds inhibits communication. Evaluators can be their own barrier to effective communication when they are overly concerned with the values of their own discipline, when they do not share the same substantive concerns as policymakers, and when they are largely unconcerned with what happens to the information they produce.

Public Policy

The public policy process can be a barrier to communication. Policy emerges hesitantly or rapidly from a sometimes unpredictable process of conviction, hunch, conflict, compromise, and fatigue. Evaluators who are baffled by the policy process may not know when or to whom to communicate. Information is only one element in the activity that generates policy. Tradition, precedent, law, and politics can and often do outweigh the importance of information produced by evaluation studies.

Policy Issues

The character of a particular policy issue may also interfere with communication. Some policy issues may be too difficult or too complex to explain to nonspecialist decisionmakers. People need a strong incentive to take the effort to make sense out of something difficult. It is easier to rely on feelings than on data. Occasionally there may be too much information available about an issue, or the issue is understood quite well by just about everyone involved. In those instances, it is difficult for new information and perspectives to be "heard." According to the majority of organizations surveyed, political feasibility and value preferences are more significant determinants of policy decisions than is research information.

Policymakers

Policymakers themselves can be constrained from using the information evaluators make available to them. Decisionmakers may be unable to act because of political, institutional, economic, or other reasons. They may be unwilling to act because of their personal predilections or doubts about the reliability or value of the information. Decisionmakers may also be uninterested in acting because the information does not support what they are already doing.

Link between Information and Potential Uses

The policy or decision implications of a study are often not obvious from a quick glance at the data. Someone must go through the process of translating evaluation data into a policy-relevant form. Communication is inhibited when the link between the evaluation and decision making is missing or ineffective. The management of the communication process may be inadequate. The goals and strategies for communicating information may be unclear or conflicting. The resources for communication may also be insufficient.

Elements of an Effective Communication Program

The respondents to the survey were also asked to describe the elements of an effective communication program. They identified and discussed five elements: knowledge of the audience, knowledge of communication methods, intelligibility of information, timeliness, and communication management.

Knowing the Audience

Effective communication requires that the evaluator know something about the people who are to receive the information. What do they want or need to know that the evaluator can tell them? How best can the audience "hear" the message?

Audiences differ in their preference for receiving information. Most managers and executives prefer verbal to written presentations. The evaluator can find out what information is relevant to the user by establishing close relationships and by becoming part of the user's information network. Involving users in the planning and production of information stimulates interest and encourages a commitment to the use of the information produced. Knowing how an audience assimilates information, who the gatekeepers, opinion leaders, and early adopters are in a policy arena, can be used to plan targeting strategies.

Knowing about Communication

Evaluators should use more than one method to communication findings, using different techniques as appropriate for different audiences. Some people will want to see the executive summary of a report; others are more interested in hearing, briefly, about the study's implications. Multiple information channels, redundancy, and duplication help to increase the likelihood that the message will be heard. Feedback from the user is critical if the evaluator wants to make certain the message was understood.

The evaluator ought also to have a reputation for producing quality work. He or she ought to sound authoritative, credible, and knowledgeable about the information being communicated. The information has to be perceived as fair, accurate, and nontrivial. It has to be easy and inexpensive for the user to obtain. The options for action have to be immediately apparent. It can also help to present opposing arguments or alternative interpretations of the data.

Intelligibility of Information

The first rule of intelligible communication is for the evaluator to have a clear idea about what is to be communicated. Next, the information has to be tailored to specific audiences. This means that the material has to be presented in the user's language. For policymakers this generally means plain English, clearly and well written or spoken, concise, attractively presented, well organized, and easy to understand. The ideas have to be well thought out and presented at a level of sophistication appropriate to the audience. The information has to be complete, but not burdened with detail.

Timeliness

Providing information to users at the right time in their planning, budgeting, and decisionmaking cycles helps to encourage audience receptivity and use. In addition to predictable information needs, people are also receptive to receiving information when their environment is changing, when they need specific information about an issue of interest to them, when a new issue appears on their agenda, or when they wish to readjust their behavior.

Communication Management

Communication management refers to the link between producing and using information. Effective communication requires planning and resources. Evaluators plan for effective communication during the design of the evaluation by having a clear idea about who the audience is, what information it wants and needs, when the information is required, and how the audience can best receive the information.

Communication management requires resources. Money is needed to hire writers, editors, publicists, and other staff skilled in communication. There is also a need for space and equipment, such as audiovisual, graphic arts, and computing equipment. Communication managers also monitor and evaluate communication activities, refine traditional communication techniques (such as briefings), experiment with new, possibly more effective techniques, and aim to reduce the costs to decisionmakers of getting and using information.

Communication as Politics

The central implication of these research findings is that communication in public policy is a political act that can influence the distribution of power and resources in society. The person sending a message is making a claim about what is real concerning a policy issue. When evaluators argue that a nutrition program reduces the number of low weight births or that the Job Corps returns more benefits to society than the program costs, they are making an implicit claim that future policy actions should be influenced by this information. They are entering the political debate.

Yet evaluators are reluctant to acknowledge their political role. Two comprehensive reviews of the field all but ignore the political implications of evaluation.[3] One evaluator who responded to the study reported above wrote that it was not his job to influence policy, it was the legislator's job. His task was to provide the legislator with the best, most objective data he could get. Although this is a respectable position to espouse, anyone who has ever collected information for a decisionmaker recognizes how rarely one encounters "objective" data. Assumptions, limitations on resources, and collection methodologies inevitably skew data. The dominant notion of the evaluator as a neutral servant of the policy process helps explain why communicating findings has been a low priority.

Three Models of Policy Communication

There are three basic models of policy communication: a political model, a policy system model, and a management model.

The Political Model of Communication

The *political model of communication* looks at information as one weapon in an arsenal that is placed at the disposal of a particular policy issue. People operating from this model assert that there is a "right" answer or approach to a policy issue. Information that supports this position is used in the policy debate. Contradictory data are ignored or suppressed. The function of communication is to persuade significant others—like legislative committees, the public, and the media—to share the communicator's perception about appropriate policy action.[4]

Evaluators have avoided the political model because of their traditional concern for objectivity and uninvolvement in power issues. Evaluators have been concerned with discovering the "truth." Once the truth is made evident, the evaluator's task is done. The information is added to the fund of data that naturally surrounds any policy issue, and decisionmakers use it or ignore it as their positions and preferences dictate. Evaluators have revealed an implicit preference for this policy system model of communication.

The Policy System Model of Communication

A *policy system model of communication* consists of the actors, institutions, issues, and structures linked together by shared policy concerns. Policy systems receive inputs in the form of demands and resources, take actions on the basis of some internal dynamic and generate outputs that affect the larger environment.[5] The system functions without the calculations and strategies that characterize more purposeful human activities. From this basic analytical perspective, answers to policy problems emerge over time in a spontaneous, incremental, and synergistic fashion. The role of communication in the policy system is to create, to maintain, and to act upon agenda items.

If the policy system functions well—and it would not exist for long if it did not—policymakers usually get all the information they need when they need it.[6] The evaluator's role is to be one of the system's sources of information. Like the Congressional Research Service responding to a congressman's request for data, the evaluator simply sends the final report off to the client, and it is up to the recipient to act on or to ignore the information. The evaluator's task is finished, and he or she can go on to the next study.

The Management Model of Communication

The *management model of policy communication* acknowledges that people and organizations have policy preferences, that they are political actors. But the management model also recognizes that decisions are made on the basis of more than information. Values, resources, timing, traditions, and other factors contribute to policy decisions. The function of communication from the perspective of the management model is neither to attempt to impose preferences on the policy world nor to ignore the political dimension of information. Communication contributes to organizational and program excellence by linking problems and solutions with resources.

The management view of communications is a synthesis of the political and policy system approach. There typically is not a single "right" answer to a policy problem. But some answers, some actions, are more appropriate than others in achieving a desired end. Evaluators can act to facilitate as well as inhibit communication about what constitutes appropriate action.

Broad policy goals have to be translated into measurable objectives. Evaluators recognize the political nature of this task when they involve decisionmakers and operating staff in planning the evaluation effort. The same is true when deciding what data to collect to measure performance and what changes can be made to improve the way a program or organization operates.

Underlying the participatory strategy of performance-oriented evaluators is the recognition that each new program or policy is a solution to some identified problem that, in turn, creates its own new problems. The power to act and the knowledge about how to act is fragmented and shared among actors at the street, mid-management, and executive levels. Resources are constrained. There is always more that could be done if the resources—personnel, money time—were available.

From a management view of policy, the function of communication is to help managers link "resources to problems worth solving at the level of action they occur, within the time available," using the means that the program or organization can control.[7] Looked at this way, the task of evaluation is to help policies evolve. There will always be problems to solve and needs to meet. But as it has been demonstrated historically, program, organization, and policy performance can be improved. Evaluators use communication to help program and organizations do the most they can with the resources available. This is the road to excellence.

An Example of the Management Model of Policy Communication

A few years ago, an evaluator for a state education department completed a study of a statewide policy that required high school seniors to pass a test to demonstrate a basic proficiency in math, reading, and writing. The evaluator's study looked at the effects of the proficiency policy on school districts' remedial education programs. Her findings indicated that a large number of districts in the state were diverting resources to help students prepare for the proficiency test. The diverted resources would otherwise have been used in remedial education programs. This meant, if the evaluation were correct, that helping students prepare for the proficiency test was becoming more important than helping students actually improve their skills.

The evaluator wrote up her preliminary findings and gave them to the director of the evaluation unit. The next move was up to him.

The director came to the department originally as a political appointee. He was no stranger to politics. His reputation in education circles was built somewhat, but not entirely, on the apparent success of proficiency policy. As a political actor, then, he could be expected to suppress the study because it shed unfavorable light on something he had worked hard to achieve.

On the other hand, there was soon to be a statewide election for the Superintendent of Education position. The evaluation director privately supported the challenger over the incumbent. He thus had an incentive to leak reports unfavorable to the incumbent's policies.

From a political perspective, the director was in a no-win situation. Leak the report and his reputation would be tarnished. Suppress the report and he would reduce the chance that his candidate for superintendent would win the election.

From a policy system perspective, the evaluation director should simply issue the report, and not be concerned with what political actors do with the information. Organizations are based on division of labor: someone collects information, someone else decides what to do with it.

But the evaluation director took a communications management approach to the dilemma. He believed, and his past actions testified that he acted on the belief, that his task was to provide quality, timely, and relevant information to aid decisionmakers. The findings about the impact of proficiency policy on remedial education programs were preliminary. In evaluator's language, this means that the conclusions were rough approximations, based on a sketchy analysis of the first computer printouts. The potential policy and political impact of the study required that the data be subjected to additional and more rigorous analysis before the director could be confident about the study's validity.

Perhaps more importantly, however, there was no practical use for the information. Proficiency policy was not an active item on any policymaker's agenda. Even if the study were completely accurate, there was nothing decisionmakers wanted to or could do at that time to influence how school districts were using their resources. That condition might change after the election or when budget appropriation time came around. But presently, in the director's judgment, communicating the study's findings would have added more unnecessary "noise" to an already crowded information environment.[8]

Conclusion

In this chapter I have looked at communication as an integal part of a four-step process that evaluators can use to help an organization or program become more results oriented. Each of the four steps is important; however, successfully identifying performance objectives, assessing performance, and helping improve performance depend fundamentally on communication.

I have argued that communication is a political act. Evaluators are asserting a claim about what is real regarding problems or solutions. Evaluators who neglect the power implications of what they do risk continuing to have their work ignored by decisionmakers.

Evaluators tend to adopt the natural model of policy communication largely because of their ethos of objectivity. This approach to communication ignores the political value of information and is one explanation for the common complaint that evaluation is rarely useful to decisionmakers.

The policy management model of communications encourages evaluators to retain their tradition of accuracy, reliability, and objectivity. But the model also encourages evaluators to acknowledge their political role. This does not mean that evaluators have to become propaganda agents for their agencies. But it does require evaluators to help managers link data and information with available resources in order to improve performance. Being political does not mean surrendering objectivity. It does mean thinking strategically about how communication can be used to make others aware of which programs and organizations work well and about what realistically can be done to improve performance.

The central message of this chapter is that effective communication is a purposive—not an incidental—activity. Evaluators can improve their ability to communicate in the same way they improve their other evaluation skills: becoming aware of their current practices, experimenting with alternative methods, and evaluating the results.[9]

Notes

1. See chapter 4 above for an extended discussion of this issue.

2. For details about the methodology used in the survey and the findings, see Christopher Bellavita, "What Do Information Producers Do To Disseminate Their Products?" prepared for the National Institute for Education, January 1981. Copies are available from NIE or from the author.

3. Charles B. Wright, "Evaluation Research," *International Encyclopedia of Social Science* (MacMillan: New York, 1968), Vol. 5, pp. 197–202; and Stuart S. Nagel, "Policy Evaluation Methods," *Encyclopedia of Policy Studies* (Marcel Decker: New York, 1983), pp. 65–91.

4. Arnold Meltsner, "Don't Slight Communications: Some Problems of Analytical Practice," *Policy Analysis,* 5(Summer 1979).

5. David Easton, *A Framework for Political Analysis* (Prentice-Hall: Englewood Cliffs, NJ, 1965).

6. J. Knott and A. Wildavsky, "If Dissemination is the Solution, What is the Problem?" *Knowledge* 1(September 1979).

7. Aaron Wildavsky, *Speaking Truth to Power* (Boston: Little, Brown, 1979), p. 23.

8. For other examples of how the evaluation director used communication to improve the utility of evaluation, see A. Meltsner and C. Bellavita, *The Policy Organization* (Beverly Hills: Sage, 1983).

9. For other examples in this book about the impact of communication on the utility of evaluation, see chapters 4, 11, 19, 20, and 21. On policy communication in general, see L.E. Lynn (Ed.), *Knowledge and Policy, the Uncertain Connection* (Washington, D.C.: National Academy of Sciences, 1978); and C.E. Lindblom and D.K. Cohen, *Usable Knowledge* (New Haven, CT: Yale University Press, 1979).

19

The Job Corps: Congressional Uses of Evaluation Findings

Joseph S. Wholey

In the early 1980s, evaluation played a significant role in congressional decisions to maintain funding for the Job Corps in the face of Reagan administration attempts to eliminate or to curtail the program. The story goes on as this chapter is written. The Reagan administration again seeks to eliminate the Job Corps and a number of other domestic programs, and evaluation information is again being used in congressional decisions on the fate of the Job Corps.

Initiated twenty years ago under the Economic Opportunity Act, the Job Corps is a relatively high-cost training program designed to improve the employability of disadvantaged youth, all of whom are from poor families and most of whom are school dropouts. In addition to skills training, the Job Corps offers comprehensive services, including basic education and health care, in approximately 100 centers, most of which are operated by private contractors. By the early 1980s, the Job Corps was enrolling nearly 100,000 youth each year, at an annual cost of approximately $600 million. The Job Corps has frequently been questioned because of its high cost per training slot ("it would be cheaper to send them to Harvard"), because of issues related to administration or to particular centers, and as a symbol of the liberally oriented "War on Poverty."

The Reagan administration's efforts to reduce federal domestic expenditures have included proposals for large cuts in Job Corps funding. Though Congress agreed to a 60 percent reduction in federally funded employment and training programs between early 1981 and mid-1983, Congress maintained Job Corps funding at approximately $600 million per year. Congressional decisions not to accept the administration's Job Corps proposals appear to have been influenced by evaluation evidence that demonstrated that the program is effective and that its benefits to society outweigh its high cost.

This chapter examines a major evaluation of the Job Corps and the use of that evaluation by Congress.[1] The evaluation demonstrated that (1) Job Corps participants had better postprogram experiences than comparable youth not enrolled in the program, (2) those enrolled in the Job Corps for longer periods had much better results, and (3) Job Corps' economic benefits to society exceed the high cost of the program. Though many factors influence budget decisions, the positive evaluation findings played a significant role as Congress decided to maintain Job Corps funding and enrollment levels in a different budget environment.

Job Corps Evaluations

Over the years there have been several evaluations of the Job Corps. For most of these evaluations, inadequate data or inadequate analytic methods made it difficult to estimate the extent to which the program was producing intended effects, and left study findings open to serious question.

In 1976, after a period in which the program was redirected and then stabilized, the Employment and Training Administration's (ETA's) Office of Policy, Evaluation and Research contracted for a major longitudinal evaluation of the benefits and costs of the Job Corps. This evaluation, which took six years and cost more than $2 million, compared the postprogram experience of a large sample of Corpsmembers participating in the program in the spring of 1977 with the experiences of a comparable group of disadvantaged youth who had not been in the Job Corps. The comparison group members were selected from school dropouts and employment service applicants in areas of the country that were similar to the areas from which Corpsmembers came, but in which the Job Corps did not recruit extensively. Baseline surveys were done in the spring of 1977; follow-up surveys were conducted at periods of 9, 24, and 54 months after the baseline survey to document postprogram experiences on a variety of relevant measures. The last survey included more than 3,900 youth, represented nearly 70 percent of the baseline observations, and included an average of forty-eight months of postprogram experiences of Corpsmembers.

In 1980, an interim report from this evaluation found that the Job Corps had a positive, sizable effect on participants in the first twenty-four months and estimated that the program's economic benefits to society were greater than its costs.[2] Estimates based on the interim evaluation indicated that the Job Corps returned $1.39 for every $1.00 expended on program services.[3]

In 1982, after the experiences of participants and comparison group members had been tracked for an additional thirty months, the final report from the evaluation stated that:

> During the first four postprogram years, we find that Job Corps is at least moderately successful in achieving its desired effects: (1) increasing employment and earnings, (2) improving labor-market opportunities through work

experience, military service, higher education and training, better health, and geographic mobility, (3) reducing dependency on welfare assistance and other public transfers, and (4) reducing criminality.[4]

The measured effects included the following (on a per-Corpsmember basis, including military jobs, and averaged over the four-year observation period):

1. An increase in employment (more than three weeks per year).
2. An increase in earnings of approximately $655 per year (more than 15 percent).
3. A very substantial increase in the probability of having a high school diploma or equivalent (a 27 percentage point increase).
4. Fewer serious health problems (a reduction of more than one week per year).
5. Less dependence on welfare (a reduction of two weeks per year).
6. Less dependence on unemployment insurance (a reduction of nearly one week per year).
7. No effect on arrests, but a significant shift from more to less serious crimes (fewer thefts and more traffic offenses).[5]

The evaluators concluded that:

8. A substantial positive correlation exists between the estimated Job Corps impacts and the proportion of the Job Corps completed. Impact estimates for those who completed the program were generally more than twice the overall program average, partial completers made only small gains, and early program dropouts made little or no gains over comparable nonparticipants.
9. The program's economic benefits to society were estimated to be approximately $7,400 per participant in 1977 dollars, in comparison with costs of approximately $5,100. Because more than 40,000 youths enrolled in Job Corps during 1977, net social benefits were estimated to be more than $90 million for that year.
10. A substantial part of the economic benefits of the Job Corps (approximately $2,900 per Corpsmember) were associated with reduction in criminal activity by Corpsmembers, particularly murder, robbery, and larceny (including substantial reductions of these and burglary during the program).
11. Additional unmeasured, intangible benefits would increase the estimates of net benefits to society if economic values were assigned to them; for

example, reductions in the psychological costs of crime for actual and potential victims and participants' satisfaction from working rather than receiving welfare.

12. Economic benefits exceed costs under a wide range of alternative assumptions, estimated effects, and values, without including any of the unmeasured benefits. As long as displacement in the labor markets that Corpsmembers enter was not severe and the observed crime reductions were at least minimally valued, Job Corps was estimated to be an economically efficient investment.[6]

Mathematica's Job Corps evaluation was impressive in its successful effort to maintain contact with participants and comparison group members over a four-year period. Equally impressive was its presentation of findings under a wide range of alternative assumptions; for example, alternative assumptions as to the persistance of the effects measured over the four-year period and alternative assumptions as to the discount rate that should be used for assigning present value to benefits to be received in future years. At the request of the Office of Management and Budget (OMB), the Department of Labor asked several reviewers to critique the Job Corps evaluation. Though the reviewers raised several technical questions and noted possible uncertainties (particularly about possibly inadequate control for selection bias in construction of the comparison group), the reviewers commended the evaluation as generally meeting such questions as well as the current state of the art permitted and concluded that the basic evaluation findings were strong and credible.[7]

Dissemination and Use of the Evaluation Findings

The findings of the 1980 interim evaluation of the Job Corps were widely disseminated by the ETA's Office of Policy, Evaluation and Research. The findings from the interim evaluation (which were confirmed in the longer time period covered in the final report) were made known, not only to the Job Corps staff and the contractors operating Job Corps centers, but also to the key officials in the Department of Labor and in the OMB, to congressional committee staffs, to key members of the House and Senate, and to the press. Any use of evaluation findings by private contractors has not been examined and is not covered here.

The OMB was not influenced by the evaluation, considering the Job Corps to be a high-cost program whatever its merits. OMB, which had long been a critic of Job Corps "wastefulness," regarded the program as an obvious target given the new administration's strong desire to reduce the federal role in, and federal expenditures for, social programs. OMB pressed for reduction of the Job Corps on grounds of the program's high unit cost. In addition, OMB stressed that most enrollees left the Job Corps quickly and that the program's benefits were concentrated on relatively new participants.

Early in 1981, as the Reagan administration was taking office and talk of budget outs was everywhere, the *Washington Post* published an editorial on the Job Corps under the title, "A Social Program That Works." *The Post* characterized the Job Corps as effective: "Not an automatic ticket to the middle class but a long step in the right direction."[8]

On February 26, 1981, a key conservative republican, Orrin Hatch, took the Senate floor to encourage his colleagues to maintain the Job Corps. Hatch had been impressed by a Job Corps center in his state that was operated by a private contractor. He had been reassured that the center was representative. His staff had been made aware that a credible evaluation study showed that the Job Corps produced significant, lasting benefits. After quoting *The Post* editorial and referring to his recent visit to the Clearfield (Utah) Job Corps Center, Hatch continued:

> As the new chairman of the Senate Labor and Human Resources Committee, I am more committed than ever to insure the continuation of *The Post's* description of what "a social program can hope to achieve." Here at last, in that process of achievement, is a Government training program that provides jobs and saves more dollars than it expends. . . .

After describing both the national program and the Clearfield Center, he continued,

> These students who have enrolled in the Job Corps, according to both government statistics and an ongoing independent study by a private and independent research firm, have markedly increased their employment and earnings, reduced their dependence on welfare assistance and other public transfers, reduced criminality, reduced extramarital children, delayed family formation in females, and almost doubled the likelihood of entering the armed forces.

> Are these benefits worth the cost when measured against an average student staying six months with an average center operational cost of $3,800 per student? The comprehensive evaluation of the social benefits and costs back up observations that, indeed, the public investment in Job Corps is economically efficient. . . .

Senator Hatch concluded:

> To reduce inflation, I totally subscribe to federal budget cuts which will improve the economy. However, it would be foolhardy to reduce the Job Corps which is doing that already. . . .[9]

On March 1, 1981, the *Washington Post* reported that, "[T]he Job Corps, originally slated for a major reduction, has been largely spared after pleas from Congress."[10] Aside from attempts to achieve across-the-board cuts in Department of Labor programs later in 1981, the administration postponed its attempts to achieve major reductions in Job Corps funding. The Omnibus Budget Reconciliation Act of 1981 signaled major surgery for most programs funded under the Comprehensive Employment and Training Act (CETA), including elimination of the Public Service Employment program, but produced no change in the Job Corps.

In 1982 Congress again used information on Job Corps effectiveness in deciding to maintain the Job Corps. In its report on the Job Training Partnership Act of 1982 (P.L. 97–300), which made substantial program changes in replacing CETA, for example, the Senate Committee on Labor and Human Resources stated that:

> Title IV B of the Comprehensive Employment and Training Act authorizing the Job Corps is retained unamended.[11]

On the House side, the Committee on Education and Labor stated that:

> Because of the exemplary success which the Job Corps has demonstrated over a number of years in making the hardest-to-employ youth employable, the Committee believes that it is most important to continue this program without the disruption engendered by unnecessary changes in authorizing provisions. Therefore, most existing provisions of law are extended with little or no change.[12]

In 1982 Congress again rejected administration proposals for substantial reduction of Job Corps funding.

After President Reagan was re-elected in 1984, the administration again attempted to eliminate the Job Corps. Though congressional action on the administration's FY 1986 budget has not been completed as this is written, Senator Hatch, generally a supporter of federal budget restraint, has again opposed the administration's efforts to eliminate the Job Corps. Introducing a resolution to express the sense of the Congress that the Job Corps is effective and should not be eliminated, he stated that he had originally been opposed to the Job Corps but had become a supporter because the Job Corps is a benefit rather than a cost to society:

> The Job Corps, I once thought, was not much more than a handout for youth so we could start their welfare dependence much earlier in life.
>
> After I was elected a senator from Utah and was assigned to the Labor and Human Resources Committee, I began to learn much more about the Job Corps. I studied most of the reports on the effectiveness of the program and

the long-term success of its students. Perhaps more importantly, I was invited to visit the Clearfield Job Corps Center operated by the Management and Training Corporation. I was greatly impressed by what I saw and by the enthusiastic responses of the students. It was clear that the Job Corps was not a handout program at all, but a hand-up program designed to give youth a chance to learn lifetime skills.

After summarizing the findings of the Mathematica study and the findings of a study by the Upjohn Institute for Employment Research, Senator Hatch stated that:

> In short, I support the Job Corps because it works. We can count the results, measured by those young people who become fully, contributing members of our society rather than welfare junkies.

Senator Hatch concluded:

> I want to join Senator Cranston and other bipartisan supporters of the Job Corps in urging that budget reductions which may be necessary this year to control the federal deficit be made in the Job Corps Program as a last resort. If budget cuts are required for economic or equity reasons, they should not damage the essential elements of the Job Corps concept, namely its aim to provide life skills as well as job skills for those youth who are most in need.[13]

Budget Outcomes

Key Senate conservatives, who are ordinarily skeptical of federal social programs, have given considerable weight to evaluation findings that demonstrate the effectiveness of the Job Corps and its value to society. Their support of the Job Corps, based at least in part on its "demonstrated effectiveness," appears to have tilted the balance in favor of maintaining Job Corps funding.

The incoming Reagan administration moved quickly to change the direction of the federal government. Within four weeks of Inauguration Day, 1981, the new administration introduced a "Program for Economic Recovery" that included $35 billion in reductions from the expenditure levels in the FY 1982 budget that the outgoing Carter administration had just proposed. Three weeks later, the new administration produced a revised budget that included another $14 billion in proposed expenditure reductions.

Congress was strongly influenced by the administration's constant pressures to reduce spending in domestic programs: proposed rescissions for FY 1981, a revised budget for FY 1982, actual and threatened vetoes of appropriations that exceeded administration proposals for FY 1982, and proposals for further reduction for FY 1983 and FY 1984. In the Omnibus Budget Reconciliation Act of 1981 and the series of four continuing resolutions that financed the Department of Labor in FY 1982, Congress agreed to substantial reductions in employment and training programs (see table 19–1). Faced with actual and threatened vetoes, Congress made across-the-board cuts in FY 1982 appropriations for the Department of Labor but restored some of these cuts later in the fiscal year. Overall, the administration achieved a 60 percent reduction in funding for employment and training programs between January 1981 and July 1983.[14]

But both Orrin Hatch (chairman of the Senate Committee on Labor and Human Resources) and Dan Quayle (chairman of that committee's Employment and Productivity subcommittee), senators who supported many of the administration's proposed budget reductions, rejected the proposed cuts in Job Corps funding. Though Congress agreed to deep reductions in federally funded employment and training programs in response to Reagan administration proposals, Congress has maintained funding for the Job Corps at approximately $600 million per year. For FY 1982 Congress agreed to deep cuts in general employment and training programs and elimination of the Public Service Employment program, but slightly increased Job Corps funding. For FY 1983 the Administration proposed cutting Job Corps funding to $387 million,[15] but Congress again increased Job Corps funding. As the Congressional Budget Office has reported,

> This program—which has proven effective for those who complete it—has not undergone the more substantial reductions in real funding that have been made in most other employment programs for the disadvantaged.[16]

Conclusion

Information on program effectiveness was used in congressional decisions to maintain Job Corps funding and enrollment levels. Dealing with a very difficult client population, the Job Corps had been shown by a credible evaluation to be effective in terms of its objectives and to return more than its cost to society. An expensive longitudinal evaluation was needed to demonstrate the effectiveness and value of the Job Corps. The evaluation produced clear evidence that the Job Corps increases employment and earnings, increases the likelihood of subsequent education and training, reduces criminal activity, and reduces the need for public assistance and unemployment benefits.

The Job Corps' demonstrated effectiveness—and favorable benefit-cost ratio—appear to have been persuasive to key legislators otherwise disposed to reduction or elimination of social programs. Their support was pivotal in

Table 19–1
Trends in Federal Support for Selected Employment and Training Programs

	Total Obligations ($ Millions)				
	1980	1981	1982	1983	1984
CETA/JTPA Block Grant	3,342	3,692	2,108	2,179	3,301
Job Corps	401	573	583	617	596
Public Service Employment	1,660	750	0	0	0

Source: Budget of the United States Government: Fiscal Years 1982–1986; Employment and Training Report of the President, Fiscal Years 1980 and 1981.

getting Congress to maintain the Job Corps despite the administration's desire to curtail the program during times of wide agreement on the need for budget stringency. The availability of information demonstrating program effectiveness—information that is lacking for most programs—apparently led to a more positive decision for the Job Corps than would have occurred if that information had not been available.

Again in 1985, as the Job Corps is threatened with termination, key conservatives are joining more liberal senators in a bipartisan effort to save a program of demonstrated effectiveness. While many factors influence budget decisions, evidence of a program's effectiveness can sometimes play an influential role.

Notes

1. This chapter expands on observations included in Joseph S. Wholey, "Executive Agency Retrenchment," in Gregory B. Mills and John L. Palmer (Eds.), *Federal Budget Policy in the 1980s* (Washington, D.C.: The Urban Institute, 1984), pp. 295–332. Information on the budget environment and on budget and program outcomes is reprinted with the permission of The Urban Institute Press. I am indebted to Seymour Brandwein for his critical comments and many constructive suggestions on the points made in this and earlier presentations.

2. Charles Mallar et al., "Evaluation of the Economic Impact of the Job Corps Program: Second Follow-up Report," Report prepared for the U.S. Department of Labor, Employment and Training Administration, Office of Policy, Evaluation and Research (Princeton, N.J.: Mathematica Policy Research, 1980).

3. Estimates by the National Council on Employment Policy based on the interim report just cited. See "CETA's Results and Their Implications, a Policy Statement by the National Council on Employment Policy, September, 1981," U.S. Congress, House, Committee on Education and Labor, Subcommittee on Employment Opportunities, "Oversight on CETA Reauthorization," Hearings, 97th Congress, 1st session, November 1981, pp. 154–162.

4. Charles Mallar et al., "Evaluation of the Economic Impact of the Job Corps Program: Third Follow-up Report," Report prepared for the U.S. Department of Labor, Employment and Training Administration, Office of Policy, Evaluation and Research (Princeton, N.J.: Mathematica Policy Research, 1982) and Office of Research and Evaluation, "Evaluation of the Economic Impact of the Job Corps Program: Management Summary" (Washington, D.C.: U.S. Department of Labor, Employment and Training Administration, November 1982).

5. *Ibid.*

6. *Ibid.*

7. Information provided by Employment and Training Administration staff, April 1985.

8. Orrin Hatch, "The Job Corps," *Congressional Record,* February 26, 1981, pp. S 1600–S 1601.

9. *Ibid.*

10. The *Washington Post,* March 1, 1981, p. A4.

11. U.S. Congress, Senate, Committee on Labor and Human Resources, 97th Congress, 2nd session, Senate Report No. 97–469, 1982, p. 8.

12. U.S. Congress, House, Committee on Education and Labor, 97th Congress, 2nd session, House Report No. 97–537, 1982, p. 29.

13. Orrin Hatch, "Favoring the Continuation of the Job Corps Program," *Congressional Record,* February 20, 1985, pp. S 1610–S 1611.

14. Congressional Budget Office, "Major Legislative Changes in Human Resources Programs Since January 1981: Staff Memorandum," Report prepared for Speaker Thomas P. O'Neill (Washington, D.C.: August 1983).

15. U.S. Congress, House, Committee on Education and Labor, "Oversight Hearings on 1983 Budget Request," Hearings, 97th Congress, 2nd session, March 1982, p. 194.

16. Congressional Budget Office, "Major Legislative Changes in Human Resources Programs since January 1981," Staff Memorandum, p. 67.

20
Communicating the Value of Tennessee's Prenatal Program

Jean D. Smith

I n 1981 the Tennessee Department of Public Health undertook an evaluation of a five-year, federally funded prenatal services program that had been operating in selected sites in the state. The original focus of the evaluation was expanded when it became clear that the results of the evaluation could be used in communicating the value of the prenatal programs to executive and legislative budgetmakers to support proposals to secure state funds to replace federal grant funds. The focus was again widened when, in the fifth month of the study, prenatal program staff were directed to produce a plan for expanding prenatal services.

Examination of the period from June 1981 to July 1982 reveals the impact of the evaluation process on program and policy levels. An examination of activities in subsequent years illustrates the possible consequences of an inability to communicate the program results.

The Evaluation

The program evaluated was a federally funded demonstration program, "Toward Improving the Outcome of Pregnancy" (TIOP), which provided prenatal service through local health departments in seven areas of Tennessee. The evaluation team included two contractor staff members and the author.[1] The evaluation included: (1) an evaluability assessment, which was completed in one month and which resulted in agreement on high-priority program objectives that were realistic and measurable,[2] (2) a rapid-feedback evaluation completed in five months (an evaluation step that was not included in the contract but was added after the first round of interviews with managers and policymakers in order to provide information needed in the budget process),[3] (3) a full-scale evaluation, completed in 13 months, and (4) follow-up assistance in developing a statewide prenatal program and information system.

Each step in the evaluation involved extensive communication with the program and management staffs. These staffs were involved to a much greater degree than they had anticipated in the evaluation process. The fact that these staffs were caught up in the continuous interaction and were able to shape the evaluation was crucially important to the success of the evaluation. The speed with which the evaluability assessment was completed and the addition of the rapid-feedback evaluation, timed to allow its use in budgeting, gave the evaluation a relevance it would not have otherwise had. The evaluation contract began June 1, 1981, and included evaluation of the demonstration program in terms of the objectives in the grant proposal, evaluation of the efficiency and effectiveness of the demonstration program, and recommendations on the expansion of the program. The chronology from that point, was as follows:

July 8, 1981

The evaluability assessment was completed.[4] The intended prenatal care program was described and performance indicators were defined and agreed on by program and management staffs. The agreed-on program performance indicators included, for example, costs of the program, number of patients served, trimester of pregnancy in which prenatal care was initiated, birthweight of the infant, and neonatal and infant mortality rates. The evaluation was facilitated by a Work Group comprised of local, regional, an central office program level staff; a Policy Group comprised of management staff at the regional, sectional, bureau, and departmental levels; the Deputy Commissioner of Public Health; and the health department's budget analyst in the Department of Finance and Administration.

In addition to securing agreement on the program objectives and performance indicators, the evaluability assessment resulted in agreement on the types of data most desired by the Work Group and the Policy Group and the points of focus of the evaluation. The evaluators had by this time determined that, in order to be useful in the next budget cycle, evaluation information was needed by mid-November. If the state were to assume the funding of the prenatal demonstration projects when the five-year federal grant ended in June 1982, supporting data would be needed by November 1981.

The evaluability assessment involved a number of decisions of the Work Group and the Policy Group, such as whether the resources, activities, intended outcomes, goals, and assumed causal connections in the prenatal program were accurately described, and what priorities should be given to analyzing and summarizing new data. Although these decisions were crucial to the success of the evaluation, few members of either group realized the full significance of the steps they took. Guided by the evaluation team, they did make the choices they were asked to make. Their feeling that the outcome of the evaluation was logical or right and useful carried with it the impression that it was inevitable. There was, in the end, no apparent consciousness on the part of most of the members of these groups, of the complexity and meticulousness of the evaluation process. This had the advantage of ensuring ownership of the evaluation results. It had the disadvantage of failing to inspire, particularly in the Policy Group members, an awareness of the significance of the evaluators' role, thus making important follow-up steps more difficult.

Three tasks were required under the evaluation contract: (A) evaluation in terms of the original program objectives, (B) evaluation of the efficiency and effectiveness of the demonstration program, and (C) recommendations for the application of the findings to other maternal and child health programs. The evaluability assessment foreshadowed almost every subsequent development in the evaluation and planning process. The lack of interest among members of the Work Group and Policy Group in the original program objectives (such as geocoding to locate high-risk patients) was noted; the agreement on the interest of both groups in determining the effectiveness and efficiency of the demonstration program was stressed; and there was a statement that the evaluators would work on Task C, follow-up programs, as resources permitted. In fact, after decisions were made to develop a statewide prenatal program in Tennessee, the evaluators provided a great deal of assistance in developing the plan for the statewide prenatal program, in carrying out a prenatal program management conference, and in providing other assistance during the first year of the statewide program. A broadly written clause in the contract provided the flexibility to adapt to changing needs.

September 1981

The Governor's Task Force on Mental Retardation, chaired by the governor's wife, issued a report in which the principal focus was prenatal care. The governor's wife, Honey Alexander, later crusaded and lobbied for the state appropriation of funds for the statewide prenatal services program. These funds were identified by legislators as "Honey's money."

October 28, 1981

The evaluation priorities had been decided by the Work Group and the Policy Group, and they had been briefed on the findings to date. The Work Group and the Policy Group had indicated that they preferred an evaluation focusing on the efficiency and the effectiveness of the demonstration prenatal program, rather than on the original objectives included in the grant proposal. In addition, as time and resources permitted, they requested the evaluators to make recommendations on ways the department could build on the base established by the demonstration program. The two groups had also indicated that they preferred that the evaluators concentrate on the analysis of existing data, rather than on generating new data.

November 5, 1981

By this time, the departmental policymakers who had budgetmaking responsibilities had been involved in the evaluation for five months. The Policy Group had met three times to review the progress of evaluation. The bureau director had assisted in making decisions about the types of data to be produced in the evaluation. Included were the kinds of data required for program expansion requests. The Maternal and Child Health staff were directed to write a plan for the implementation of a statewide prenatal services program. The plan was to be completed by December 1981. Funds for implementing the plan were included in the proposed departmental budget. A nurse-midwife, who had nursing responsibility for the prenatal demonstration program, and the author were given the task of writing the plan. At this point the planning and evaluation processes were productively melded. If this had not happened, if the relationship of these two processes had not been recognized and a steady exchange of information between planners and evaluators had not occurred, the effectiveness of both the evaluation and the planning would have been seriously impaired.

Results of the Evaluation

November 18, 1981

The rapid-feedback evaluation, titled "Interim Evaluation,"[5] was completed. This report provided the first comprehensive data on the operation of the TIOP demonstration program. The TIOP program was found to have had the important effect of reducing the proportion of infants born with low birthweight (below five and one-half pounds). The data indicated that only 6.9 percent of infants born to TIOP patients weighed less than five and one-half pounds at birth, while approximately 8 percent of all infants born in Tennessee during the same period were of low birthweight. TIOP program outcomes also compared favorably with those of patients enrolled in Tennessee's nutrition program for Women, Infants and Children (WIC), in which 8.2 percent of the births were low birthweight, and with WIC patients who were also Food Stamp recipients, among whom 9.2 percent had low birthweight infants. This last comparison was particularly important since the income status of the women who were enrolled in TIOP was probably most comparable with the incomes of those enrolled in both WIC and the Food

Stamp program. The difference in birthweights among infants born to these low income women could be attributed to the prenatal care received by the TIOP patients. This finding was clear and probably the most significant in medical terms since appropriate birthweight is the best single indicator of the subsequent physical and mental development of the infant. From this point, birthweight became the most important outcome indicator to those planning the proposed expanded prenatal program. The interim evaluation report included all of the information and recommendations needed and used in departmental planning for an extended prenatal program, including costs, efficiencies, priority indicators, management suggestions, and proposed next steps. The principal evaluator had, by this time, begun talking to program and management staffs about a "prenatal czar," urging the state to establish an effective management structure for the expanded program.

December 4, 1981

A revised draft of the State Prenatal Plan was completed by Maternal and Child Health staff. The first draft had been reviewed by representatives of the State Public Health Regions. The evaluation and management sections of the plan were incomplete.

December 18, 1981

Regional implementation plans were submitted by public health regional staffs. The department was basing its plan on a proposed $2 million appropriation.

December 29, 1981

The principal evaluator emphasized the relationship of the evaluation and management aspects of the State Prenatal Plan and agreed, as a part of the evaluation contract, to draft a prenatal program management plan. The management plan included the following objectives for the statewide prenatal program: early entry into prenatal care, reduction in the percent of low birthweights, reduction in neonatal death rates, maximizing Medicaid reimbursements to the local health departments for prenatal care, and securing the support of private physicians for the program. These objectives derived directly from the evaluation of the demonstration program. This plan was incorporated, after state review and comments, as a section of the State Prenatal Plan. During this month, as a result of negotiations with physicians, $200,000 of the proposed state appropriation was allocated to regional prenatal centers, leaving $1.8 million for the proposed prenatal program.

January 6–8, 1982

The principal evaluator briefed members of the Work Group and the Policy Group on the Interim Evaluation and on the status of the evaluation. Decisions were imminent on the department's budget requests. The staff and management of the department remained hopeful that the full $2 million would be included in the governor's budget for FY 1982–83. During a 9 A.M. meeting with the health department's budget analyst in the Department of Finance and Administration on January 8, 1982, the evaluators were told that the department's request for funds to implement a statewide prenatal program would not be included in the governor's budget. Only $500,000 would be recommended to continue the existing demonstration projects in FY 1983. The total for the following year would be $200,000 to $300,000. The budget analyst discussed various relationships between prenatal services and the Medicaid program and the possibilities for securing matching funds from Medicaid for prenatal services. He concluded, however, by stating that the Governor's Task Force on Prevention of Mental Retardation had the political leverage to secure funds and that support from that group for the proposed prenatal program would be most effective.

Immediately after the meeting with the budget analyst, the evaluators assembled the central office staff members of the Work Group to discuss the information given by the budget analyst and the meeting to be held that afternoon with the Commissioner and Deputy Commissioner of Public Health. It was suggested that the principal staff person for the Governor's Task Force on the Prevention of Mental Retardation should be informed of the proposed reduction in the budget request for prenatal services. This staff person might report the budget reduction to the governor's wife, who chaired the task force.

In the afternoon meeting, which included the Commissioner and Deputy Commissioner of Public Health and the Director of the Bureau of Health Services, there was spirited discussion of the proposed reduction in the department's request for funding. The deputy commissioner and the bureau director, both of whom had been closely involved in the evaluation to date, cited the program achievements revealed in the evaluation report and urged the commissioner to use various strategies to assure the restoration of the prenatal program funds. The commissioner expressed the view that the case had been put forward in its strongest form and that further efforts would be met with a negative reaction in the Department of Finance and Administration.

At the conclusion of this meeting, the evaluators believed that no further attempts would be made to press the case for prenatal services. This was on Friday. On the following Monday, the prenatal services staff were told that the department's full budget request of $2 million for prenatal services had been restored. The evaluators never learned which of the strategies discussed during that Friday were actually followed. Each of the proposed strategies included an emphasis on the demonstrated effectiveness of the prenatal program as documented in the interim evaluation.

Fiscal Year 1983 was a year of retrenchment in Tennessee state government. The new $2 million prenatal program was unique that year, when many programs were being cut and the rest were struggling to maintain current services. Although budget decisions are based upon many factors, all of which may be said to influence the outcome, it appears that the results of the interim evaluation may have been one of those factors in the decision to propose a statewide prenatal program.

January 19, 1982

The evaluation tasks now included assistance in the development of a reporting system. It was decided that the quickest and easiest way of initiating a data system was to add a very small number of items, including birthweight of the child, to the input form being used in the state's Family Planning system. It was later decided, however, that such a system would be unsatisfactory. A new reporting system was to be designed with "highest priority" for implementation.

April 1982

Planning for a Prenatal Management Conference was begun. The purpose of the conference, as proposed by the principal evaluator, was to allow regional and local demonstration program staffs to explain their "best practices" in achieving the program objectives of inducing women to enter prenatal services early in their pregnancies, reducing the proportion of low birth weights, and securing the cooperation of the private medical community. In addition, during this time period, an allocation formula was developed that would be used initially to distribute funds according to need and later to reward program improvement and good program performance. The need formula was used to distribute the $1.8 million appropriation in 1982. In 1983 one performance indicator for which data were available (the number of patients served) was added to the formula for distributing an additional $1.8 million. There has been no increase in the level of funding since that time, and other parts of the formula relating to program achievement and program improvement have not been used.

June 30, 1982

The final evaluation report on the demonstration program was completed. Significantly, the title was "Toward Improving the Outcome of Pregnancy:

Implications for the Statewide Prenatal Program."[6] The findings were now even more positive—the percentage of low birthweight babies born to program participants was lower than in the total population and the percentage appeared to be declining. A Director of Prenatal Services had been designated and the responsibilities of the different program levels defined. The report outlined the eight steps considered necessary to the production of a demonstrably efficient, demonstrably effective prenatal program:

1. Defining the prenatal program and defining who is responsible for managing the program.
2. Agreeing on a set of realistic, outcome-oriented program objectives and program performance indicators in terms of which the program would be assessed and managed.
3. Establishing a system for assessing program performance in terms of the agreed-upon program objectives and performance indicators.
4. Establishing standards of expected program performance in terms of the agreed-upon program objectives and performance indicators.
5. Establishing systems for using information on program performance and regional and local variations in performance to stimulate improved program performance.
6. Achieving efficient, effective program performance, in terms of the agreed-upon project objectives, performance indicators, and performance targets.
7. Communicating program performance and results to policymakers and to the public.
8. Demonstrating the value of program activities to policymakers and to the public.[7]

The report stated that the first four of these eight steps had been accomplished, and that the remaining steps were within the resources and ability of the department. The program was halfway to what Wholey has called "results-oriented management," the purposeful use of resources and information to achieve measurable progress toward program outcome objectives related to program goals.[8] The state had accomplished this before the expanded program was actually implemented. It is doubtful that a new program could have been undertaken with better omens of success. The evaluation report stated that, "All that is needed now is the will to make it happen."

July 1, 1982

The prenatal program was implemented throughout Tennessee. The program objectives and the planned management structure derived directly from the evaluation.

August 24–25, 1982

The Prenatal Management Conference was held in Nashville. The widely attended conference, with the principal evaluator as reporter, served several purposes. The governor's wife, the Commissioner of Public Health, and the Director of the Bureau of Health Services all expressed their enthusiasm for the program. There was no doubt among the conference participants that they were involved in a program with a very high priority. The results of the evaluation were discussed and staff members of regional and local demonstration projects that had been shown by the evaluation to be most successful in some aspect of the program appeared on panels to share their program methods with others. Staff from one project explained how they succeeded in encouraging women to enter prenatal care early; staff from another project discussed their success in reducing low birthweights among their patients; staff from a third project detailed their procedures for securing private physicians' cooperation in the program; and staff from still another project explained how they had increased their Medicaid reimbursements.[9] These presentations served both as recognition for the staffs of effective projects and as examples of ways to achieve what had emerged through the evaluation process as the major program objectives.

Characteristics of Successful Evaluation

The evaluation of the prenatal demonstration program had three major impacts beyond the relatively modest one of assessing the success of the program staff. First, the evaluation influenced the decision to request funding for a statewide prenatal program. Second, the evaluation was used to shape the expanded prenatal program. Third, the evaluation was used to shape the organization and management of the statewide program.

   Reflecting on this experience, it is possible to identify elements that seem to have contributed to the success of the evaluation. These elements related to the characteristics of the progam evaluated, characteristics of the staff and managers of the program, and characteristics of the evaluation process itself.

Characteristics of the Program Evaluated

Five characteristics of the program appear to have been important:

1. The program had high priority in the eyes of policymakers and managers.
2. The program recipients were easy to identify.
3. The outcome measures were fairly easily identified and agreed upon. Birthweight is an intermediate outcome indicator and was a compromise between ultimate outcome indicators (such as infant mortality rate),

which policymakers tended to prefer, and process indicators (such as number of patients served) to which program staffs were accustomed. Birthweight was an outcome that program staffs believed they could influence.

4. Successful outcome was easy to determine. Birthweight had medical legitimacy as an indicator and overrode the measures on which the demonstration program had had less success. In addition, comparable data for nonproject populations were available. There was little ambiguity in the results.

5. A data collection system had been in place from the beginning of the demonstration projects. Quarterly reporting forms included the information needed to assess program performance on the principal indicators.

Characteristics of Management

Six characteristics of management also appear to have been important:

1. The evaluation had high priority among managers, especially after the push for a statewide program began.

2. There was commitment by management to use the evaluation. A great many decisions were being made during the period described. These decisions could have been based on the sorts of information that influence most budget decisions, many of which are more fortuitous than reality based. Instead, there was a willingness to base program decisions on the best information available. A tie was secured between evaluation and program planning.

3. During the evaluation period, there was continuity of management.

4. There was consciousness, on the part of a few key staff, of the evaluation process and of the significance of the components of it.

5. There were simple incentives provided to the staff carrying out the work. These included increased and appropriate responsibility for important work, some recognition for work done, and the ability to influence important decisions.

6. A data collection system was designed that would provide information on program performance. Plans to implement a data processing system were given high priority.

Characteristics of the Evaluation Process

Finally, five characteristics of the evaluation process appear to have been important:

1. The evaluation included every person needed to build consensus on what the program was, what it should achieve, and how it should be managed.

2. The on-site evaluator was able to facilitate an appropriate flow of information from staff and management to the consultant and from the consultant to staff and management.

3. The evaluation was flexible and easily adapted to changing needs and conditions without losing sight of the important aspects of the original work. The timing of the evaluability assessment and the rapid-feedback evaluation was critical.

4. The evaluators reiterated the need for certain decisions necessary in planning an efficient and effective program. The objective voice in the middle of the hectic budgeting and planning process is both rare and valuable.

5. The emerging results were communicated to managers and policymakers in a timely and convincing way so that the results became the basis for budgetary and planning decisions.

Epilogue: Loss of Momentum

In FY 1983, as the new statewide prenatal program was launched, the prenatal program lost status. New policy initiatives, changes in personnel, and changes in data processing priorities all slowed the progress of the prenatal program.

July 1982

Shortly after the prenatal program was funded, planning was begun in Tennessee for what was to become the governor's "Healthy Children" Initiative. The goal of the initiative was to assure that every child born in Tennessee would be healthy and remain healthy through at least the first five years of life. The Department of Public Health was given primary responsibility for developing a plan for the initiative. Prenatal services were, of course, an important component of the initiative. Because the initiative included the coordination of planning among all state agencies serving children, the planning for the initiatives was located in the central staff of the Bureau of Health Services. The prenatal program was located in the Maternal Health Services section of that bureau. Decisions about priorities and budgets were made within the context of the broader initiative.

At the end of July 1982 the manager of the Maternal Health Services section left that position. This position was not filled, and the Director of Child Health Services, who acted as Interim Director of Maternal Health Services, resigned at the end of 1982. A new director of the combined Maternal and Child Health Services was appointed in January 1983.

June 1983

A prenatal program status report indicated that little additional progress had been made in the eight steps described above as necessary for a demonstrably effective program.[10] The report suggested that two factors largely accounted for the lack of achievement in program performance and communicating this performance to policymakers and the public. First, the report noted that,

> With the recent changes in bureau and section leadership and the development of plans for the Department's Healthy Children Initiative, the division of central office prenatal program management roles and responsibilities has become less clear.[11]

Second, momentum had been lost for developing the computerized reporting system for the prenatal program. No computerized reports were yet available, and no manual system had been maintained that would provide information on program achievement. There was no convincing evidence that program objectives were being met; and the formula for allocating prenatal program resources based on local program achievement and program improvement could not be implemented. In contrast with the dynamic developments at the beginning of the statewide prenatal program, there has been a much slower expansion of the program in succeeding years. Table 20–1 illustrates this flattened growth. In the absence of further information on prenatal program performance, the funding increases declined from over 300 percent in the first year of the statewide program to less than 1 percent in the third year of the statewide program. The number of patients served has remained

Table 20–1
Tennessee's Prenatal Program: Funding and Patients Served

	FY 1982	FY 1983	FY 1984	FY 1985
State Appropriation	$0	$1,905,300	$1,858,000	$2,169,300
Other State Funds (Reallocation of Fees)	0	17,200	1,517,200	1,646,100
Federal Grant Funds	622,200	732,100	981,300	560,100
Total	$622,200	$2,654,600	$4,356,500	$4,375,500
Prenatal Patients Served	3,085	11,365	11,280	6,495[a]

Source: Reports provided by the Tennessee Department of Health and Environment, March 1985.
[a]First six months of FY 1985.

fairly constant since the first year of the statewide program. Central office staff responsible for planning and monitoring the program has declined from five to one and one-half positions.

Conclusion

Being involved in an effective evaluation process is a heady and exhilarating experience. The evaluation of the demonstration prenatal program in Tennessee succeeded beyond the most extravagant expectations of the evaluators. The results of the evaluation were unexpectedly convincing: the effectiveness of the program was demonstrated beyond question. The evaluation results were not only related to the demonstration program evaluated; they were also used in shaping and increasing the credibility of the statewide prenatal program. The evaluation gave strength, momentum, and direction to the program planners and policy staff. The evaluation was a part of the budget deliberations and resulted in establishing realistic objectives and a reporting system as an initial part of the new program. Achievements of this kind are rare and exciting and should be examined closely for the lessons to be learned from them.

This example also confirms that organizations respond to a variety of pressures besides those which the evaluator brings to bear. It is unlikely that full success will be achieved or that, if success is achieved, there will be no further program changes.

In the Tennessee prenatal program, few of the adverse changes that occurred could have been prevented. Given a second chance, more urgency might have been given to moving forward the work on the data system. And while that system was being developed, the manual reporting system used in the demonstration program might have been maintained. The prenatal staff had not felt that a dual reporting system would be tolerated by the regional and county staffs, but in retrospect it appears that they should have insisted upon that course. Solid numbers might have provided stepping stones across the changing waters.

Notes

1. At the time of the study, the author was a health planner on the staff of the Maternal and Child Health section, Bureau of Health Services, Tennessee Department of Public Health.

2. Joseph S. Wholey and Margaret S. Wholey, *Evaluation of TIOP and Related Prenatal Care Programs: Proposed Approach to Parts A, B, and C of the Evaluation,* Report prepared for the Tennessee Department of Public Health (Arlington, Virginia: Wholey Associates, June 1981).

3. Joseph S. Wholey and Margaret S. Wholey, *Evaluation of TIOP and Related Prenatal Care Programs: Interim Report,* Report prepared for the Tennessee Department of Public Health (Arlington, Virginia: Wholey Associates, November 1981).

4. Wholey and Wholey, *Proposed Approach to Parts A, B, and C of the Evaluation.*

5. Wholey and Wholey, *Interim Report.*

6. Joseph S. Wholey and Margaret S. Wholey, *Toward Improving the Outcome of Pregnancy: Implications for the Statewide Program* (Arlington, Virginia: Wholey Associates, June 1982).

7. *Ibid.,* pp.21–22.

8. Joseph S. Wholey, *Evaluation and Effective Public Management* (Boston: Little, Brown, 1983), pp.3–32.

9. Joseph S. Wholey, *Tennessee's Prenatal Program: Report on the 1982 Management Conference,* Report prepared for the Tennessee Department of Public Health (Arlington, Virginia: Wholey Associates, December 1982).

10. Joseph S. Wholey, *Managing Tennessee's Prenatal Program: Present Status and Next Steps,* Report prepared for the Tennessee Department of Public Health (Arlington, Virginia: Wholey Associates, June 1983).

11. *Ibid.,* p.III–I.

21
WIC: Positive Outcomes for a Demonstrably Effective Program

Joseph S. Wholey

Established as a two-year pilot program in 1972 and officially started in FY 1974, the Special Supplemental Food Program for Women, Infants and Children (WIC) is a U.S. Department of Agriculture (USDA) program that provides food supplements and nutrition counseling to low income pregnant women, nursing mothers, infants, and preschool children who are determined to be at "nutritional risk" according to criteria established at state or local levels. The WIC program is designed to operate in assocation with local health clinics and hospitals, not as a freestanding program.

In the first three years of the Reagan administration, the USDA's Food and Nutrition Service was under pressure from the White House and the Office of Management and Budget (OMB) to reduce spending on nutrition programs and incorporate the WIC program into a Maternal and Child Health block grant. Although Congress agreed to substantial cuts in other nutrition programs between 1981 and 1983, Congress resisted Reagan administration's proposals for reduction or elimination of the WIC program and instead increased WIC appropriations substantially.

This chapter discusses the policy uses of an accumulating body of research and evaluation studies that indicated the value of the WIC program in improving participants' nutritional and health status.[1] Though these studies may not have been fully conclusive (a more definitive $5 million, five-year national WIC evaluation is to be released in 1985), the studies appear to have been sufficient to demonstrate the value of the WIC program prior to and during congressional decision making on the continued existence and size of the WIC program. Though many factors influence policy decisions (the WIC program had enjoyed strong bipartisan support in the Congress prior to 1981), evidence of WIC's "cost effectiveness" appears to have been useful when the program's funding and existence were threatened in a harsh budget environment.

WIC Evaluations and Related Research

A substantial body of research throughout the world, including a number of studies using sophisticated research designs, demonstrates that supplementing diet with calories, protein, and other nutrients increases infants' birthweight, reduces the percentage of low birthweight infants (infants weighing less than 5 pounds, 8 ounces), and improves the nutritional status of young children.[2] Since the inception of the WIC program, many WIC evaluations have been completed at local, state, and national levels. These evaluations indicate that the WIC program improves participants' nutritional and health status, reduces the percentage of low birthweight infants, and reduces newborn infants' hospital costs.[3] Though each of the evaluations had limitations, by 1981 the available evidence suggested that the WIC program was effective.

In 1976, under a contract with the USDA, the University of North Carolina School of Public Health completed an evaluation of the impact of the WIC program on the health and nutritional status of participants. This evaluation concluded that:

> Pregnant women who participated in the WIC program gained more weight during pregnancy than the women in the initial population.
>
> An increase in infants' average birthweight was associated with the WIC program. The impact of the program was greater on black and Hispanic infants than on white infants.
>
> An increase in average hemoglobin concentration and a reduction in the prevalence of anemia was shown for women who were pregnant more than twenty-eight weeks and for infants and children.[4]

While the University of North Carolina study was still underway and subsequently, the General Accounting Office (GAO) and others identified many problems and limitations in this and other nutrition program evaluations—in particular, problems in health standards and nutrition standards, lack of suitable comparison groups, and poor data collection methodology.[5] In 1975, in reauthorizing the WIC program, Congress responded by mandating the establishment of an advisory committee to

> study the methods available to evaluate successfully and economically, in part or in total, the health benefits of the Special Supplemental Food Program . . . [and] determine and recommend in detail how, using accepted scientific methods, the health benefits of the Special Supplemental Food Program may best be evaluated and assessed.[6]

In 1977 the Advisory Committee on Nutrition Evaluation, which included members representing the various health professions, summarized and critiqued prior nutrition evaluations and developed four proposals for more definitive evaluation of the WIC program. Agreeing that a randomized experiment would be ethically unacceptable, the committee recommended:

> An evaluation of the nutritional status of WIC program participants, using existing anthropometric and hematological data collected at the time of entrance to the program and after participation. (It was estimated that this evaluation would take approximately one year and cost approximately $200,000.)

> A system for periodically evaluating the nutritional and health status of WIC program participants using a standardized protocol and some customarily used indicators of nutrition and health status. (It was estimated that this evaluation would cost approximately $250,000 in the first year and $200,000 per year thereafter.)

> An in-depth, longitudinal evaluation of the effects of WIC participation on the nutrition and health status of selected participants using a variety of more precise measures and rigidly controlled and standardized procedures. (It was estimated that this evaluation would cost approximately $1.75 million and take a minimum of three years.)

> An evaluation of the extent to which the WIC program reaches those in greatest need of program benefits. (This evaluation would take three years and cost approximately $750,000.)[7]

The committee believed that higher quality, higher cost evaluation efforts would be required to assess the nutritional and health benefits of the WIC program.

In response, the USDA prepared and made available summaries of federal, state, and local WIC evaluations for the sessions of Congress beginning in 1978 and worked with the Department of Health, Education, and Welfare (HEW) to expand the Center for Disease Control surveillance system to additional local health clinics and thus provide a continuous assessment of WIC participants. By January 1981, as the Reagan administration was coming into office, the department's Food and Nutrition Service disseminated an evaluation summary based on the studies that had been completed up to that time. The evaluation summary concluded that:

1. A substantial body of evidence indicates that the WIC program has a positive and significant effect on program participants.

2. Participation in WIC is associated with a positive and significant increase in birthweight and with a reduction in the incidence of low birthweight.

3. Preliminary data from a study completed in January 1981 indicated that the WIC program significantly reduces neonatal mortality.

4. The WIC program results in significant medical savings, primarily by decreasing the number of low birthweight infants.

5. The WIC program has been associated with improvements in nutritional status in infants and children. Infants and children participating in WIC had accelerated rates of growth and decreased rates of anemia.[8]

During the same time period, however, a number of critics continued to state that the effectiveness of the WIC program had not been conclusively demonstrated. In 1979, for example, the GAO stated that:

[R]eliable assessments of the special supplemental food program's overall results and benefits have not been made. . . .

The broader evaluations of the program that have been made, while providing some information that may be useful, have not always been reliable. The more limited studies, including those conducted by various states, generally are of uncertain quality and reliability.[9]

In testimony before the Senate Subcommittee on Nutrition, Dr. George Graham of Johns Hopkins University stated that:

We don't know whether the programs have produced the results that are expected of them. They probably have, but it is extremely difficult, as has been recognized by this committee, by the General Accounting Office, to really know whether results can be attributed to programs.[10]

In later testimony before the same subcommittee, Dr. Graham stated that:

I'm here to support cuts in the WIC program. And more important, its disappearance into the maternal and child health block grants to the states.

In [many WIC] programs, probably the majority, nutritional risk has been interpreted very loosely. . . . As a result, pregnant women who are normal or already obese and infants who are growing at a greater than normal rate have been enrolled, often forming the majority of the participants. . . .

Perhaps the most valuable role of the WIC program has been its ability, when coordinated with proper health services, to attract and hold many pregnant women into regular prenatal care, with its known benefits, and infants into regular health supervision.

. . . I think that as the program exists now, it could easily be cut in half, in that many, many of the participants do not qualify as being at nutritional risk.[11]

In his written statement, Dr. Graham went on to say that:

> Observations in underdeveloped nations had earlier suggested that severe malnutrition in infancy and early childhood resulted not only in physical stunting but also in significant degrees of mental retardation: a number of carefully executed studies have since failed to substantiate both assumptions, and suggest instead that the inferior mental performance is most likely the result of intellectual deprivation in the poor environments in which malnutrition usually develops. . . .
>
> . . . The United States continues to experience an undesirable high incidence of low birthweight, due primarily to premature labor and delivery, very particularly among the black population. . . . No convincing evidence has been developed to relate premature delivery to nutritional deficiences.[12]

Dr. Graham went on to question most of the WIC evaluations completed up to that point in time.

In testimony before the Senate Committee on Agriculture, Nutrition, and Forestry, Eleanor Chelimsky of the GAO stated that:

> In sum, our finding is that the information available from the WIC evaluations is insufficient for making general or conclusive judgments about whether the WIC program is effective or ineffective overall. On the other hand, the information does indicate the likelihood, in a limited way, that WIC may have positive effects in some areas. . . .
>
> In summary, evidence—of highly varying quantity and quality—is available to support a range of inferences about the WIC program, but no definite conclusions. . . .[13]

Despite such caveats, WIC enthusiasts are to be found at all levels of government and in the medical community. Contrary to experiences in many programs, supporters of the WIC program have eagerly sought evaluation to provide stronger evidence of the benefits of WIC. In 1977 and 1978, the need for more definitive evaluation of the WIC program was repeatedly expressed in statements by independent advisory groups and testimony by WIC supporters.[14] In reauthoring the WIC program in 1978, Congress authorized the use of up to one-half of 1 percent of WIC appropriations (not to exceed $3 million per year) for evaluating WIC program performance, evaluating health benefits, and administration of pilot projects.[15] The USDA then contracted for the more definitive national WIC evaluation mentioned above. This evaluation, which is to be released in 1985, includes four studies:

> An ecological study of the effects of the WIC program on outcomes of pregnancy (including birthweight and infant mortality rates) for the period 1972–80.

A nationally representative longitudinal study of pregnant women who are in WIC or who are WIC-eligible nonparticipants.

A cross-sectional study of children of women in the longitudinal study.

A study of the degree to which WIC foods substitute for foods that would have been purchased or are shared with family members.[16]

This evaluation will provide evidence of the effectiveness of the WIC program on a national scale; in particular, evidence of WIC's effectiveness in improving outcomes of pregnancy.

Dissemination and Use of Evaluation Findings

In the late 1970s and early 1980s, WIC evaluation findings were widely disseminated and used in congressional decision making. Those involved in health and nutrition programs joined advocacy groups and the medical community in strong support of WIC, presenting evidence of WIC program effectiveness at congressional committee hearings and in other areas. Congress used this evidence in making decisions to continue and expand the WIC program.

In May 1978, in its report on the Child Nutrition amendments of 1978 (P.L. 95–627), the House Committee on Education and Labor noted that:

> During its consideration of the WIC program the committee found a body of persuasive evidence which indicates the positive aspects of the program and its potential impact on our nation's nutritionally deprived women, infants, and children. The overwhelming support that the WIC program inspires at all levels further reinforces the committee's view that there is a critical need for its continuation.[17]

During the same period, the Senate Committee on Agriculture, Nutrition, and Forestry noted that:

> Data collected independently by State WIC programs in such States as Arizona, Oregon, and Louisiana during the years 1974 to 1977 show that WIC participants demonstrated a substantial reduction in anemia, a reduced incidence of low birthweight infants, and improvement in both underweight and overweight participants.[18]

By April 1980, at hearings before the Senate Subcommittee on Nutrition, Carol Tucker Foreman, Assistant Secretary of Agriculture, testified that:

[WIC] is amazingly cost effective. In our 1981 budget, it contains a substantial increase for the program, primarily because several recent studies have demonstrated the value of the WIC program. One study conducted at the Harvard School of Public Health in four WIC projects in Massachusetts found that the incidence of low birthweight among infants whose mothers participated in the WIC program during the prenatal period was markedly less than among infants whose mothers, although eligible for the WIC program, did not participate.

The reduction in incidence of low birthweight led to much lower hospitalization costs. The study estimated that each dollar spent in the prenatal components of the WIC program resulted in a $3 reduction in hospitalization costs, since the number of low-birthweight infants who had to be hospitalized was significantly reduced.

And I brought with me today a chart that reflects results of a study conducted by the Waterbury, Connecticut, Health Department in conjunction with the Yale Medical School where they found substantial reductions, as you will see, in infant mortality rates among WIC participants as opposed to mothers from similar groups who did not participate in the WIC program.[19]

At the same hearing physicians, WIC participants, and representatives of advocacy groups testified on the improvements in health and nutrition status that were associated with the WIC program and on the need to expand the program to meet unmet needs.

By January 1981, as the Reagan administration came into office, the WIC program was very highly regarded in Congress, having a reputation for being both cost effective and free of recipient fraud and abuse. When the Reagan administration proposed substantial reductions in the WIC program in 1981 and 1982, Congress rejected the administrations' proposals and instead increased WIC appropriations substantially.

In March 1981, at hearings before the House Subcommittee on Elementary, Secondary, and Vocational Education, representatives of advocacy groups and of those involved in WIC used evidence of WIC program effectiveness in urging rejections of the Reagan administration's proposed reduction of WIC appropriations from $900 million for FY 1981 to $720 million for FY 1982. Representing Bread for the World, an advocacy group, Barbara Howell stated that:

> WIC is well targeted and cost effective with a success rate rarely achieved in any federal program. . . .
> A recent study by Harvard School of Public Health found that every $1 spent on nutritious food for pregnant mothers saved $3 on costs of incubators, medicine, [and] special health care after birth.[20]

Deirdre Viera of the Children's Foundation noted that:

Numerous studies have shown the effectiveness of the WIC program. The results of these studies are contained in a USDA report . . . released to the Congress in January.[21]

Viera then reviewed some of the highlights of the evaluation summary discussed earlier, submitting the entire Food and Nutrition Service report for the hearing record.[22]

At the same hearing, Milton Kotelchuck of the Massachusetts Department of Public Health reviewed a recent statewide study that attempted to overcome methodological problems in past studies and showed small but positive effects associated with WIC participation: reductions in the incidence of low birthweight from 8.7 percent of the control sample to 6.9 percent of all births in the WIC program, a reduction in neonatal mortality, and more positive pregnancy outcomes for WIC mothers who participated for longer periods.[23] In addition, Richard Blount, WIC project director in the Missouri Division of Human Resources, testified that:

> The WIC program is much more than a supplemental food program. In Missouri and across the nation, it is a vital and integral part of our total preventive health system and nutrition education program. . . .
>
> A number of states [have] reported that WIC has definitely caused an increase in the number of persons receiving maternal and child health services. Prenatal patients are entering health clinics one to two months earlier than they did before WIC. This earlier health assessment of infants and children results in earlier detection of other health needs that can be treated. Immunization has increased. Coordination between health services as well as health and social services providers has increased. WIC has contributed to the establishment of new health services in areas previously without health services.
>
> These impact statements represent the conclusions of state health personnel, including physicians, nurses, nutritionists, WIC, and maternal and child health directors and local personnel on the firing line who responded to the national survey and conducted state surveys of their own.[24]

Dr. Calvin Woodruff, representing the American Academy of Pediatrics, testified that:

> The academy has supported the WIC program since its inception as part of our commitment to insuring adequate nutrition to pregnant and lactating women and infants in greatest need. Such nutrition is indispensable to proper mental and physical development during formative stages of growth. . . .
>
> . . . WIC has produced impressive results in the most vulnerable populations—pregnant and lactating women and infants in their first year of life . . . .

All studies appear to indicate that WIC not only has led to marked improvements in the health of its participants, but that it is a cost-effective program as well.[25]

Evidence of WIC program effectiveness was used in the Senate in 1981 and 1982, as senators and staff from both parties protected WIC while other nutrition programs were being cut substantially. Eileen Kennedy's "Harvard Study," which indicated that WIC saved $3 for every $1 expended on the prenatal component, was repeatedly cited.[26] Testimony along these lines was presented to the Senate Subcommittee on Nutrition in February 1982, as witnesses opposed the Reagan administration's proposal to terminate funding for the WIC program and incorporate nutrition services in an expanded Maternal and Child Health block grant to the states. Speaking for the American Academy of Pediatrics, for example, Dr. Alan M. Mauer opposed reductions in WIC funding and supported continuation of the WIC program as a categorical program administered by the USDA. Speaking for the Association of WIC Directors, Douglas Paterson also opposed the inclusion of WIC in the Maternal and Child Health block grant. Paterson noted that:

. . . WIC's continued support has only been possible because we have been able to prove the importance of our contributions on health delivery. Only because WIC has been identifiable and we have been able to evaluate its effectiveness has its support been possible.[27]

Legislative and Budget Outcomes

The WIC program survived both the Reagan administration's attempts to obtain substantial cuts in the WIC budget and the administration's attempts to fold WIC into the Maternal and Child Health block grant (with reduced funding for the combined program). On the contrary, between FY 1980 and FY 1985, Congress increased WIC appropriations substantially.

The Omnibus Budget Reconciliation Act of 1981, which cut other nutrition programs, authorized increasing appropriations for the WIC nutrition program. The Senate Committee on Agriculture, Nutrition, and Forestry rejected a Reagan administration proposal to reduce WIC appropriations from $900 million in FY 1981 to $720 million in FY 1982, and instead authorized increased WIC funding for FY 1982 and subsequent years. In the report accompanying the budget reconciliation bill, the committee stated that:

WIC is the fastest growing of all child nutrition programs. It was [sic] grown in less than eight years from a $20 million pilot program . . . to a $900 million program serving over two million participants.

While acknowledging the merits of WIC, the Committee also recognizes the need for program restraint. The Committee therefore recommends authorizing appropriations of $998 million in FY 1982, $1,060 million in FY 1983, and $1,126 million in FY 1984.[28]

On the Senate floor, in the debate on the budget reconciliation bill, Senator Patrick Leahy, ranking democrat on the Nutrition Subcommittee, commended Senator Robert Dole, the nutrition subcommittee chairman, for "his thoughtful leadership and gracious cooperative spirit in developing proposals in these areas." Senator Leahy continued:

> In the area of the special supplemental feeding program for women, infants and children (WIC), the President had proposed severe reductions. Under his proposal, hundreds of thousands fewer needy persons would have been served than are served now. With the help of many other members of Congress, we were able to retain authorization levels for WIC that would not require a significant cut in caseload. With its proven record of success and cost effectiveness, major reductions in the WIC program would have been a tragedy.[29]

The Omnibus Budget Reconciliation Act of 1981 tightened eligibility requirements for food and nutrition program recipients and reduced levels of support for eligible individuals. For FY 1982 through FY 1985, legislative changes reduced the Food Stamp program approximately 13 percent and reduced the Child Nutrition programs approximately 28 percent, in comparison with "current services" baseline expenditures.[30] Approximately one million people lost eligibility for food stamps as a result of program changes adopted for FY 1982 and FY 1983.[31]

Reductions in the Food Stamp program held the number of households receiving food stamps roughly constant between FY 1981 and FY 1982, during a deepening recession.[32] Participants in the School Lunch program decreased by three million children from FY 1981 to FY 1982, including a reduction of two million children paying the full price for their lunches. Participation in the Free Lunch program has since grown to approximately the FY 1981 level, while participation by those paying reduced prices of full service has not recovered.[33] When budget cuts were needed, Congress cut programs that were considered wasteful or inefficient in helping those most in need.

After holding WIC appropriations level at $900 million in FY 1982, Congress expanded the WIC program in subsequent years. WIC expansion was one of the program improvements included in the Jobs Bill of 1983 (for example: between FY 1980 and FY 1984, WIC appropriations grew by 85 percent).

Fiscal year 1980: $736 million

Fiscal year 1981: $900 million

Fiscal year 1982: $900 million

Fiscal year 1983: $1160 million

Fiscal year 1984: $1360 million

Participation in the WIC program was reduced in some months in 1981, while major program changes were under consideration and the Food and Nutrition Service delayed in reallocating unspent WIC funds, but WIC enrollment stabilized by the end of 1981 and has grown since then.[35]

Conclusion

Arguments of program effectiveness were used in congressional decision making as Congress kept the WIC nutrition program separate from the Maternal and Child Health block grant program, resisted WIC program cuts in FY 1982, and expanded the WIC program in subsequent years. There have been many evaluations of the impacts of the WIC program. There is evidence that the WIC program improves nutrition, increases infants' birthweight, results in healthier babies, and saves health care dollars.

WIC's effectiveness has been demonstrated to the satisfaction of members of Congress and congressional staffs, who consider WIC a "shining star" in comparison with other nutrition programs. The "cost effectiveness" finding, that WIC saves $3 for every $1 expended on the prenatal component, has been widely and repeatedly cited in Congress since 1980. Senator Robert Dole, who for many years has had the greatest influence in the Senate with regard to nutrition programs, summarized the congressional view of the WIC program in a recent statement on the floor of the Senate:

> Perhaps more than any other federal nutrition program, WIC has a strong performance in both Houses of Congress. WIC has earned this high regard because it is free from fraud, waste, and abuse that continues to mar the image of the Food Stamp Program, for example.
>
> WIC is a true nutrition program whose benefits are tailored to meet the special nutrition needs of the recipients it serves. Evaluation studies indicate the WIC program has been cost effective in both health and dollar terms. A major study at the Harvard School of Public Health found that each $1 spent in the prenatal component of WIC saves $3 in hospitalization costs due to the reduced number of low-birthweight infants requiring expensive neonatal care.[36]

While many factors influence legislative and budget decisions (resources for effective programs have often been reduced), evidence of a program's effectiveness can play a useful, constructive role in legislative decision making.

Notes

1. This chapter expands observations included in Joseph S. Wholey, "Executive Agency Retrenchment," in Gregory B. Mills and John L. Palmer (Eds.), *Federal Budget Policy in the 1980s* (Washington, D.C.: The Urban Institute, 1984), pp.295–332. Information on the policy environment, on legislative and budget outcomes, and on nutrition program impacts is reprinted with the permission of The Urban Institute Press. I am indebted to Robert Behn and Laurence Lynn for their comments on the points made in earlier presentations.

2. "Evaluation of the Effectiveness of WIC" (Washington, D.C.: U.S. Department of Agriculture, Food and Nutrition Service, Office of Policy, Planning and Evaluation, 1981). Also see "Evaluation of the WIC Program: Predesign Activities, Phase I, Final Report," Report prepared for the U.S. Department of Agriculture (Research Triangle Park, N.C.: Research Triangle Institute, 1981).

3. *Ibid.*

4. J.C. Edozien, "Medical Evaluation of the Special Supplemental Food Program for Women, Infants, and Children," Report prepared for the U.S. Department of Agriculture (Chapen Hill, N.C.: University of North Carolina, School of Public Health, 1976), summarized in "Evaluation of the Effectiveness of the WIC Program."

5. Comptroller General of the United States, "Observations on the Special Supplemental Food Program" (Washington, D.C.: U.S. General Accounting Office, RED–75–310, 1974).

6. P.L. 94–105.

7. Advisory Committee on Nutrition Evaluation, "Evaluating the Nutrition and Health Benefits of the Special Supplemental Food Program for Women, Infants, and Children." Report to the Congress (Washington, D.C.: U.S. Department of Agriculture, Food and Nutrition Service, FNS–165, 1977).

8. "Evaluation of the Effectiveness of the WIC Program."

9. Comptroller General of the United States, "The Special Supplemental Food Program for Women, Infants, and Children (WIC)—How Can It Work Better?" (Washington, D.C.: U.S. General Accounting Office, CED–79–65, 1979), p.iv.

10. U.S. Congress, Senate, Committee on Agriculture, Nutrition, and Forestry, Subcommittee on Nutrition, "Food and Nutrition Program Optional Consolidation and Reorganization Act of 1979," Hearings, 96th Congress, 1st session, December 1979, p.29.

11. U.S. Congress, Senate, Committee on Agriculture, Nutrition, and Forestry, Subcommittee on Nutrition, "Oversight on Federal Nutrition Programs," Hearings, 97th Congress, 2nd session, February 1982, pp. 94–98.

12. *Ibid.*, p.232.

13. Eleanor Chelimsky, U.S. General Accounting Office, "Evaluation of WIC's Effectiveness," Statement before the Committee on Agriculture, Nutrition, and Forestry, U.S. Senate, March 15, 1984, pp.4, 8. Also see Comptroller General of the United States, "WIC Evaluations Provide Some Favorable But No Conclusive Evidence on the Effects Expected for the Special Supplemental Program for Women, Infants, and Children" (Washington, D.C.: U.S. General Accounting Office, PEMD–84–4, 1984).

14. See "Evaluation of the WIC Program: Predesign Activities, Phase I Final Report," pp. 7–9.

15. P.L. 95–627.

16. "The National WIC Evaluation" (Washington, D.C.: U.S. Department of Agriculture, Food and Nutrition Service, Office of Analysis and Evaluation, October 1983).

17. U.S. Congress, House, Committee on Education and Labor, 95th Congress, 2nd session, Report No. 95–1153(I), 1978, p. 3.

18. U.S. Congress, Senate, Committee on Agriculture, Nutrition, and Forestry, 95th Congress, 2nd session, Report No. 95–884, 1978, p. 11.

19. U.S. Congress, Senate, Committee on Agriculture, Nutrition, and Forestry, Subcommittee on Nutrition, Hearings, 96th Congress, 2nd session, April 1980, p. 3.

20. U.S. Congress, House, Committee on Education and Labor, Subcommittee on Elementary, Secondary, and Vocational Education, "The Administration's Fiscal Year 1982 Budget Authorization for Child Nutrition," Hearings, 97th Congress, 1st session, March 1981, p. 121.

21. *Ibid.,* p. 355.

22. *Ibid.,* pp. 361ff.

23. *Ibid.,* pp. 388–393.

24. *Ibid.,* pp. 412–413.

25. *Ibid.,* pp. 415–416.

26. E.T. Kennedy et al., "Evaluation of the Effects of the WIC Supplemental Feeding Program on Prenatal Patients in Massachusetts" (Boston: Harvard School of Public Health, Doctoral Thesis, 1979), summarized in "Evaluation of the Effectiveness of WIC.

27. U.S. Congress, Senate, Committee on Agriculture, Nutrition, and Forestry, Subcommittee on Nutrition, "Oversight on Federal Nutrition Programs," Hearings, 97th Congress, 2nd session, February 1982, p. 88.

28. U.S. Congress, Senate, Budget Committee, 97th Congress, 1st session, Senate Report No. 97–139, June 1981, p. 88.

29. U.S. Congress, *Congressional Record,* July 31, 1981, p. S 9006.

30. Congressional Budget Office, "Major Legislative Changes in Human Resources Programs Since January 1981: Staff Memorandum," Report prepared for Speaker Thomas P. O'Neill (Washington, D.C., August 1983).

31. Linda E. Demkovich, "Feeding the Young—Will the Reagan 'Safety Net' Catch the 'Truly Needy'?" *National Journal,* April 10, 1982, pp. 624–629.

32. "Annual Historical Review of FNS Programs, Fiscal Year 1983" (Washington, D.C.: U.S. Department of Agriculture, Food and Nutrition Service, 1984), p. 38.

33. *Ibid.,* p. 42.

34. Information provided by Food and Nutrition Service staff, March 1985.

35. See "Annual Historical Review," p. 40.

36. U.S. Congress, *Congressional Record,* June 25, 1984, p. S8152.

22

Performance-Oriented Evaluation: Prospects for the Future

Christopher Bellavita
Joseph S. Wholey
Mark A. Abramson

Over the past 20 years, citizen confidence in our major institutions has peaked and then declined. We have gone from the hopeful days of the civil rights revolution and the War on Poverty to the darker days of a divisive war in Vietnam, Watergate, political attacks on bureaucrats, and a plethora of tax limitation measures.

As our society has become more complex and interdependent, our need for joint action has increased. The tasks that we must accomplish together have become more challenging. At the same time, however, public willingness to undertake and to finance joint action has declined. In a major recession, our nation was unwilling to expand many programs even when real needs were clear. At a time when joint problems demand joint solutions, citizens turn increasingly to their own interests.

As a nation we are accumulating deficits that could destroy us. Our federal government continues to buy more goods, services, and "income transfers" than we as taxpayers are willing to finance. At state and local government levels, where deficit financing cannot be the norm, services are being reduced, even as public needs increase. In government and in the nonprofit sector, our leaders are less and less able to persuade taxpayers and potential donors about the value of the services their organizations provide.

Part of the problem has been inflated rhetoric, as programs were oversold to gain political and financial support. Part of the problem has been lack of effective political and institutional leadership. Certainly evaluators are not responsible for solving all of the problems of the society. But evaluators do have a part to play in seeking solutions.

Evaluators have functioned well as critics, pointing out where and when organizations have failed to meet their objectives or have produced negative side effects that outweigh positive accomplishments. Evaluators will continue to function well in this "critic" role, but their role must encompass more than criticism.

It has been argued that evaluators have contributed to the public's negative image of government by accentuating their role as critics. In interviews conducted by The Center for Excellence in Government, evaluators were mentioned prominently as one of the contributing forces to the negative image of government. The center was told[1]:

> In a funny way, modern policy science and evaluation has contributed to the problem of the public's perception of government. Social scientists take a piece of legislation and they measure its impact too soon. They tear up the roots before anything has had time to grow. Social scientists are just plain wrong sometimes . . . All social scientists do is measure things in quantitative terms and they measure it too early to boot.
>
> Look at the HMO program. It has been criticized but the critics haven't looked at the entire program. HMO's have had a great impact over the last twenty years in the health care system but social scientists are calling it a failure when it was actually a success.
>
> *A University Official*

> Since the 1960s, we have program evaluation types all over the government. They provide a rigorous attempt to study government. But they have given prominent attention to the defects of government and may have undermined confidence in government. But there are many things which government has done well and has made a difference. The black community has made major improvements in health and education over the last twenty years.
>
> Nobody has done the same type studies on the Department of Defense when it had wings of planes falling off. Instead, it was easier to say that the Job Corps wasn't placing enough people. All of this contributes to the public's low image of government and contributes to the general criticism of government.
>
> *A Business Executive/Former Federal Official*

Although evaluators clearly should not be asked to be cheerleaders for government, there is a legitimate point that they can play a more positive role in both shaping public opinion about government and helping agency managers run their programs. Although there have been instances where evaluators have helped policymakers and managers decide realistically what their programs can do, there need to be more instances of evaluators playing this constructive role. Evaluators have also helped policymakers and managers improve their programs while those programs were underway, but it is argued that this role should become the norm for evaluators, rather than the exception. Finally, evaluators have provided timely, convincing evidence about program effectiveness in the past and should continue to play that role.

Excellence has been getting a great deal of attention. Although the concept could quickly become a cliché, it is important to understand that what underlies the "search for excellence" is the basic belief that programs and organizations *can* improve their performance. In the business sector, the concept of excellence is relatively easy to define, progress is relatively easy to measure, and examples are relatively easy to find. In the public and nonprofit sectors, however, the definition of excellence is more elusive, and credible examples of excellent organizational performance are more difficult to locate.

As a developing profession, evaluators are working to establish standards that can guide future work and clarify the types of contributions evaluators can make. To have something to offer, evaluators must preserve their credibility and independence. But independence need not conflict with cooperation and service. We hope evaluators can more often act to help produce examples of high performance in government and nonprofit organizations. For the balance of this century, we need to give greater attention to the constructive roles that evaluators can play helping programs, organizations, and society itself make the transition from its current struggle with malaise to excellence.

As the cases described in this book illustrate, evaluators are well on the way to helping produce solutions to the problems of the 1980s. Things are not equally bleak everywhere. Local school districts throughout the country are re-examining missions and practices. Organizations at all levels of government and in the nonprofit sector are treating program and fiscal accountability as instruments to help improve performance. Human service, criminal justice, transportation, training, and research and development programs have learned how to learn from past experiences. Program development, implementation monitoring, and evaluation methods have been refined to the point where evaluators are more frequently contributing to program success.

But the cases described in this book also reveal the continuing evolution of the evaluation profession. The dominating image of the evaluator as an objective, fact-oriented, methodologically sophisticated, emotionally uninvolved scientist is being replaced by a new image. We now have enough examples of effective evaluation and effective evaluators to begin to describe some of the characteristics of an evaluation function that is oriented to high organizational performance.

The Evaluator's Environment

Evaluators need to understand the environment they work in. The environment influences the opportunities evaluators have to make a positive difference in program and organizations, and it also places constraints on what evaluators can accomplish. In the public and nonprofit sectors, information on performance is not the only factor guiding decisionmakers' actions. Many times performance information is not even an especially significant ingredient in a decision. But the contribution information makes to decision making can be increased if evaluators are able to provide decision-oriented data in usable forms.

There are several enduring features of the evaluator's environment that influence the potential utility of evaluation. Evaluations have multiple clients. The funding agency, program staff, managers, policymakers, clients, and the public all have a stake, to varying degrees, in an evaluation. Clients may have multiple, conflicting objectives: some apparent, others hidden.

Evaluators work under time and resource constraints. Decisionmaking processes follow their own unique timeliness. To be effective, evaluators need to adapt their schedule to the decisionmaker's clock and not expect decisions to be placed on hold until new data arrive.

The 1980s clearly is an age of fiscal resource constraints. This environment challenges evaluators to find other resources for their work. Money for evaluation is scarce. But new ideas, methodologies, communication techniques, and other approaches to evaluation are not scarce. They are waiting to be used.

Finally, it is important to acknowledge that people still feel threatened by evaluation. There are few programs or organizations that look forward to being judged, whether the judge comes from inside or from outside the organization. Information about performance is needed by decisionmakers. But evaluators cannot afford to ignore the fact that their work creates mistrust and at times fear. This need not be the case, however. It is the evaluator's responsibility to demonstrate by actions the constructive and supportive uses of evaluation.

The Evaluator's Role

Effective evaluators, that is, evaluators who make significant contributions to excellence, are often involved in programs and organizations more as participants than as outsiders. The evaluator's role is shifting away from a narrow analytic, objective report of facts toward an expanded role that incorporates the traditional focus with a more service-oriented, supportive problem-solving approach to evaluation. The basic task of the evaluator—to inform the decisionmaking process—remains unchanged. But the way the evaluator carries out that task is evolving.

The complex, interdependent environment the evaluator lives in highlights the limitations of the traditional evaluator's role. Being an outsider means not fully understanding the nuances, personalities, and issues that often color program and organizational realities. Sensitive evaluators eventually can discover those elements and gauge their signficance, but at a cost in time. Evaluators who come to an enterprise with an open, cooperative, and facilitative stance, evaluators who believe in the basic ideas and intentions of the program or organization, can gain access to resources closed to the traditional evaluator.

The new evaluator is a *program advocate*—not an advocate in the sense of an ideologue willing to manipulate data and to alter findings to secure next year's funding. The new evaluator is someone who believes in and is interested in helping programs and organizations succeed. At times the program advocate evaluator will play the traditional critic role: challenging basic program assumptions, reporting lackluster performance, or identifying inefficiencies. The difference, however, is that criticism is not the end of performance-oriented evaluation; rather, it is part of a larger process of program and organizational improvement, a process that receives as much of the evaluator's attention and talents as the criticism function.

To successfully carry out their role, evaluators must also become *team players.* they must share responsibility for evaluation with policymakers, managers, and staff in deciding evaluation questions; monitoring programs; and collecting, interpreting, and using data. Further, they must contribute their analytical skills to help decisionmakers and staff test and modify ideas for program and organizational improvement. Being a program advocate means joining with like-minded others to build program and organizational success.

The Evaluator's Skills

Performance-oriented evaluators need skills not typically taught in evaluation training programs or courses. Evaluators need first the ability to function effectively in the midst of ambiguity, uncertainty, and complexity. Evaluators need to be able to conceptualize issues and concerns early in the evaluation process and to be able to translate those concepts into researchable questions whose answers can help inform decision makers. Evaluators need to understand how organizations function; they need knowledge in substantive fields; they need to grasp the details of the programs and innovations they are evaluating; and they need a thorough grounding in policy and implementation theories. It is the rare evaluator who possesses knowledge in all of these domains. Thus evaluators need to be able to develop and to maintain effective working relationships with people who *do* have the required knowledge—staff, managers, and policymakers.

Evaluators need negotiation skills. Clients and other people involved with an evaluation frequently have different ideas about what should be researched, how long the evaluation should take, and the amount of resources to allocate to evaluation. Negotiation skills can be used to resolve these issues and, in the process, help build the team relationships that are the foundation of successful evaluations.

Evaluators working in the public or nonprofit sector need a bias for the pragmatic. There are always more tasks that could be done, more data that could be analyzed, and more questions that could be asked. Evaluators need the capacity to separate what "can be done" from what it would be "interesting" to do, and to stick rigorously to the resulting work plans.

Evaluators who work on operational or volatile issues need the flexibility and skill to respond quickly to information requests. Evaluators have a storehouse of traditional analytical tools and methodologies that can be useful in a variety of settings. But the pressing needs of decisionmakers can require of evaluators the intellectual courage to adapt traditional techniques to current contexts and to create new techniques as the situation warrants. Evaluators need to take risks without undue concern about the reaction of their discipline.

Finally, evaluators need to develop and to hone their communication skills. Three communication skills in particular will play a key role in the future evolution of the evaluation profession: speaking, visual communication, and listening. *Speaking* skills are an integral part of team building, negotiating, collecting data, and presenting evaluation findings. The increasing use of computer graphics foretells the role that *visual communication* can play in evaluation. Seeing a bar graph that displays the variations in a program's performance across geographic jurisdictions, for example, often gives a clearer message than columns and rows of numbers. *Listening,* being able to take in both the content and the sense of another's communication, is arguably the single most important communication skill for an evaluator. Listening is a mode of communication that is applicable to practically everything an evaluator does.

The Evaluation Process

There are times when the traditionally deliberate and methodological evaluation process is appropriate. When long-term impacts are sought, when deadlines and immediate decisions are not an issue, and when resources are relatively plentiful, evaluation need not be a hurried activity. When time and resources are at a premium, however, some modifications need to be made in the standard ways of conducting evaluations.

Existing data sources should be used before evaluators create new information systems or request staff and others to collect data that are not already being gathered. Evaluators can look for rough approximations instead of precise answers and can reduce sample sizes for the sake of timeliness. Triangulation, blending qualitative and quantitative data, and other techniques can be used to minimize the likelihood of gross errors. Methodologies that are simple should be preferred over ones that are complex. Evaluators should pursue data collection strategies that emphasize quality over quantity of data, inexpensive over expensive data collection strategies, and clear performance measures over the complex and the subtle ones.

The emphasis on speed, rough approximations, and relevant performance measures need not adversely affect the quality of the evaluation product. An evaluation whose findings are timely, relevant, and approximate is more useful to a decisionmaker than an evaluation that is precise but late or that looked at the wrong questions. Working closely with people who have more intimate knowledge of the program is another protection against major errors.

The Evaluation Product

Evaluations should be useful to managers. There is probably no more important criterion for a performance-oriented evaluator. An evaluation is useful if it provides information about issues a manager can influence. Evaluations are useful when findings are presented in a clear, intelligible manner.

Evaluations are not like detective stories or movies where the punchline comes at the end. Final reports and exit briefings ought not to be the places where significant findings are revealed for the first time. Evaluators should continually be sharing their insights, findings, and conclusions with staff, managers, and policymakers. Clients should not be surprised by the contents of evaluation reports or briefings.

Finally, evaluators' ideas about how programs and organizations can be improved should not ignore political, organizational, or fiscal realities. Evaluators should aim first to provide ideas that require no new personnel, data collection requirements, or spending. Recommendations that do require new resources are more likely to be adopted if evaluators can show how existing resources can be reallocated without reducing a program or organization's effectiveness in other areas.

Conclusion

The ideas presented above are preliminary thoughts, gleaned from the concepts and experiences described in previous chapters. Obviously, the suggestions will not work equally well in all contexts. But the environment that government and nonprofit organizations find themselves in today demands different approaches to evaluation. Performance-oriented evaluation is one strategy that has demonstrated its utility in real-world situations.

Clearly more work needs to be done. Now let us work together to define what high performance and excellence mean in public and nonprofit contexts. Let us work to help improve agency and program performance. Let us work to enhance public confidence in those agencies and programs that perform well.

Note

1. Mark A. Abramson, *The "Excellence in Government" Debate,* Washington, D.C.: The Center for Excellence in Government, 1984.

Index

About the Contributors

Alan P. Balutis is director of the Office of Management and Organization at the U.S. Department of Commerce (DoC). He was the first recipient of the Annual Commerce Award for Outstanding Administrative Management and was recently awarded a Silver Medal, the Department's second highest honor. He is the author or co-author of four books, more than twenty-five articles, and numerous conference papers on governmental reorganization, legislative reform, budgeting, and internship programs.

Alain J. Barbarie has been with the Public Service of Canada for the past eleven years. In 1980–81 he worked at the International Institute for Applied Systems Analysis (IIASS) in Vienna on Decision Support Systems. He subsequently returned to Canada to the Ministry of State for Science and Technology as a policy advisor. He later joined the Office of the Comptroller General of Canada, where he has worked in the field of program evaluation and in particular the evaluation of R&D programs. In 1984, he worked on a task force on Federal Policies and Programs for Technology Development.

Bill B. Benton is the executive vice president for Urban Systems Research and Engineering Inc., Washington, D.C., an applied research and consulting firm that provides services in a variety of areas including social services, income security, health care delivery, housing, and community development. He holds a doctorate in Public Administration from the University of Southern California, Washington Public Affairs Center.

Previously Dr. Benton served as assistant secretary and deputy secretary of the Maryland Department of Human Services; deputy director for the Office of Planning Research and Evaluation, Office of Human Development Services, Department of Health and Human Services; and senior research associate at the Urban Institute. As visiting director of the New Zealand Department of Social Welfare, he designed and implemented a system of management indicators.

Larry S. Beyna was a senior member of the study team conducting the evaluation of the Civil Services Reform Act in the Department of Health and Human Services. He is currently a partner in the firm of James Bell and Associates, Inc., which specializes in program evaluation and development.

Kenneth L. Bickel serves as marketing strategist in the fraternal department of Aid Association for Lutherans, Appleton, Wisconsin, working in strategic policy development for AAL's fraternal programs. Prior to this, Bickel designed and conducted numerous evaluations of AAL's various fraternal benefit programs. Active in the community human service agency network, Bickel has also been involved in evaluation training and consultation projects with community nonprofit organizations.

Anabel Burgh Crane is deputy director, Division of Planning and Evaluation, Health Resources and Services Administration. Her previous health-related positions were with the Health Resources Administration and the U.S. Office of Economic Opportunity. She has held positions that involve evaluation as a major responsibility since 1977. Ms. Crane has a Master of Public Administration degree from Syracuse University.

Wayne Gray received his Ph.D. from the University of California at Berkeley in 1979. From 1980 to 1983, he worked for the Army Research Institute's (ARI) Monterey unit. At Monterey, he became involved in the implementation of tactical training programs such as REALTRAIN and MILES. Since August 1983, he has worked for ARI Alexandria on the Smart Technology for Training Team. In that capacity, he has assisted the Army Engineer School in designing, developing, implementing, and monitoring the army's first large-scale effort to apply computer-based training to officer education. Dr. Gray's current interest involves designing, developing, evaluating and, of course, implementing artificial intelligence technology into army training.

Ann H. Hastings directed the final year of the evaluation of the Civil Services Reform Act in the Department of Health and Human Services, which was conducted for the government by Advanced Technology, Inc. Dr. Hastings is currently co-owner of Scanlon & Hastings/A Management Services Group, which specializes in providing research, evaluation, strategic planning, and decision support services to public and nonpublic organizations.

Thomas A. Horan is a program analyst for the Orange County Transit District. His primary research interest concerns using an organizational perspective to improve the design, implementation, and evaluation of government programs. He is also actively involved in regional transportation planning. He has a Master's degree in public policy from Claremont Graduate School, where he is currently a doctoral candidate in the psychology department.

Mike Jewell is a program analyst in the Office of the Secretary, Department of Health and Human Services. He has extensive experience in formulating and implementing research and evaluation plans. In addition to serving as project officer on a number of contracted evaluation studies, he has taken a lead role in established quick-turn-around contract mechanisms for use in the Office of the Secretary.

Stephen A. Kapp (M.S.W., Michigan) is a research associate in benefit research at Aid Association for Lutherans in Appleton, Wisconsin. In this position, in which he designs and conducts evaluation research projects, Kapp has been able to observe and facilitate the utilization of evaluation findings after the research has been completed. His interests are in the on ongoing uses of program evaluation at the program and organizational levels. He also has experience in evaluation in juvenile delinquency, and community-based services at the agency level.

John P. King is associate vice president for planning, Research and Information Systems at Longwood College, Virginia. Dr. King has served with the Virginia Department of Mental Health, taught at Virginia Tech and other universities, and has written about strategic planning and evaluation.

Dr. Michael S. Knapp, an educational sociologist with the Social Sciences Department at SRI International, has specialized over the past six years in studying the implementation and effects of federal and state policies in local institutions, primarily in education but also in other areas of human service. He takes special interest in the development of appropriate methods for evaluation research, including local documentation strategies, multiple-site qualitative designs, and designs that combine qualitative and quantitative elements. Dr. Knapp is currently directing a national study of the federal education block grant, Chapter 2 of the Education Consolidation and Improvement Act of 1981, under the sponsorship of the U.S. Department of Education.

Martin Kotler's twenty-two years in government and consulting have involved a broad base of experience in both running and evaluating health programs. His health-related programmatic expertise includes a range of areas such as alcohol and drug abuse, primary care, occupational counseling, health resources training and development, mental health education/risk reduction programs, and health maintenance organizations.

Steve Lillie is a health policy analyst and evaluator with the U.S. Department of Health and Human Services. In addition to conducting several short-term evaluations, he has worked to develop approaches to assessing the effectiveness of evaluation offices in the department.

Steven Maynard-Moody is assistant professor of public administration and research associate in the Center for Public Affairs at the University of Kansas. His work has appeared in the *Administrative Science Quarterly, Administration and Society, Policy Studies Review, Policy Studies Journal, Evaluation Review,* and numerous edited volumes.

Michael C. Musheno is professor of justice studies, political science, and public affairs at Arizona State University. He has taught at several universities, including the City University of New York, the University of Minnesota, and the University of Kansas. His research on public policy, organizational behavior, and justice-related issues has appeared in a number of academic journals including *Law and Society Review, Administrative Law Review, Social Science Quarterly, Administrative Science Quarterly, Political Methodology, Policy Studies Journal,* and *Policy Studies Review.* His coauthored books include *Criminal Justice: Law in Action, Public Policy, and Police Discretion,* and *Criminal Justice: A Public Policy Approach.* He is currently studying how notions of social justice impact on organizational behavior in public service bureaucracies.

Carole M. P. Neves is a senior policy analyst at Urban Systems Research and Engineering, Inc. She obtained her Doctorate in Public Administration and Policy from the Center for Public Administration and Policy, Virginia Polytechnic Institute and State University. Previously she was a member of the technical staff at the Mitre Corporation, Washington, D.C., and worked as a professor and journalist in São Paulo, Brazil, where she resided for nearly a decade.

Dennis Palumbo is professor of public affairs at Arizona State University. He has taught at a number of universities, including Michigan State, Hawaii, Pennsylvania, City University of New York, Indiana, and Kansas. He has published in the *American Journal of Politics, Public Administration Review, Urban Affairs Quarterly, Social Science Quarterly, Crime and Delinquency, Evaluation Review, Policy Sciences,* and the *Policy Studies Review.* Author or coauthor of several books (the most recent being *Criminal Justice: The Law Is Action,* John Wiley, 1985), he currently is editor of the *Policy Studies Review* and working on a book entitled *Introduction to American Public Policy.*

Mary Ann Scheirer is a senior behavioral scientist with Westat, Inc., in Rockville, Maryland. She is a social psychologist applying social systems analysis to research on the implementation of organizational, technical, and social changes. Her earlier work on the implementation of innovations was published as *Program Implementation: The Organizational Context* (Sage, 1981).

Liese Sherwood-Fabre received her Ph.D. from Indiana University, Bloomington. Part of the research presented here originally developed as part of her graduate research in pretrial release services. She became involved in the Department of Health and Human Services' evaluation of civil service reform during the project's final year while a policy research associate with HHS. She is currently working as a survey statistician with the International Statistical Programs Center at the Census Bureau, where she is continuing her interests in program evaluation at the international level.

Jean D. Smith, a planner in the Office of Policy Planning in the Tennessee Department of Mental Health and Mental Retardation, has been involved in planning, evaluating and managing state programs for more than eighteen years. Trained as a sociologist, she began her work in Tennessee state government in the state's Appalachian Development program. She was instrumental in securing passage of the Tennessee Child Development Act, and served as assistant director of the Office of Child Development created by that legislation. For the past few years, Ms. Smith has worked primarily in planning and evaluating health programs for mothers and children.

Dr. Marian S. Stearns, director of the Social Sciences Department at SRI International, has conducted numerous evaluations of federal and state education programs and consulted on public policy decisions over a 15-year period. She manages an interdisciplinary group at SRI that does survey research, planning and evaluation studies, and consulting under contract with public and business organizations. The areas of research and consulting include education and the economy, application of technology in education and training, human services programs, and special populations (refugees, handicapped).

James F. Wolf is the director for Northern Virginia Programs and a Professor of the Center for Public Administration and Policy, Virginia Polytechnic Institute and State University. He obtained his Doctorate in Public Administration from the Washington Public Affairs Center, University of Southern California. He has designed and coordinated training, management, and executive development programs for federal, state, and local government officials. In addition to having taught courses at the Washington Public Affairs Center, University of Southern California, he directed the Intergovernmental Management Program.

About the Editors

Joseph S. Wholey is professor of public administration at the University of Southern California and member of the Virginia Board of Social Services. He has served as deputy assistant secretary for planning and evaluation and as director of evaluation in the Department of Health, Education, and Welfare; director of program evaluation studies at the Urban Institute; technical staff member in the Department of Defense's Weapons Systems Evaluation Group; chairman of the Arlington County Board; chairman of the Washington Metropolitan Area Transit Authority (METRO); and president of Hospice of Northern Virginia. His most recent book is *Evaluation and Effective Public Management*.

Mark A. Abramson is presently director of the Center for Excellence in Government in Washington, D.C. Before joining the center, Mr. Abramson was a program evaluator in the Office of the Assistant Secretary of Planning and Evaluation in the U.S. Department of Health and Human Services. Previously, Mr. Abramson was a research associate at the National Academy of Sciences on a project examining social research and development. He is the author of the *Funding of Social Knowledge Production and Application* (National Academy of Sciences) and numerous other articles on the subjects of program evaluation and government management. He received his B.A. degree from Florida State University and holds graduate degrees from New York University and Syracuse University.

Christopher Bellavita is an assistant professor of public administration at the University of Southern California. He teaches organization behavior and public policy at USC's Washington Public Affairs Center. He is the coauthor of *The Policy Organization*.